Banking on Change

Banking on Change:

Democratising finance in South Africa **1994–2004**

David Porteous with Ethel Hazelhurst

DOUBLE
STOREY
a juta company

First published 2004 by Double Storey Books, a division of Juta & Co. Ltd,
Mercury Crescent, Wetton, Cape Town

© 2004 FinMark Trust

ISBN 1-919930-85-X

All rights reserved

Page design and graphs by Jenny Sandler
Layout by Claudine Willatt-Bate
Printed by ABC Press, Epping, Cape Town

Contents

Foreword by Trevor Manuel		vii
Preface		ix
Abbreviations		x

Chapter 1: Introduction — 1
    Case study: The Financial Sector Charter: behind the scenes — 18

Chapter 2: Transaction Banking — 21
    Case study: Standard Bank's E Plan: the first wave — 46
    Case study: Sekulula: Social grant payments: 'It's easy now' — 50
    Case study: Teba Bank: mining the rural areas — 54

Chapter 3: Savings — 57
    Case study: People's Benefit Scheme: the missing link — 70
    Case study: Financial Diaries: household decisions — 73

Chapter 4: Micro Lending — 77
    Case study: The Micro Finance Regulatory Council: policing the frontiers — 93
    Case study: African Bank Investments Limited: the Henry Ford of micro credit — 96

Chapter 5: Small, Medium and Micro Enterprise Finance — 100
    Case study: African Contractor Finance Corporation: hidden pitfalls — 114
    Case study: Rural Finance Facility: democratic management — 118

Chapter 6: Housing Finance — 121
    Case study: The Community Bank: building society Mark 2 — 139
    Case study: CashBank: gobbled by Goliath — 143
    Case study: Gateway Home Loans: showing SA a new way home — 147

Chapter 7: Insurance — 150
    Case study: Home Loan Guarantee Company: the Starship Enterprise — 163
    Case study: Burial societies: social capital — 167

Chapter 8:	**SA Financial Institutions and the Region**	170
	Case study: African Life Assurance: exploring the region	182
Chapter 9:	**Conclusion**	184
Appendix 1:	Stokvels: making social cents	193
Appendix 2:	Village banks: democratic banking?	196
Appendix 3:	The macro picture: why saving matters but has declined	200
Appendix 4:	Was there a credit bubble in the late 1990s?	203
Appendix 5:	SMME definitions	208
Appendix 6:	Government support entities	212
Appendix 7:	Regional integration mechanisms	216
Appendix 8:	Financial literacy	222
	Glossary	225
	References	228
	Index	238

Foreword

by Trevor Manuel

Anyone walking into one of Johannesburg's shiny banking malls or sitting across a boardroom table in the offices of one of Cape Town's insurance giants will quickly understand why the South African financial sector enjoys a reputation for international standards and sophistication.

Yet this is only half the story.

Should that same person look to the townships or rural areas, it would be hard to ignore the fact that millions of South Africans have little or no access to financial services.

This goes to the heart of what President Thabo Mbeki has described as the divide between the First and the Second Economy in South Africa: the structural manifestation of poverty, underdevelopment and marginalisation of large sections of our people. Lack of access to appropriate savings or transactional products, coupled with poor financial literacy and consumer education, compounds the divide between the haves and the have-nots.

A financial system that does not serve the needs of all South Africans is a dysfunctional financial system. It is an anomaly that requires urgent redress.

Yet it is not possible to be clear on the path of renewal without first understanding where we have come from.

This is what the authors have helped us to do. Their book describes the status of access to financial services in South Africa in 2004, on the ten year anniversary of the transition to democracy. It analyses key developments and innovations that have broadened access to financial services since 1994. It documents trends for public policy-makers and financial institutions alike.

What is clear is that the South African financial sector has for a long time been struggling with the challenges of information asymmetry. Functioning as it should, the financial system will lead to an efficient allocation of capital through collecting and disseminating information on risk and reward. However, in cases where such information is scarce, or perhaps even skewed, the financial system can lead to a debilitating under-allocation of resources to certain sectors.

This book seeks to place in perspective all the innovations and developments in the sphere of access to financial services designed to try and address these fundamental problems over the past decade of freedom. The authors succinctly describe to the informed but non-expert reader which strategies have been successful and which have failed—and most importantly, why.

Lastly, the book also suggests policy directions for the next decade of freedom. Here there is much to be optimistic about.

The Financial Sector Charter has added a deep social dimension to the functioning of the financial system. It goes to the core of how the financial sector will address the urgent need to make business sense of a more sustainable, inclusive and equitable future. The sector has committed to increase access to financial services to 80% of people in the LSM1–5 categories by 2008. The sector will also increase targeted lending to SMMEs, agricultural enterprises, development infrastructure and low-cost housing. In this, the base year of the Financial Sector Charter, the book provides a benchmark against which to measure progress. Furthermore, its insightful review of knowledge and experience will assist in ensuring that rapid progress is made in achieving the sector's goals for access and targeted lending.

There is no conflict or contradiction in the twin goals of ensuring a South African financial system which remains world-class and one which is inclusive of all our people. The long-run sustainability and competitiveness of the South African financial sector is intricately intertwined with its ability to broaden its reach to all sectors of the South African economy.

I am confident that, ten years from now, readers of David and Ethel's book will have cause to remark on how much progress has been made.

Trevor A Manuel
Minister of Finance

Preface

FinMark Trust is an independent trust based in Johannesburg, South Africa. Its mission is 'Making Financial Markets Work for the Poor' in the countries of southern Africa. FinMark Trust is funded by an accountable grant from the UK's Department for International Development (DFID).

I had the privilege of being first Chief Executive of the Trust from inception in 2002 until mid-2004. During this time, FinMark Trust commissioned wide-ranging research on the issues of access to financial services. This book arises from in part from a desire to package the many pieces of underlying research, most of which are available through the FinMark Trust website, into a coherent whole. But it also seeks to go further. South Africa in particular is a country in which the debates on access to financial services have been heated and frequent. This was of course linked to the arrival of democracy in 1994 and the subsequent process of democratising the society as a whole.

The book aims to participate in and influence the wider debate on how best to advance access. While much progress has been made in many areas, there is still much to debate and much to explore. The book also seeks to cast a spotlight on the innovations and innovators of the past decade. This is in the hope that the stories from the rich spectrum of experiments, some successful, some failed, will contribute towards the next generation of innovation ahead.

Our thanks are due to many people who have contributed to this book. A number of subject experts reviewed particular chapters and gave us their views: Charles Chemel, Jeremy Leach, Stephan Malherbe, John Orford, Kecia Rust, Johan de Ridder, Doubell Chamberlain, Hennie Bester. Others agreed to read the manuscript and helped us to enhance the story-line: Richard Stovin-Bradford, Stephan Malherbe, Hugh Scott and Gerhard Coetzee. To all of these, our thanks; of course, all remaining errors and omissions remain our responsibility alone. Finally, our thanks to the trustees of FinMark Trust who supported the project throughout: Nkunku Sowazi (Chair), Ethel Matenge-Sebesho, Bob Tucker and Mutle Mogase.

David Porteous
Johannesburg
July 2004

Abbreviations

Abil	African Bank Investments Limited
Absip	Association of Black Securities and Investment Professionals
ACFC	African Contractor Finance Corporation
ACSA	Accumulating Savings and Credit Association
AEC	African Economic Community
ALA	African Life assurance
AML	anti-money laundering
AMPS	All Media & Products Survey
ANC	African National Congress
ART	anti-retroviral therapy
ATM	automated teller machine
AVP	Anicap Venture Partners
BBA	basic bank account
BEC	Black Empowerment Commission
BEE	Black Economic Empowerment
BIFM	Botswana Insurance Fund Management
BIH	Botswana Insurance Holdings
BLNS	Botswana, Lesotho, Namibia and Swaziland
BMR	Bureau of Market Research
BRCS	Bay Research and Consultancy Service
CAT	charges, access and terms
CGAP	Consultative Group to Assist the Poorest
Cisna	Committee of Insurance, Securities and Non-banking Financial Authorities
CLO	collateralised loan obligation fund
CMA	Common Monetary Area
Comesa	Common Market for Eastern and Southern Africa
Cosatu	Congress of South African Trade Unions
CPI	consumer price index
CPS	Cash Paymaster Services
CR	Community Reinvestment
CTF	counter-terrorist finance
DBSA	Development Bank of Southern Africa
DFI	development finance intermediaries/institutions
DFID	(UK) Department for International Development
DG	Director General
DRC	Democratic Republic of the Congo
DTI	Department of Trade and Industry
ECI	Ebony Consulting International
ESAAMLG	Eastern and Southern African Anti-Money Laundering Group
ESAF	Eastern and Southern African Banking Supervisors Group
Esop	employee share ownership plan
FAIS	Financial Advisory and Intermediary Services
FATF	Financial Action Task Force

FICA	Financial Intelligence Centre Act
FIP	Finance and Investment Protocol
FM	*Financial Mail*
FNB	First National Bank
FSA	Financial Services Association
FSB	Financial Services Board
FSC	Financial Sector Charter
FSC	Financial Services Co-operative
FSCC	Financial Sector Campaign Coalition
FSM	financial summary measure
GCC	Group Credit Company
GDP	gross domestic product
GEM	Global Entrepreneurship Monitor
GSM	Global System for Mobile Communications
HANIS	Home Affairs National Identification System
HDI	historically disadvantaged individual
HDP	historically disadvantaged person
IDC	Industrial Development Corporation
IDT	Independent Development Trust
IDTFC	Independent Development Trust Finance Company
IFAD	International Fund for Agricultural Development
IFC	International Finance Corporation
IFI	integrated financial institution
ILO	International Labour Organisation
IMF	International Monetary Fund
Khula	Khula Enterprise Finance
KZN	KwaZulu-Natal
LBSC	Local Business Service Centre
LFS	Labour Force Survey
LOA	Life Offices Association
LSM	living standard measure
MCO	micro credit organisation/outlets
MEA	Micro Enterprise Alliance
MERG	Macro-Economic Research Group
MFI	micro finance institution
MFO	micro finance organisation
MFRC	Micro Finance Regulatory Council
MIF	Mortgage Indemnity Fund
MLA	Micro Lenders Association
Namac	National Manufacturing Advisory Centre
Nasasa	National Stokvels Association of South Africa
NDA	National Department of Agriculture
Nedlac	National Economic Development and Labour Council
NEF	National Empowerment Fund

Nepad	New Partnership for Africa's Development
NGO	non-government organisation
NHBRC	National Home Builders Registration Council
NHFC	National Housing Finance Corporation
NLR	National Loans Register
NSBC	National Small Business Council
Ntsika	Ntsika Enterprise Promotion Agency
Nurcha	National Urban Reconstruction and Housing Agency
P2P	person-to-person
PBS	People's Benefit Scheme
PDI	previously disadvantaged person
PIN	personal identification number
PIP	properties in possession
POS	point of sale
PTA	Preferential Trade Area
Q	question in FinScope survey
RDP	Reconstruction and Development Programme
RFF	Rural Finance Facility
RFI	retail financing institution
RHF	Rural Housing Finance
RHLF	Rural Housing Loan Fund
RISDP	Regional Indicative Strategic Development Plan
Rosca	Rotating Savings and Credit Association
RoU	record of understanding
SA	South Africa/South African
SACU	Southern African Customs Union
SADC	Southern African Development Community
SAHL	South African Home Loans
SAIA	South African Short-Term Insurance Association
Saldru	Southern Africa Labour and Development Research Unit
SARB	South African Reserve Bank
Sasria	South African Special Risks Insurance Association
SEE	Survey of Employment and Earnings
SEE	Survey of Employment and Earnings
SEF	Small Enterprise Foundation
Seta	Sectoral Education and Training Authority
SME	small and medium enterprise
SMME	small, medium and micro enterprise
SSA	Statistics South Africa
UCT	University of Cape Town
UNDP	United Nations Development Programme
USAid	United States Agency for International Development
UYF	Umsobomvu Youth Fund
VAT	Value Added Tax

Chapter 1

Introduction

It is estimated that close to three-quarters of SA's adult population of 24m are 'unbanked' ... Driving the banks' efforts to satisfy this mass of 'unbanked' people is a combination of powerful political, social and economic forces. In blunt terms, the banks can no longer afford to turn their backs on the unbanked. Apart from the possible adverse political ramifications such a stance could easily threaten banks' profitability.
Simon Cashmore, *IT Review*, December 1993, p.9.

The quotation above is remarkable not for its substance but for its publication date. It was written over ten years ago, before the democratic transition in South Africa (SA), yet the sentiment could just as easily have been expressed in 2003 during negotiations over the Financial Sector Charter (FSC). To some, this shows how little the underlying issues have changed in ten years. To others, the fact that only half the population is unbanked in 2004 is a sign of great progress.

Both are right. In SA's first decade of democracy the financial sector has seen great change—and experienced great continuity. The advent of democracy opened up what was previously a protected industry to foreign entrants, and it created the opportunity for SA financial institutions to look outside of SA in search of new markets, especially in other parts of Africa. In parallel, the wider deployment of technology in the form of ATMs and debit cards brought millions more people into the banking system, and a change in the credit laws unintentionally opened the way for explosive growth in the micro credit industry.

However, the arrival of democracy raised political and social expectations and increased pressure on the financial system to provide services in key areas of social delivery, such as housing and small, medium and micro enterprise (SMME).

The situation in 1994 needs some historical context. For more than 40 years, SA had been the site of a vast social engineering project. The apartheid system, introduced in the early 1950s, had attempted to separate the 'races' in all aspects of life, including residence, association, the workplace, education and the provision of services. Official policy distinguished between several 'racial' subcategories, but the essential distinction was between those who were white—and therefore citizens—and the rest, who were not, and therefore could not fully participate in the economy. The policy was vigorously implemented for about two decades, as the National Party government tried to turn the tide of urbanisation and contain the majority of black South Africans in tribal 'homelands' and specially designated urban areas. But by the late 1970s, it had become clear even to government supporters that the system was unworkable. Laws were either ignored or gradually dropped from the statute book.

In the mid-1980s, anti-apartheid financial sanctions were applied, which placed the white government under serious pressure by the end of the decade. At that point, domestic developments were overtaken by international events. The fall of the former Soviet Union paved the way for rapprochement between the government of FW de Klerk and the liberation movement, the African National Congress (ANC), which had depended on Soviet support. Following lengthy negotiations, SA's first democratic election brought the ANC to power in 1994. And it immediately repealed all remaining discriminatory laws.

But SA was left with a dual economy, with highly sophisticated first-world financial markets and a third-world social infrastructure. And it remained a social laboratory. Driven by the overriding need to repair the social and economic damage inflicted by apartheid, government, business and civil society launched a range of social delivery, transformation and empowerment initiatives. One of the crucial arenas in the process was the financial services sector. And one aspect of the history of the past ten years is the interplay between the state and business in this sector as expectations rose and fell about what the sector could deliver.

The broader story, however, is of a decade rich in innovation and experimentation. Even where there has not been significant progress—such as in housing finance or in SMME finance—the decade has been marked by pioneering initiatives. Some have worked and many have not. But ten years of experiment and innovation is worth recounting. This book tells a story that has not been told in this way before. Not only are the episodes interesting in themselves—often with colourful characters and epic story lines—they are also important for the public record. Too often, memory is short and history forgotten. And the next generation pays the price of rediscovering what has already been learned.

In 2004, as SA celebrates ten years of democracy, it can point to great strides made on many fronts that influence the social, economic and political order in the country. Much of the emphasis of post-apartheid government, to date, has been on creating and stabilising the policy and legislative frameworks for growth and transformation. On this front, government has a credible track record. The record of delivery of basic services has been patchier; but even those who criticise the pace or nature of that delivery recognise the areas of substantial achievement.

The record is reflected in Table 1.1, which shows areas of both public roll-out (such as electricity) and private roll-out (such as cellphones). In some public arenas, government has relied on private delivery mechanisms: for example, low-income housing, initially built mainly by private developers; and social grants, which are distributed by private agencies.

Table 1.1: **Living-standard indicators**

	Note	1994	2003
Population	1	38,63m	46,43m
GDP per capita (constant 2000 rand)	2	R18 726	R21 310
% households electrified	3	65,3% (1995)	78,7%
% households with clean water	3	51,6% (1995)	68,3%
% households with mail address	4	28,8%	68,4% (2002)
% households with cellphone	5	2% (1995)	20,7% (2002)
Recipients of capital housing subsidy (cumulative)	6	0	2,1m
Social grant beneficiaries	7	2,6m (1995)	5,9m

Sources
1. Statistics SA Midyear estimates 2003 (P0302). These are estimated values for the years 1994 and 2003.
2. Statistics SA: Statistical Release GDP 4th quarter 2003 (P0441). The source data is for the full year as at December 1994 and December 2003. The GDP is expressed in real terms, constant at year 2000.
3. Statistics South Africa October Household Survey 1995 (P0317), and Statistics South Africa General Household Survey 2003 (P0318). The electrified categorisation refers to electricity for lighting, and clean water refers to drinking water.
4. SA Institute of Race Relations (2002).
5. 1995 data: Statistics South Africa October Household Survey 1995 (P0317). 2002 data: Hodge (2002).
6. Department of Housing (2004).
7. 1995 data: taken from annual budgeted figures provided by Prof. S. van den Berg of the University of Stellenbosch. 2003: data as at December 2003 from Soc Pen database.

In government's recently published *Towards a Ten Year Review* (2003), the Presidency has chronicled areas of progress and shortfall as a backdrop to its agenda for the next ten years. The subject of access to financial services is mainly implicit rather than explicit; it appears in key flashpoint areas, such as housing finance and SMME promotion, that are part of the conventional developmental lexicon. Yet these two categories are only part of a broader range of retail financial services that play a vital role in social and economic development.

The debate around access to financial services has sharpened and deepened in the past two years of negotiations, a process that led to the Charter in 2003 (see Box 1.2 on p.10). The Charter takes a much broader view of financial access, and sets five-year targets for delivery of broad-based financial access starting in 2004. So, in this base year for most Charter target measurement, we stand on the threshold of a new era of developments around access. Whether access or other targets in the Charter are likely to be reached will be discussed throughout this book. But, whether they are or not, the subject of financial access has been placed high on the political and economic agenda for the next decade.

Objectives and scope of this book and chapter

Against this backdrop, *Banking on Change* creates a context for the unfolding debates around financial access in the second decade of democracy—after 40 years of apartheid and several centuries of colonisation. The book outlines the history of the past ten years to achieve two specific objectives. It aims, first, to provide a compendium of the experiments, successful and unsuccessful, so that new initiatives can have the benefit of history. Second, it aims to establish clear benchmarks for the current status of access to, and usage of, financial services in the year in which the Charter obligations are to take effect. It is in the context of these two objectives that we look forward to seeing how the process of expanding access—or democratising finance—will continue in the next ten years.

This chapter sets the scene by addressing three questions:
- What was the bigger context of change in the financial sector?
- Why does expanded access to financial services matter?
- How does one benchmark the current reality after the changes in the financial sector since 1994?

The book does not pretend to be a comprehensive history of the SA financial system in the past decade. It focuses on the expansion of access to retail financial services at the lower end of the SA market, variously called the affordable market (in housing parlance) or the mass market (in bank segmentation terms). Access has been, and continues to be, the frontier issue for SA financial services.

The relevance of broader access

One might ask why the expansion of access to financial services deserves this level of attention, especially since other issues—education, crime and job creation—seem to be more important. There are three broad answers to this question; they will be dealt with below.

1. Growth and job creation

Expansion of access to financial services is closely associated with economic growth and job creation—both economic priorities for the country. 'Association' does not mean causality, and a wide economic literature has built up over the past decade seeking to test causality: does economic growth lead to increased take-up of financial services, or is it the increase in financial service usage that generates growth? The econometric work is by and large inconclusive, although a recent study claims that financial development leads to economic growth, and that this effect is especially pronounced for developing countries.[1]

However, even if this cannot be demonstrated econometrically within the limits of available data, there are clear micro-economic chains of causality. For example, access to finance enables the start and expansion of new small businesses, and these, in turn, create jobs. Easier access to housing finance increases demand for new housing stock, which encourages new household formation. New household formation, in its turn, leads to derived consumption demand in areas such as construction, furniture and other household durables. So it is a key driver of domestic economic activity.

Even if greater access did not have macroeconomic significance, it has clear implications for the growth of the financial sector. Data will be presented in this book to show that, in many categories of formal financial services, retail markets have stagnated over the past decade. To grow, financial institutions have to find new clients. Some are finding them beyond SA's borders, and Chapter 8 tells this story. But international expansion is never easy, and the majority will have to find ways to attract new clients in the domestic market. This too will not be easy; but there will be rewards for those who can find the appropriate products, channels and cost structure to take on new client bases.

2. Poverty reduction
Poverty reduction is a key national goal. And an increasing flow of literature from the micro-finance sector has demonstrated conceptually and, increasingly, empirically, how access to appropriate financial services helps reduce overall levels of poverty.[2]

For instance, without the protection of insurance or savings, events such as the illness of a wage-earner or the failure of a crop can push poor households over the edge of just coping, into destitution. Some form of insurance cover or savings instrument could reduce poor people's vulnerability to income shocks.

Another example: without access to productive capital it is impossible for households to create wealth. Productive capital is usually understood to be working capital for business enterprise. But perhaps more productive for the poor is human capital investment in the form of education for children. Education costs are often 'lumpy', and parents need access to some form of financial service (credit or savings) to finance fees, transport, uniforms and books even when education itself is provided 'free'.

3. Social exclusion
Social exclusion has undesirable social and political consequences: the marginalisation and alienation of large sections of the population. Governments in developed countries, such as the US and the UK, have increasingly tackled the problem of the 'unbanked' as both a symptom and a cause of social exclusion, even though a relatively small minority is unbanked.[3] In SA, too, government identifies social exclusion as a problem.[4] To many people, the financial sector in SA is an example of the two-nation divide, with a relatively well-functioning world-class sector providing for a third to a half of the population, but excluding the rest. Some argue that, in the absence of determined state effort, the growth trajectory may exacer-

bate this divide, threatening the fragile stability of the whole economic transformation effort at the centre of government's agenda for the next decade.

In addition to these headline reasons why access matters, there is also another derived reason. It matters simply because it has become a major political issue in SA. In other words: even if it had no broader impact or consequences, the fact that it is now squarely on the political and transformation agenda means that it matters—both for policy-makers and for financial institutions. In the light of this, it is appropriate to provide the context of state–private sector relations over the past decade that has brought us to this point.

Government policy towards the financial sector

Though the Presidency's *Ten Year Review* does not address access to financial services explicitly, the issue has been on the policy agenda for a long time. The complex interaction between government and the financial sector is one of the more interesting stories of the decade, since it reveals the broader interplay between politics and economics in the new SA. Political freedom won at the polls in 1994 had to be translated into economic freedom.

The ANC's pre-1994 policy positions were based on the view that banks were part of the 'commanding heights' of the economy. The Freedom Charter of 1955 spoke in ringing tones of the intention to nationalise them: 'The People Shall Share in the Country's Wealth ... the mineral wealth beneath the soil, the banks and monopoly industry shall be transferred to the ownership of the people as a whole.'

On his release in 1991, Nelson Mandela reaffirmed the basic tenets of the Freedom Charter approach. However, even before the ANC came to power, there were signs that the new government would take a more sophisticated approach to the economy. For example, the Macro-Economic Research Group (MERG) report, essentially a shadow economic-policy report published in 1993, advocated a move towards a more German-style financial system, with increased regulation in key areas. But it made no mention of nationalisation. Importantly, the report stated: 'MERG places a high priority on developing banking services for the majority of the population. All South Africans, including the poorest, must be able to keep their money safely in a bank ...'[5] To achieve this, the report recommended the creation of a 'people's bank', based on the existing PostBank. These themes were picked up in the Reconstruction and Development Programme (RDP) implemented by government.

After the new African National Congress (ANC) government took office in 1994, the interaction between government and the private financial sector oscillated through three distinct phases, which may be called the honeymoon, stand-off and rapprochement.

1. *The honeymoon* (1994–1997): given its earlier policy positions, the new government initially adopted a surprisingly conciliatory and enabling stance towards

the financial sector. For example, in the potentially explosive township housing sector, banks had substantial exposure to bad mortgages in 1994 and, as a result, had largely ceased to lend in these areas. The new government entered into a Record of Understanding with the lending banks. This agreement did not force banks to resume lending; it provided an incentive by reducing 'non-commercial' risks for lenders, through a mortgage guarantee scheme, until townships were deemed to be more stable or 'normalised'. In return, the banks jointly agreed to a lending target of 150 000 new loans in township areas. The state established new 'development' financial institutions in 1996, in the housing and SMME sectors—the National Housing Finance Corporation (NHFC) and Khula Enterprise Finance. But these were not retail institutions that would compete with the private sector. Rather, the mandates of both were exclusively wholesale, and their approach was to support and enable private investment in their respective sectors, through the banks among other means. Their subsequent experiences will be outlined in the relevant chapters.

2. *Stand-off* (1998–2002): by 1998, there were signs of increasing strain in the relationship. Each side accused the other of not fulfilling its implicit or explicit obligations. The Housing Ministry began to plan new legislation, which would increase pressure on banks to service low-income communities and borrowers. First, the Home Loan and Mortgage Disclosure Act was passed in 2000. Then a draft Community Reinvestment Bill (CR Bill) along US lines (proposed by the ANC in the early 1990s, but later shelved) was tabled in 2002. There was increasing talk of government wholesale entities 'going retail' and entering the market directly, if the private sector would not or could not lend. A formal consultancy was appointed to investigate this option for Khula in 2002. The Red October campaign, initiated by the SA Communist Party and alliance partners (together known as the Financial Sector Campaign Coalition), kicked off in October 2000 with nationwide marches to demonstrate against bank discrimination in lending. This marked a high point in popular mobilisation against financial institutions.

3. *Rapprochement* (late 2002 onwards): just as the relationship appeared to be at its nadir, a new day began to dawn. Galvanised, in part, by the desire to avoid repeating the economic meltdown that took place from 2000 onwards in neighbouring Zimbabwe, the financial sector signed far-reaching, if vague, commitments at the Nedlac Financial Sector Summit in August 2002. Standard Bank chairman Derek Cooper, speaking to the Summit on behalf of the financial sector, described the day as a 'watershed … which signifies a new beginning.'[6] While little that was concrete had happened, the spirit of the discussion changed. The dramatic loss of market capitalisation of SA mining houses, following leaks in a mismanaged Mining Charter process in 2002, also galvanised financial sector leaders into proactively signalling willingness to transform. In late 2002, the sector

initiated the negotiations with the Association of Black Securities and Investment Professionals (Absip) that led, little more than a year later, to a comprehensive Charter (see **The Financial Sector Charter**, p.18).

The Financial Sector Charter committed all designated financial institutions (essentially all regulated entities, from banks to insurers and fund managers) to achieving specific targets in a number of areas. These included: black ownership and management; procurement; and, most importantly from the perspective of this book, access to financial services and targeted investments in sectors such as housing and SMMEs (see Box 1.2, p.10). The Charter represented a voluntary commitment by the sector to transformation and black economic empowerment (BEE). Government only became involved in a supportive role towards the end of the process. Nevertheless, it pronounced itself happy with the outcome: a major sector in the economy would monitor and report on its own progress towards agreed transformation over a ten-year period. As a result, the passage of the more confrontational legislative proposals—such as the CR Bill—was suspended, pending the outcome of the Charter process.

In 2004, therefore, government–financial sector relations ended the first decade at a high point. However, the warm glow surrounding signature of the Charter soon showed signs of dissipating in the harsh reality of obstacles to and constraints on delivery. Within government, there remain conflicting views over how to engage the private sector in the provision of essential or basic services. While the National Treasury, which was the lead ministry in the Charter process, appears content to be facilitative, other ministries have chosen a more aggressive approach. Health, for instance, is forcing cross-subsidisation across medical aid schemes to increase access to affordable health care.

Underneath the apparent post-Charter conviviality, there is slowly growing tension over whether Charter objectives are appropriate and whether they can and will be achieved. This is particularly true in broad-based empowerment areas such as access, as opposed to 'narrow' areas such as ownership of financial institutions. Even if Charter targets are met, will this achievement be enough to carry the political day in the 2009 election, the first of the post-Mbeki era?

It is always interesting to speculate on counterfactual scenarios: what might have happened if no Charter had been agreed on? In other newly democratic regimes in Africa in the 1960s and 1970s, there was often a cycle of increasing state coercion of the private financial sector into socially desirable investment. When this coercion triggered resistance from the sector or the collapse of the weakened system, wholesale or partial nationalisation of banks followed. In a debilitated state, the nationalised financial sector could typically do little to promote access over time. SA policy-makers have clearly learned from these experiences that the financial sector is inherently fragile. Nonetheless, now that there is a Charter formed by negotiation and agreement, the risk of coercion could reappear if the targets are not met. Indeed, the risk may be higher than before, since the sector has now proposed its own measurement standards in all the various targeted areas, including access to financial services. The access objectives are one of the most heavily weighted components of the Charter scorecard.

> **Box 1.1: Extracts from the Nedlac Financial Sector Summit**
>
> The Nedlac Financial Sector Summit was held in August 2002, following a long period of negotiation between the Nedlac social partners—government, labour, business (here the financial sector) and civil society—which was sparked by the Red October campaign. The Summit produced a Declaration, which is given in full in www.nedlac.org.za/find/index.html. The following are relevant excerpts from the commitments made:
>
> 3.1. *Ensuring access to basic financial services*: To engage effectively in the economy, encourage savings and improve the quality of life, every South African resident should have access to affordable and convenient payments and savings facilities. Both the public and private sector financial institutions must play a role in achieving these aims.
> 3.2. The parties will jointly research the economics of basic financial services and, on that basis, establish mechanisms and timeframes for achieving universal access.
> 3.3. *Development of sustainable institutions to serve poor communities*. While the large formal financial institutions have an important role to play in providing services for the poor, they must interact with and support smaller institutions, especially co-operative banks and NGOs that can provide micro credit to the poorest households. We need to harness the energies of the existing institutions in our communities, such as stokvels and burial societies, in order to mobilise our people's savings. The smaller financial institutions serve to increase the diversity of the sector and broaden ownership.
> 3.4. The parties agree on the need for new enabling legislation for so-called second and third-tier deposit-taking financial institutions. As a start, they have agreed key principles for legislation for financial cooperatives. The legislation should ensure that these institutions operate according to cooperative principles and enjoy adequate prudential oversight.
>
> Following the Summit, a working group was formed to address detailed implementation, although its work was largely overtaken by the Charter process in 2003.

SA's financial system—now and then

Expansion of retail access must be seen in the context of broader changes within the SA financial sector. Table 1.2 shows snapshots of the financial system from the beginning and the end of the decade. The figures give some sense of the developments in the financial sector as a whole over the decade.

Box 1.2: **The Financial Sector Charter**

Negotiations around a Charter in the Financial Services Sector essentially started following the Financial Sector Summit. The Association of Black Securities and Investment Professionals (Absip) represented BEE constituencies and negotiated with the main industry bodies, especially the two largest, the Banking Council and the Life Offices Association, in a process lasting almost a year. The process started in advance of the publication of government's BEE Policy document, which encouraged sectors to produce voluntary Codes, using a balanced scorecard approach. Government, led by the SA National Treasury, became involved towards the end of the process. The Charter was signed on 17 October 2003. After initial fears in financial markets about the costs and impact, by the time the final terms were published, financial sector indices hardly moved.

The Charter (available from www.banking.org.za) is comprehensive, addressing transformation in issues of ownership, management representation and procurement. However, for the purposes of this book, the relevant sections are Sections 8 ('Access to financial services in which detailed targets are set') and 9 ('Targeted investment'). Key excerpts follow.

8.1   The financial sector acknowledges that access to first-order retail financial services is fundamental to BEE and to the development of the economy as a whole. In respect of this charter, the financial sector commits itself to substantially increase effective access to first-order retail financial services to a greater segment of the population, within LSM 1–5.

First-order retail products and services means:
- transaction products and services, being a first-order, basic and secure means of accessing and transferring cash for day-to-day purposes;
- savings products and services, being a first-order basic and secure means of accumulating funds over time. (e.g. savings accounts, contractual savings products such as endowment policies, collective investments and community-based savings schemes);
- credit for low-income housing, financing agricultural development, or establishing, financing or expanding a black SMME;
- insurance products and services being the mitigation of impact of defined first-order basic risks (e.g. life insurance, funeral insurance, burial society, household insurance and health insurance).

8.6   By 2005, the financial sector, together with Government, undertakes to establish standards to monitor access, and to design a mechanism for the ongoing evaluation and review of the impact of its initiatives on access.

Table 1.2: Financial system indicators

	Note	1994	2003
Prime interest rate (average)	1	15,3%	11,5%
CPI inflation (average)	2	8,9%	5,3%
JSE liquidity (%)	3	8,5%	42,5% (2002)
Banking:			
Bank assets to GDP	4	64,4%	113%
Loans and advances to GDP	5	58,2%	84,8%
No. of registered banks	6	44	40
Share of assets of top 4 banks	7	82,4%	82,9%
Share of retail deposits of top 4 banks	8	84,5%	94,4%
RoE of banking sector	9	18%	21,1%
Bank net lending margin %	10	4,6%	3,6%
Cost-to-income ratio (Big 4 banks only)	11	66,2%	59,4%
No. of ATMs	12	NA	10 241
No. of on-line POS devices	13	NA	91 542
No. of Internet banking clients	14	0	1,1m
Insurance:			
No. of registered insurers	15	106	168
Assets to GDP (long-term and short-term)	16	65,7%	67,6%
Long-term insurers:			
Share in assets of top 3 insurers	17	71,5%	56,2%

Sources

1. SARB. Values for January 1994 and May 2004. www.resbank.co.za.
2. National Treasury. CPI is for the metropolitan areas. Percentage change calculated from annual average index values.
3. http://tips.easydata.co.za . The latest available data is for December 2002. The preceding years also had yearly data as at December of that year.
4. SARB and Banking Genesis www.bankinggenesis.co.za. The source data is for February of the corresponding years (i.e. 1994 and 2004). The assets are expressed in real terms (at constant 2000 prices), using February '94 and '04 indices.
5. SARB and Banking Genesis. www.bankinggenesis.co.za The source data is for February of the corresponding year (i.e. 1994 and 2004).
6. This figure refers to the number of active banking licences in 1994 and 2004. Source: SARB and Banking Genesis. www.bankinggenesis.co.za The source data is for February of the corresponding year (i.e. 1994 and 2004). The assets are expressed in real terms (at constant 2000 prices), using February '94 and '04 indices.
7. Combined total banking assets of Absa group, FirstRand group, Nedcor group and Standard Bank group over total assets of the banking sector. Barnard Jacobs Mellet (2003).
8. Combined retail deposits of Absa Group, FirstRand Group, Nedcor Group and Standard Bank over total retail deposits of the banking sector. Retail deposits defined as those of individuals, unincorporated businesses and non-profit organisations. Barnard Jacobs Mellet (2003).
9. Source of RoE data: Mike Gresty (Deutsche Bank).
10. Source of Net Interest Margin data: Mike Gresty (Deutsche Bank).
11. Based on the published results of the Big Four banks only, the cost-to-income ratio changed from 66,2 in 1994 to 60,0 in 2004. This is based on published operational expenses, interest and non-interest income, and excludes translation gains, merger costs and goodwill.
12–13. Barnard Jacobs Mellet (2003). Data for 1994 not available.
14. Moneyweb. (2004). 'ABSA, FNB tops in e-banking.' 29 January; and *Business Day*, 'Banks put a brave spin on reports of account hacking.' Available at: http://www.bday.co.za/bday/content/direct/1,3523,1446908-6078-0,00.html. Data for 1994 not available.
15–17. FSB *Annual Reports* for 1994 (data as at June 1995) and 2002 (data as at June 2003), the latest available. The 1994 report relates to the period July '94 to June '95 and similarly the 2002 report relates to the period July '02 to June '03. The assets are expressed in real terms (at constant 2000 prices), using June '95 and June '03 indices.

In essence, the statistics tell the story of a sector that has grown in size and volume, even thrived in some areas, in post-apartheid SA. Average profitability for the banking sector, measured by return on equity at least, has increased somewhat to 21%, supported in part by a fall in the cost-to-income ratio from 66% to 59%.

The structure of the sector has undergone some profound changes. In the mid-1990s, two important events accelerated the entry of foreign banks into a market previously insulated from external competition. One was the liberalisation of regulations for foreign-bank licensing in 1994. The other was the 'Big Bang' at the Johannesburg Stock Exchange in 1995, which allowed banks to own stockbroking firms. New players poached lucrative existing business in the corporate and high-end banking markets from the Big Four incumbents. The result was the decline in net interest margins, reflected in Table 1.2.

Pressures began to build and, in early 2002, the country's sixth-biggest retail bank, Saambou, faced a run by depositors. This was generated initially by concerns over mounting bad debts in its micro-lending operation. When the Finance Ministry refused to sanction liquidity support to the bank, it collapsed. In the contagion that followed, the fifth-biggest retail bank, BoE, one of the oldest in the country, was saved only by a direct government guarantee, although it was forced into a quick merger with a bigger bank. Following the crisis, many smaller banks found it impossible to raise wholesale deposits. Deriving no value from having banking licences, they handed them in. So, despite a sharp rise in the number of registered banks in the mid-to-late 1990s, there was a net decline in the number of banks over the decade. The high concentration of retail deposit-taking and other lines of business in the hands of the Big Four resumed.

The overall effect of margin squeeze on the banking sector—although largely in their corporate and wholesale business—cannot be underestimated. Figure 1.1 breaks down the impact on overall bank profitability, measured by return on assets. If banks had made their money only through intermediation (i.e. the lending margin), net profitability of the sector would have been 65% lower in 2004. Instead, the industry overall is marginally more profitable than it was in 1994. Figure 1.1 shows that the shortfall on intermediation has been compensated for by cost cutting (also reflected in the fall in the cost-to-income ratio in Table 1.2); and by increased non-interest (i.e. fee) revenue. The latter was achieved both by introducing new fee-earning products (such as Internet banking) and by increasing fees on existing products.

However, the factors that have insulated the profitability of the sector may not endure. In 1994, SA banks were far from international best-practice cost-to-income norms; but most of the bigger banks are now converging below the accepted 60% level. The substantial improvement implies that there is not much more fat to be cut. And the reliance on high fees limits the size of the market—and leaves the sector vulnerable to new-generation competitors with low-cost infrastructure. These factors will affect existing banks' participation in access developments in the next decade.

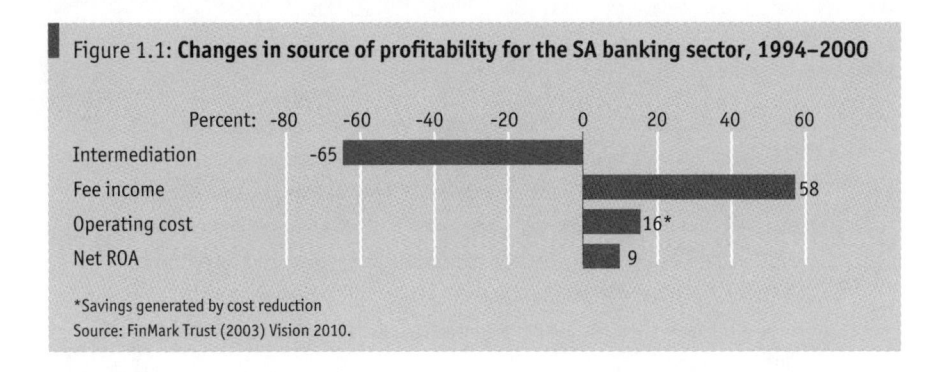

Figure 1.1: Changes in source of profitability for the SA banking sector, 1994–2000

	Percent
Intermediation	-65
Fee income	58
Operating cost	16*
Net ROA	9

*Savings generated by cost reduction
Source: FinMark Trust (2003) Vision 2010.

Definitions and measurements of access

The concept of broader access is easy to espouse but harder to define; and, without definition, it is difficult to monitor and measure. Access to a service is clearly not the same as usage of that service: for one thing, there may be people who have access but choose not to use a service. Usage cannot be forced on unwilling consumers, who will make their own decisions to use a product based on its value proposition once they have access to it. But access clearly has to go beyond theoretical availability of a product. *Effective* access has to take into account at least three dimensions:

- Geographic access: whether a consumer is near enough to a point of service, which depends more on cost—whether in travel time or expense—than distance alone;
- Affordability: whether a target consumer can reasonably afford a product; and
- Product features: whether conditions are attached to eligibility of clients or their use of the product which effectively rule out a particular group of consumers.

In the Charter, the definition of effective access was made even more specific within these three broad categories, as reflected in Box 1.3 on p.14.

Today, there are no accepted procedures in place to measure effective access, as defined above, other than the distance that can be measured using Geographic Information Systems (GIS) and census data. Most available data measures product usage. This means that, although the focus is on access, usage numbers will be reported throughout this book. Usage is, however, a proxy for effective access under certain conditions: after all, the real test of effective access is that people will want and be able to take up a product. Nonetheless, Charter monitoring will require measurement tools that are much more finely tuned than those that are currently available.

Two main data sources are used throughout this book to measure usage: first,

> **Box 1.3: Charter definition of effective access as agreed in October 2003**
>
> 2.22.1 being within a distance of 20 km to the nearest service point at which first-order retail financial services can be undertaken, and includes ATM and other origination points, except in the case of the products and services of the long-term assurance industry, where effective access, including physical access, will be in terms of the availability of these products and services, and in terms of proximity or accessibility of financial advisers to community-based infrastructure;
> 2.22.2 being within a distance of 20 km to the nearest accessible device at which an electronic (other than ATM) service can be undertaken;
> 2.22.3 a sufficiently wide range of first-order retail financial products and services to meet first-order market needs, which are aimed at, and are appropriate for, individuals who fall into the All Media & Products Survey (AMPS) categories of LSM1–5;
> 2.22.4 non-discriminatory practices;
> 2.22.5 appropriate and affordably priced products and services for effective take up by LSM1–5; and
> 2.22.6 structuring and describing financial products and services in a simple and easy to understand manner.

the All Media & Products Survey (AMPS), which is the only source of relatively time-consistent, high-level product usage figures; and, second, FinScope 2003, one of the most comprehensive national household surveys to date—exclusively on financial service needs and usage. FinScope, launched in 2003, provides depth of analysis of the current situation; while AMPS provides breadth of trend coverage but cannot do more. As FinScope is repeated, the depth of analysis will extend to trends over time. Because of the reliance on these sources, they are described more fully in Box 1.4.

The 'landscape of access' approach
This book tells the story of retail access following the 'landscape of access' approach developed by FinMark Trust. This approach divides retail financial services into four basic categories:
- *Transaction banking*: the service offered by banks which allows day-to-day transactions, in particular electronic payments to and from accounts; this category includes current accounts and most debit and ATM-card accounts;
- *Savings*: an external store of value for a client who intends to set aside money for a future purpose. This differs from transaction banking, in that usually savings accounts are not accessed for day-to-day purposes; included in this definition are common products such as bank savings accounts, unit trusts, pension and provident funds, endowment funds and

Box 1.4: **Data sources in this book**

AMPS (All Media & Products Survey) is the biannual large-scale survey managed by the SA Advertising Research Foundation but undertaken, on contract, by private market research agencies. AMPS interviews around 34 000 households and has done so since 1974. AMPS is the major source of longer-term trended data in SA. Its focus is on media and consumer product usage, with financial services only one component of a comprehensive questionnaire. The sampling base used is that of the University of South Africa's Bureau of Market Research (BMR). AMPS has developed the Living Standard Measure (LSM) as a basic market segmentation algorithm. This measure categorises a respondent into one of ten groups, based on observable characteristics, largely to do with durable goods ownership. These groups largely track household income but provide another view of the market. LSM1 people are overwhelmingly in rural, very poor households; whereas LSM10s are SA's urban elite. LSM1–5 are generally poor households by international standards, living on less than $2 per head per day; and this group is the focus of Charter access targets. For more information, see www.saarf.org.za.

FinScope is the national household survey of financial service needs and usage, developed by FinMark Trust. Following a pilot of 1 000 households in urban areas in 2002, the first national survey took place in mid-2003. A sample of 2 984 households was interviewed using a sample frame of 600 enumerator areas, drawn from the Census 2001 sample frame. FinScope is funded by a syndicate of institutions, currently coordinated and underwritten by FinMark Trust. FinScope is to become an annual benchmark survey. Weights are applied to survey results to generate national figures. As an example of precision for the sample size, where half of respondents responded to a question, the true result will be ±1.8% of the given answer, at a 95% confidence level. Linked to FinScope is the development of a Financial Summary Measure (FSM) based on factors related to financial service usage and profile, which is designed to complement LSMs in financial services. For more information, including the questionnaire used in 2003, see www.finscope.co.za.

even informal products such as stokvel or savings club membership. Note that the product category cuts across various types of providers: banks, insurers, fund managers and others all provide savings products;
- *Credit*: the provision of an amount of money to a borrower in return for future repayments; this is a very broad category which spans all forms of consumer credit, from mortgages to micro loans, with credit cards, hire purchase and retail credit in between; and
- *Insurance*: the provision of cover against a defined risk event or events in return for the payment of a premium. This category includes conventional products such as life insurance, funeral cover, short-term insurance and membership of informal quasi-insurers such as burial societies. Note that insurance companies do not offer only insurance—many offer savings products as well.

This landscape can be usefully summarised in a radar diagram, where each axis represents the proportion of adults using at least one product in each category. Figure 1.2 shows the landscape of access, based on AMPS numbers for 1994 and 2003 for the limited products available. Note that it does not show any numbers for credit, since reliable usage statistics are not available.

For context, in 2003 only, Figure 1.2 also shows the numbers from FinScope 2003 that are not directly comparable for various reasons. First, FinScope samples adults 18 years and older, whereas the AMPS universe is adults of 16 and older, where the larger denominator reduces the percentages. Second, FinScope numbers include informal product usage, such as burial society and stokvel membership, which are not included in AMPS. Third, FinScope product definitions are broader and more contemporary than AMPS in several respects—for example, PostBank accounts are included in FinScope banked numbers but not in AMPS banked numbers. At root, the two major surveys have different perspectives and objectives. But they yield headline results at a product level, which are broadly comparable, reinforcing the general conclusions.

Note that the credit usage statistics attributed to FinScope in Figure 1.2 are in fact drawn from the number of unique credit-active individuals in 2003, according to the country's largest credit bureau, TransUnion ITC. Since this would capture only formal credit usage, it may understate the credit usage figure.

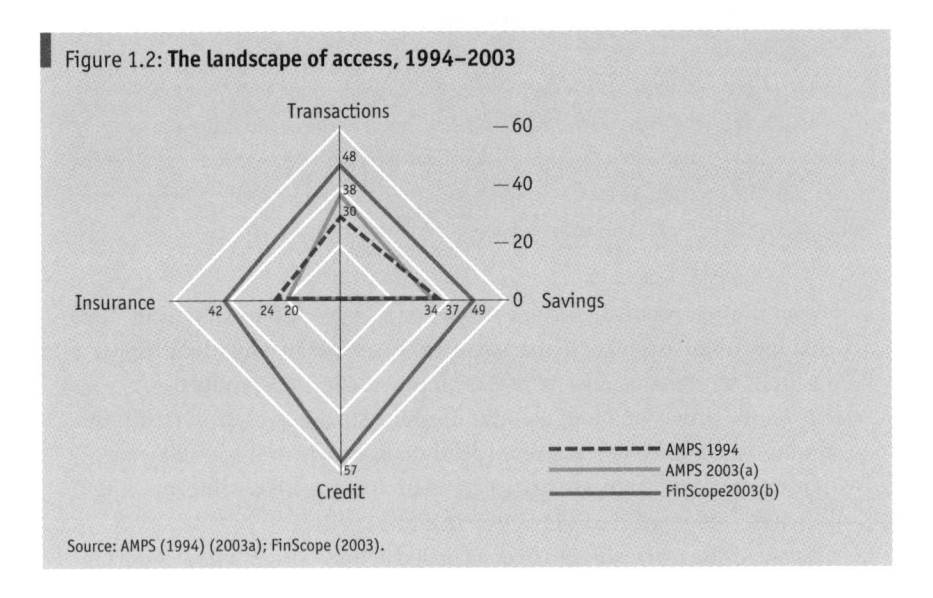

Figure 1.2: The landscape of access, 1994–2003

Transactions: 48, 38, 30
Insurance: 42, 24, 20
Savings: 34, 37, 49
Credit: 57

- - - - - AMPS 1994
———— AMPS 2003(a)
———— FinScope2003(b)

Source: AMPS (1994) (2003a); FinScope (2003).

The use of the landscape as a controlling image for the main story of this book is deliberate. It places the emphasis on the client view of retail financial markets, based on underlying needs, rather than on an organisational view that would focus on what each organisational type has done. Furthermore, the landscape directs attention to key questions of this book: how widely used is a product category? And, ultimately, how might the usage pattern (or shape of the diamond above) change over time?

Chapter outline

Each following chapter of the book addresses a different product category, or arm of the diagram above, starting from the top and moving clockwise around the grid. Because of its importance, both in the history of the past ten years and its strategic significance for the future, the broad category of 'credit' is split into sub-sectors: housing finance, SMME finance, and micro credit; these are discussed in three separate chapters.

The penultimate chapter deviates from the product-based emphasis. It considers the regional dimension: the increasing engagement in the South African Customs Union and the Southern African Development Community region by SA financial institutions, post-1994.

In each chapter, we attempt to benchmark the state of access, or at least of usage, in 1994, and compare it with the case in 2003. In this, we face data limitations. We knew much less about financial usage, let alone access, in 1994 than we do now; so 1994 figures are often inadequate or not fully comparable. But the relative abundance of more recent data helps at least to establish the benchmarks for the next decade. Using these benchmarks together with further analysis of what has happened in each sector, each chapter concludes with a view on the way forward for access in each area. Each chapter contains both boxes for factual material, which add to what is available in the body of the text; and case studies, which spotlight relevant examples of innovation, and give the views of the people responsible for them.

The final chapter seeks to draw together the threads of the various stories of change over the past ten years and look for common themes. These themes form the basis for last words about access to financial services beyond 2004.

Endnotes

1 See Calderon & Liu (2003).
2 For a good summary of empirical evidence of the effectiveness of micro finance, see Littlefield et al. (2003).
3 See for example, for the UK, HM Treasury (1999); and for the US, Berry (2004).
4 Presidency (2003, p.29).
5 MERG (1993, p.246).
6 Speech delivered at the Nedlac Financial Sector Summit, 20 August 2002.

CASE STUDY:
The Financial Sector Charter: behind the scenes

Kennedy Bungane

Jacko Maree

'If having a vote is proof of political citizenship, then access to financial services is an ID card, establishing economic citizenship,' says Kennedy Bungane. A director (BEE financing) at Standard Bank, Bungane represented the Association of Black Securities and Investment Professionals (Absip), the Black Business Council and other professional organisations in negotiations leading up to the Charter. He continues to represent them in his present capacity on the Charter Council, where he is responsible for reviewing progress towards Charter targets. Access is only one of six charter issues (see Box 1.2 on p.10), but it is one that Bungane sees as critical.

The charter process started formally at the Nedlac Financial Sector Summit in August 2002. 'From the industry point of view there were two catalysts,' says Jacko Maree, CE of Standard Bank and chairman of the Banking Council of SA through the 16 months of the negotiations. 'One was the Summit; the other was the debacle around the mining sector charter.' In the same month as the Nedlac summit, an early draft of the Mining Charter was leaked to the public. The financial markets reacted negatively to the news, wiping billions of rands off the value of mining shares in the days that followed. 'We wanted to avoid this situation and it was one of the reasons we decided to move proactively,' says Maree.

Government, too, took care to avoid a repetition. According to the *Financial Mail* (*FM*), the Department of Trade and Industry (DTI) abandoned a drafting process started months earlier, in consultation with the industry and in parallel with the mining charter.[1] The result of this shift in strategy in both private and public sectors was the FSC, a voluntary agreement negotiated between government and the private sector to promote BEE. The signatories are, on the one hand, the industry associations, including the Banking Council of SA, the Life Offices Association (LOA) of SA, the SA Short-Term Insurance Association (SAIA), the Association of Collective Investment Schemes, the Bond Exchange of SA, and the JSE Securities Exchange SA; and Absip on the other hand. Signed in October 2003 and implemented as from January 2004, the FSC sets targets, among other things, for expanding the spectrum of financial services available to the poor.

The process was painstaking and often painful. 'We took the Charter very seriously and the people we appointed to the task group were either at CE level or just below,' says Maree. 'Between August and the end of 2002, we met at 7.30 every Thursday morning. If I was abroad, I would phone in and get hooked up for the meetings.' Representatives from the banking sector were drawn from the four major banks (Absa, First National Bank, Nedcor and Standard), and also from Investec and African Bank Investments Limited (Abil). Over the weeks, the insurance industry, represented by the LOA and SAIA, was drawn into the process.

'In October [2002] we met Gill Marcus [then Reserve Bank Deputy Governor responsible for banking supervision] to report progress,' says Maree. 'We briefed the governor [Reserve Bank Governor Tito Mboweni] in December. And we met [Finance Minister] Trevor Manuel in January.' By that stage the financial services sector had completed a draft Charter.

Absip became involved in the process at the suggestion of the DTI, the department responsible for BEE strategy, says Bungane. 'The Minister (then Alec Erwin) felt we needed to have a black voice in Charter discussions,' he explains.

In November 2002, Absip hosted a black executives' consultative conference on the Charter. 'This *imbizo*[2] was well attended by a variety of senior people within the sector,' says Bungane. 'It defined key principles that Absip was going to spearhead in the negotiations. It was followed by "talks about talks", with the Banking Council and the LOA, and we found we all had parallel processes going. We realised they must converge and, in December 2002, we established rules of engagement.' The key trade associations involved in the sector met formally with Absip for the first time in February 2003 and started the process of merging the various versions of the draft charter.

'We met the Minister the following week and he impressed important principles on all of us: the importance of access to banking and the importance of human-resource development as key pillars to the FSC. He also impressed on us that we would not be allowed to play around with the stability and competitiveness of the sector,' says Bungane.

The sheer number of participants and the range of issues to be addressed complicated negotiations. 'There would be 30 or 40 people at a meeting and they wouldn't always be the same people,' says Maree. 'Meetings were massive and would go on for hours, without getting anywhere. At the same time, various task groups were gathering data on specific topics, so the process was unmanageable.'

An important milestone was reached in July 2003 with a two-day *bosberaad*[3] in Olwazini, in Muldersdrift, near Johannesburg. 'We arranged professional facilitators and we started to cut through the tangle, identifying points of agreement and of disagreement,' says Maree. 'The meeting was still large and unwieldy, so we decided to form a core group of people: three from industry and three from Absip.' On the industry side were Maree, LOA chairperson Peter Moyo, and SAIA director Adam Samie. Absip representatives were Bungane, Absip president Modise Motloba and Absip member Mutle Mogase.

The *FM* records that some of the most 'heated discussions' took place behind the scenes when representatives reported back to their own constituencies.

Lesetja Kganyago, then the Treasury deputy DG, attended core group meetings. 'He was not a negotiating party, he was an observer,' says Maree. 'But he also gave us valuable input about government's approach to BEE and so on.'

'With regard to access, there were a number of sticky issues, like: "how do you define access?"' says Bungane. 'We agreed that effective access must speak to affordability, geographic accessibility, as well as to service and products—which must not just be a cut and paste of existing products. Institutions have to consider why there isn't take-up of existing products.

'There was a huge debate around universal standards of access. We were very impressed with the well-defined standards in the telecoms industry. We wanted to develop similar standards to measure impact in the financial sector.'

In banking, the access debate centred on how to achieve critical mass quickly. Economies of scale are essential if a low-cost product is to be viable. In insurance, says Bungane, the debate related to broadening cover to the risks of living, 'from the existing narrow perception that all there is to give LSM1–5 is funeral cover'. In the case of collective investments: 'These have traditionally been positioned as a luxury reserved for those that have,' he says.

'We looked at whether financial literacy is part of access or part of corporate social investment. And if it is part of access, what constitutes promoting financial literacy? Is it distributing leaflets in Xhosa and Zulu and Tsonga? And then how do you measure the impact of that?'

However, Bungane is upbeat about progress: 'Even talk of a basic bank account is huge progress; it's a paradigm shift because banks are not just extending their current accounts; they are doing the account together. There is progress because we have been able to impress on government the need to re-look at regulations pertaining to second- and third-tier financial institutions—such as community banks and cooperatives.' (See Chapters 3 and 6.)

An important achievement, says Bungane, is that access has been placed within empowerment strategy. 'This underlines that BEE is not just about the transfer of shareholdings from white hands to black hands; it's about more. It's about bridging the divide between the first and second economies in this country. It's about setting up initiatives that would alleviate poverty, which is the biggest threat to democracy and stability.' ∎

Endnotes

1   24 October 2003.
2   A forum for enhancing dialogue and interaction.
3   Out-of-town meeting; literally 'council in the bush'.

Chapter 2

Transaction Banking

Introduction

Economic activity is driven by a multitude of day-to-day transactions. In terms of value, they are overwhelmingly electronic. But money from family is the major source of monthly income for over a quarter of SA households.[1] And most SA households still transact in cash. This means that the largest *volume* of transactions (mainly in small values) is in cash. Only households with salaried members receive most of their income via their bank account.

The heavy reliance on cash has effects at both the household level and at the macroeconomic level. Households are exposed to the risk that cash will be stolen or lost, and this risk is high in a society where over a third of the population report that they often or sometimes feel unsafe from crime in their own home.[2] For the economy as a whole, electronic transactions confer great benefits. A study by Global Insight shows that the savings created by substituting electronic payments for cash are as much as 1% of gross domestic product (GDP). A simulation of the US economy showed that a 10% shift of cash into deposits or similar reserves increased GDP by more than 1% a year.[3] And the benefits are not limited to consumer spending. Most retail savings and insurance products rely on the banking system to collect small investments and premiums cost-effectively. In this sense, transaction banking is the backbone of the whole financial sector.

Without access to this transactional capability, the poor cannot benefit from the efficiencies of an electronic payment system and are unable to become fully fledged participants in the economy. Although it is possible to have a relationship with a bank without having a transaction account, this applies to only a tiny minority of people. So, in this chapter and this book, 'banked' people are those with a transaction account of some type—whether it is a sophisticated product such as a current/chequing account, or a simple one such as the now widespread ATM-card-based account.

Ten years ago, ATM cards were not as widespread as they are today. The story of how card-based accounts spread to almost half the adult population is one of the more interesting financial service stories of the past ten years. In 2004, we also have the benefit of vastly better data on who is still unbanked and why.

Once again, in 2004, we are on the threshold of major changes. They will flow from a number of developments. One will be the cooperative solution, proposed under the Charter by the big banks, in the form of a basic bank account for poorer customers. Another driver will be competition from new technology, such as the growth of wireless communications, which challenges traditional boundaries of banking and creates new channels for products. And a third force for change will be legislation to encourage new entries to the sector.

So this sector promises to be one of continuing action in the decade ahead.

Who is unbanked and why?

Profile 1994–2004

AMPS data provides the only known consistent series of financial usage data on transaction banking over the past ten years (and longer). Even then, there are certain definitional problems. For example, the category of 'savings/transaction account' covers a wide range of account types. And 'transmission accounts', offered in 1994, have essentially been phased out as a product category. An 'ATM card' is not so much a product category as a channel to a range of banking products—from current accounts to home loans—via ATMs or Point of Sale (POS). But the predominant use made of an ATM card is to gain access to a transactional account, whatever other accounts may be linked to it. So an ATM card is a proxy for a wide class of transaction account usages. Figure 2.1 shows the AMPS numbers in key transaction-related usage categories. Figure 2.2 breaks them down into the main underlying categories.

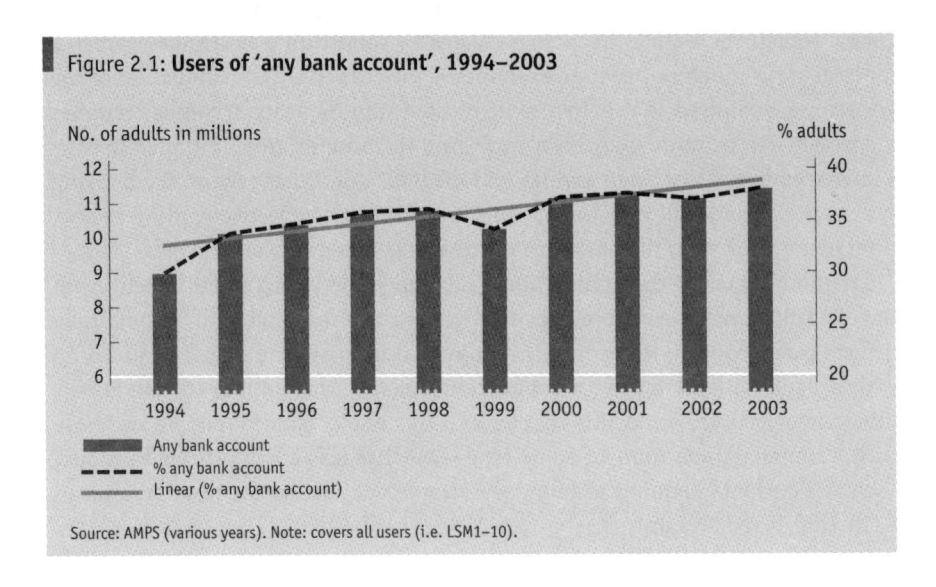

Figure 2.1: **Users of 'any bank account', 1994–2003**

Source: AMPS (various years). Note: covers all users (i.e. LSM1–10).

An interesting picture emerges. Figure 2.2 shows the retail market for high-end, transaction banking products, such as a current account or even a credit card (also used widely to transact) has been stagnant. In fact, it has even declined somewhat over the past ten years. However, as the trend line in Figure 2.1 illustrates, the number of people with any type of bank account has increased by over 3,6m or close to 50%—from some 7,8m to 11,4m today. Even allowing for population growth, the proportion of the adult population (16 years and older) with a bank account has increased quite substantially: from 26% to 38% today, according to AMPS.

AMPS numbers in fact undercount the banked—for one thing, they exclude

Figure 2.2: **Breakdown of users by product, 1994–2003**

No. of adults in millions

- Current account
- Credit card
- ATM card

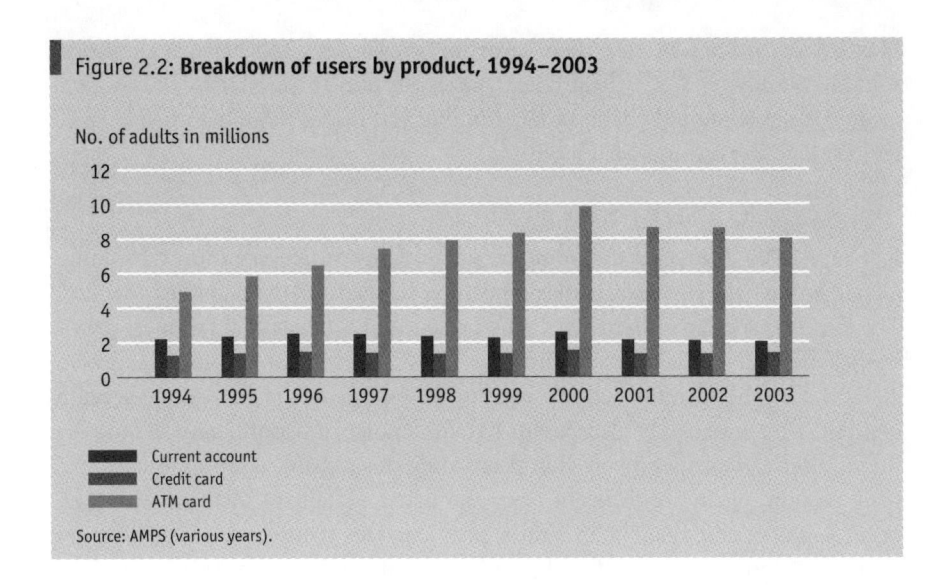

Source: AMPS (various years).

over a million PostBank customers. FinScope estimates the proportion of adults with bank accounts at 48%; but the FinScope population is based on adults of 18 and older. This excludes the 16- and 17-year-olds, who are less likely to be banked and therefore would pull the overall percentage downward. To compare, however, we may make the extreme assumption that none of this group has a bank account, which adds another two million people (aged 16 and 17 years) to the denominator. In that case, the FinScope proportion that is banked would fall by over three percentage points to 44,8%. The true number of the personally banked is therefore somewhere between the AMPS figure of 38% and the FinScope figure of 48%, depending on who and how you count. But, however you count, the headline finding is that the proportion of SA adults who are banked has increased dramatically from around a quarter in 1993. This has been one of the more remarkable changes in the financial services arena in the last ten years.

The change has been driven by the roll-out of new basic transaction accounts, mainly accessed by an ATM card, with the consequent decline of the book-based account. Today, FinScope estimates that almost 12m (90% of the banked) use ATM cards, whereas only 1,3m still use savings books, most of them PostBank customers. To put this in perspective, 20 years ago fewer than one million people reported having ATM cards.[4]

Today, most of the bank-issued ATM cards have graduated from being proprietary ATM cards, which could be used only at ATMs, to debit cards with international brands such as Mastercard Maestro or Visa Electron. This means that the cards can also be used to make purchases at the almost 100 000 POS devices in stores nationwide. However, FinScope results show that only a tiny minority (fewer than 6% of ATM card holders) use debit or credit cards to buy groceries regularly.[5]

Most ATM card holders use their cards for withdrawals and balance enquiries. And, at the low end, a typical client makes around three ATM withdrawals a month; has one monthly debit order running; and makes more than two balance enquiries on the account each month.[6]

Who is banked and who is unbanked?

FinScope 2003 segments the adult population into three significant banking-related groups: the currently banked, the never banked and the previously banked. The first two speak for themselves. The presence of a substantial group of previously banked people was first identified as significant in pilot FinScope surveys in 2002, and has been confirmed subsequently. It represents the almost one-seventh of adults who once had bank accounts but, for a range of reasons, have abandoned them. Clearly, the issues involved in persuading this unbanked group to take up a bank account again are different from the issues pertaining to those who have never had one; and as Table 2.1 shows, people in this group have a very different profile. The proportions (of the almost 27m adults in the country) in each of the three groups are shown in Figure 2.3.

Figure 2.3: **Banked and unbanked**

Previously banked
36%

Currently banked
51%

Never banked
13%

Source: FinScope 2003.

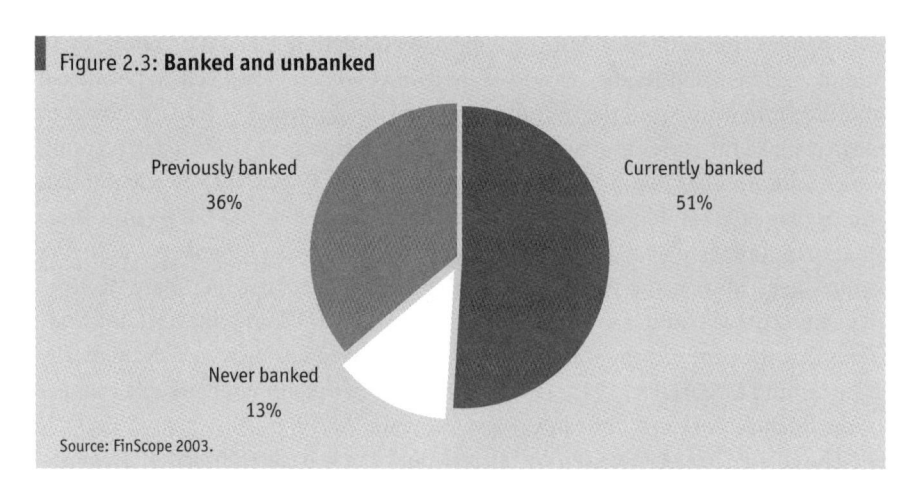

Table 2.1 shows the proportions across a variety of demographic and economic groupings: age, race, location, relative wealth and employment. In many ways, the results are not surprising, since they mirror SA's historical legacy of poverty and disadvantage. The currently banked are:

- Wealthier (almost four-fifths of LSM6–10 are banked);
- Urban (two-thirds of metro adults are banked, compared with only one-fifth of rural adults);
- Formally employed—85% of the banked are employed; and
- Older—a majority of the elderly (65+) are banked, but only a third of the much larger young group (18–24 years).

Table 2.1: **A profile of the banked and unbanked**

% are the percentage of each row who fall into one of the column categories

	Total no. of people	Currently banked	Previously banked	Never banked
Age				
Young (18–24)	5,4m	36%	4%	60%
25–65 years old	19,7m	55%	15%	30%
Old (65+)	1,8m	58%	24%	18%
Race				
Black	19,9m	43%	15%	42%
White	3,6m	94%	3%	3%
Coloured	2,5m	48%	18%	34%
Asian	0,9m	74%	12%	14%
Gender				
Male	13,5m	52%	15%	33%
Female	13,4m	50%	13%	37%
Location				
Urban metro	11,1m	64%	14%	22%
Rural	9,1m	31%	15%	54%
Living standard				
LSM1–5	17,4m	36%	17%	47%
LSM6–10	9,5m	79%	7%	14%
Employment status				
Employed—full-time	8,7m	85%	4%	11%
Informal sector	2m	40%	20%	40%
Unemployed	8,1m	17%	22%	61%

Source: FinScope 2003, Q2b

Perhaps more surprising (to some) are the following facts:
- Black clients currently make up the majority (60%) of the individual clients of the banking system;
- 40% of people who claim to be informally employed, and 16% of people who claim to be unemployed, have bank accounts; and
- Over a third of the poor (LSM1–5) are banked.

Why previously banked?

One SA adult in seven had a bank account at one stage, but no longer does. The reasons for this relate mainly to poverty (81% of the previously banked are LSM1–5) and unemployment, which affects nearly half of this group. In fact, over a third of the previously banked say they often or sometimes go without food, a proportion similar to that among the unbanked and a clear indicator of poverty. Abandonment therefore is not usually a voluntary or discretional closing of an account.

The hard-core 'never banked' group comprises almost 10m people. They are likely to be young (33%), black (88%), rural (52%), poor (LSM1–5: 86%) and unemployed (52%). However, 4,4m of the never banked belong to a household in which the household head is banked, so that, on a household basis, the proportion of the banked is higher still. Many of the never banked are young people whose parents have an account. However, they may be in geographically divided households, separated from the banked parent and therefore unable to make use of the family bank account. And many parents may not encourage this form of shared access anyway.

In addition, several categories of unbanked people (both previously and never banked) can be considered indirectly banked, to some extent, through several ways of using or sharing someone else's bank account:

- Almost 900 000 of the unbanked report actually using someone else's bank account.
- Two million of the unbanked belong to stokvels or burial societies, which have bank accounts in which to deposit the savings of the group.[7] However, the nature of these informal mechanisms is more akin to savings or insurance, as discussed later, than to offering members access to transaction facilities.

Finally, in another measure of 'closeness' to the banking system, almost a quarter of unbanked people report that their parents have or had a bank account. Whether or not this gives them any effective access, it does mean that they are not 'first generation' banking clients, which may make the transition to being banked easier.

FinScope 2003 probed the reasons given by unbanked people for not having bank accounts. The dominant reasons related to the absence of a regular or sufficient income (see Figure 2.4). Very few (3%) said that they did not need an

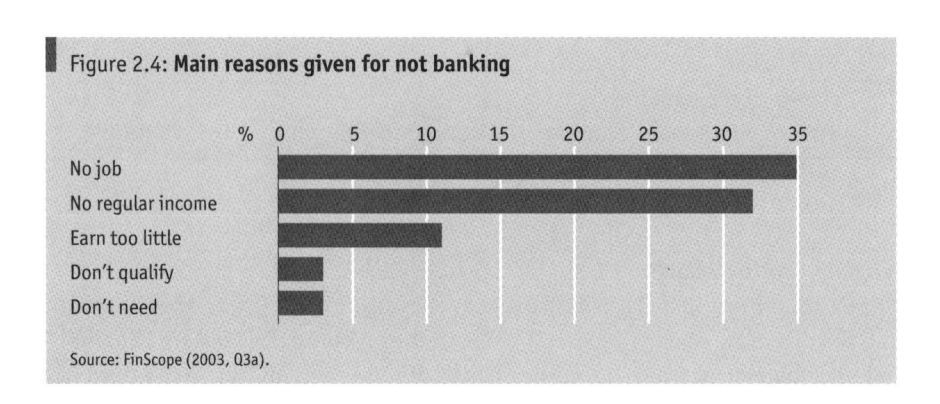

Figure 2.4: **Main reasons given for not banking**

Source: FinScope (2003, Q3a).

account. This suggests that unbanked people see a bank account as having value, if it were accessible to them. There were few who said that they were disqualified, other than by lack of income.

Table 2.1 demonstrates the close correlation of banked status with employment status. Both supply-side and demand-side influences have contributed to the correlation. Banks have historically targeted their accounts only at formally employed clients; in fact, some accounts require the client to produce a payslip as evidence of regular employment in order to open them. At the same time, consumers of banking services associate bank accounts with the payment of salaries. And when they lose a job, their need to have an account may fall away, as may their ability to maintain the required minimum balance or to service the monthly fees.

International benchmarks

Although the international data is quite patchy, and often not fully comparable, Table 2.2 shows that the current proportion of people banked in SA is comparable with middle-income, developing countries such as Mexico and Brazil. By some measures, SA is even a little ahead. The surprising pervasiveness of bank accounts is borne out in other ways: in the in-depth Financial Diaries of the Poor study currently under way,[8] for example, which finds that even poor households in a rural area are quite likely to be banked.

Table 2.2: **International data on banking**

Country	GDP per capita	% banked	Year of data
US	$35 200	78%	2003
UK	$23 920	91–94%	1999
Mexico	$6 150	37%	2003
Brazil	$2 910	43%	2003
SA	$2 590	48%	2003
Kenya	$360	6%	2002
Lesotho	$325	1%	2002

Sources:
US: Urban survey of 2000 people in three cities, 2003: Berry (2004). Household level: 91% (Federal Reserve Board (2003).
UK: Financial Services Authority (2000, p.21).
Mexico: Urban survey of 1 200 people in Mexico City, World Bank.
Brazil: Kumar (2003).
Kenya: Quoted in Porteous (2003e) from Kenyan sources.
Lesotho: Genesis (2004a), based on FinScope BNLS and supply-side numbers.
GDP per capita: All from Economist *Pocket World in Figures 2004*, except Lesotho (National Accounts 2002).

Remittances and social grant payments
Transaction bank accounts are the most important product type in the transaction space. However, another important aspect is the payment of remittances, including social grants. Flows of remittances from migrants in developed countries back to developing countries dwarf foreign-aid flows and are now second only to foreign direct investment.[9] Remittances, therefore, have a big impact on poor economies. Unlike many developing countries, SA is in fact a net remitting nation, with workers in SA sending money back to families in other African countries. However, remittances are a major issue in SA because of the pervasiveness of the state social-grant system.

A research report for FinMark Trust by Genesis called *African Family, African Money* investigated the options available for people to remit funds domestically to an unbanked recipient;[10] clearly if the recipient were banked, a deposit could be made across the counter of a bank directly into the recipient's account.

The report considers the formal and informal options available and in use. Among the formal products are postal orders and telegraphic transfers. In 2002, the SA Post Office introduced its PIN-Express product, which is similar to money transfer products provided by large international operators such as Western Union in other countries.[11] This product type relies on the allocation of a PIN number, communicated from remitter to recipient, which enables the recipient to withdraw the money at any Post Office branch. Informal mechanisms of remittance include sending money with friends or with taxi drivers on known routes. The costs to the sender also vary widely: to send R250 could cost from R11 for a simple postal order (sent by normal mail) to R21 for the PIN-Express product; and R29 if the postal order is sent by registered mail (as is advised). Costs in the informal market vary widely—from free to R20 and more to the taxi driver. Clearly, so do the risks.

FinScope numbers suggest that, after banks (this, of course, applies only where the recipient is banked), the most popular means of remitting money in SA today is via family and friends—around 10–12% of people use this method to send or receive money remotely. Of those who rely on family and friends, three quarters are unbanked. The Post Office is a distant second, used by only 5% of people; with taxi drivers a minority choice of 1% of the population.[12] The report concludes that 'The ability to transfer funds around the country is less of a constraint than is sometimes thought.'[13]

Today in SA, almost one-sixth of the population (more than eight million people) receive a monthly grant payment of some sort from the government, ranging from R160 (child care) to R700 (old-age pension). The number of recipients continues to grow rapidly, as the child care grant is extended in the face of the HIV/AIDS epidemic. The effective use of the welfare net is a key aspect of government's poverty alleviation agenda. Of the eight million or more recipients, over six million are paid in cash each month. Paying out to six million people, via 8 000 paypoints, across the country, many in rural areas, is a major logistical feat. It is carried out mainly by private-sector contractors Cash Paymaster Services (CPS), owned by Net1 Aplitec (linked to Nedbank) and AllPay, owned by Absa. They use innovative biometric technology to recognise the fingerprints of beneficiaries. At the estimated average cost to government of around R22 per payment per month, the payment of social grants is big business.

The critical question is, of course, why government should not persuade beneficiaries to open bank accounts to which it can make cost-effective electronic transfers. This has been done recently in the US and UK for grant beneficiaries. The cost savings to government can even be used to subsidise the costs of opening the bank accounts, if necessary.

A pilot of this sort is already under way in Gauteng with the Sekulula debit card, which gives access to an Absa bank account issued by AllPay (see **Social grant payments**, p.50). In 2003, the Eastern Cape Department of Social Development announced similar deals with First National Bank (FNB) and Standard Bank,[14] which allowed beneficiaries two free withdrawals a month. Government policy is to encourage this move to bank accounts. However, beneficiaries are not all prepared to open the accounts, even if they are effectively free.

The sheer size of the beneficiary group, and the fact that they receive a guaranteed monthly payment, make them an attractive segment within the unbanked group for banks to target. The creation of the new SA Social Security Agency, in 2004, to manage grant payments across all provinces should result in economies of scale and more cost-effective service across the country.

The growth of low-end transaction bank products

The growth in transaction accounts linked to ATM cards, which has brought millions of lower-income people into the banking system over the past decade, has been driven by strong forces largely on the supply side—banks and employers—rather than by customer demand. Indeed, as Table 2.3 on p.34 shows, many customers resent being forced to use new technology. The growth in card adoption has happened in several waves.

Traditionally, in SA, banks did not provide transaction services for low-income people: more than a decade ago, the majority of clients with ATM cards were white, according to AMPS. However, as the economy grew and became more complex, certain financial service needs were identified. Finding a cost-effective, formal mechanism for the transmission of funds to families of miners in rural areas, even beyond the borders of SA, was an important early driver in the mass provision of financial services in southern Africa. Specialist agencies such as Teba (since 2000 Teba Bank) were formed in part to undertake this key function (see **Teba Bank**, p.54).

Another development that brought banks into the mass market was the move by corporate clients, from the mid-1980s, to automate their payroll processes; and, in particular, to end the payment of cash wages to workers. Employers sought to reduce both their administration costs and the risk of crime. So they pushed large numbers of lower-income employees into the banking system to receive their salaries or wages. Initially, banks did not see this market as a profitable business opportunity. Even when technological advances, such as widespread ATM roll-out, reduced the cost of transacting, the profits were still not as good as those derived from other areas of activity. Just over a decade ago, low-income banking was typically a fringe activity undertaken on an experimental basis. Most notable among the experimental groups was Standard Bank's community banking division, formed in 1989 to explore ways of lending and transacting at the low end.

Box 2.1: **Chronology of key events**

1994	E Bank launched
	Community Bank launched
1995	People's Bank launched by Nedbank
1996	Community Bank closes; Absa launches Nu-Bank; E Bank absorbed into Standard Bank
2000	Absa buys majority stake in UniFer and merges it with its low-end Nu-Bank
2002	Failure of Saambou and Unibank
2003	Sekulula pilot launched in Gauteng

The first wave

The first wave of change in transaction banking began when Standard Bank made a focused and sustained move into the mass market, through the launch of a separate E Bank in 1994 (see **Standard Bank's E Plan**, p. 46). Focused around E Plan, a card-based transaction product with a savings pocket built in, E Bank grew fast in numbers of clients. This was due to the migration of existing customers from other products and also to new customer sign-up through dedicated Auto E centres. These limited-function branches did not handle cash across the counter but were sales and support outlets, where new clients were given hands-on training and support in the use of ATMs. This convenient provision of consumer education to unbanked clients was an important part of the take-up of E Plan. The essential business logic of E Plan was to make a small profit on each small transaction, and let the volume of transactions aggregate into a substantial bottom-line outcome. This logic had been borne out by 1998, and the success of E Plan attracted international low-end acclaim and attention, including from the World Bank,[15] as an example of innovation.

During those early days, other approaches were tried: Community Bank was launched in 1994 as a low-end full-service bank; but it packed up within less than two years (see **The Community Bank**, p.139). One reason for failure related to the supply-driven features of this era: successful transaction models were established by those (such as E Plan, Teba Bank and even CPS and AllPay in the social grant arena) with good relationships with paying entities: employers and government. These relationships brought the benefit of scale quite fast. Other transaction banking entities such as Community Bank or Unibank (which failed in 2002, having tried to introduce its own debit card) lacked these entrées and could not make headway in the mass retail arena.

The second wave
Apart from the large number of E Plan clients (today close to three million), the real significance of E Plan lay in its demonstration effect. After concerns about the negative bottom-line impact of poorer customers among banks at the start of the decade, E Plan proved that the low-income transaction market could be profitable. Consequently, other banks showed a greater interest in developing their offerings at the low end of the market.

This fight for competitive space characterised the second wave of change as other major banks essentially followed the E Plan example. Absa's Flexi Banking and FNB's Smartsave suite of products shared similar features: card-only account access, often with some savings or other features (such as funeral insurance) built in. Indeed, the emergence of bancassurance (banking/assurance) and the transition of micro lending from payroll collections to bank account collections increased the number of transactions per account, and thus the revenue potential of transaction banks. To the new customer, the convenience of electronic payment of accounts was part of the value proposition.

Competition for market share drove the sharp increase in ATM users in the mid-to-late 1990s. Most formally employed people are likely to have been offered bank accounts, at that time, often through their employer's banker; today, 85% of those who claim to be employed full-time have bank accounts.

State-owned banking institutions also played a role, albeit a minor one. PostBank has a suite of savings and transaction products, used by around 1,2m active customers, most of whom are black, and 40% of whom are rural. However, despite the undoubted potential of the countrywide network of over 2000 post offices for wider distribution of financial services, state strategy with respect to PostBank remains uncertain in 2004.

In developed countries, postal banks have tended to evolve into privatised banks, as in Nordic countries; or they have become competitive agency payment providers to a range of private-sector financial institutions, as in the UK and Australia. In developing countries, postal banks, many of which are corporatised, still tend to play a more basic role in savings mobilisation.[16] SA's model in this respect needs to be urgently clarified if PostBank is to play a major and constructive role in the next decade.

On a regional level, Ithala, the subsidiary of the provincial development corporation in the province of KwaZulu-Natal, started offering retail book-based savings products, focusing particularly on rural areas. Today, it has over 40 branches and well over 500 000 savings clients, who are now being offered card-based accounts.

No other state-owned institutions have provided retail transaction services over the decade. In this, SA is somewhat unusual among the ranks of otherwise similar developing countries, where state-owned banks play a much larger role. In Brazil, for example, the Caixa Econômica Federal (or Federal Savings Bank) alone has over 18m low-income customers. It has a widespread network of points of presence including, in 2003, some 2000 branches, 6000 ATMs and 2000 agents and some 9000 lottery outlets.[17] The Caixa's new card-based basic bank account product, called Conta Caixa, was designed to target the unbanked. In 2003 it attracted the attention of the BBC, which headlined its bulletin: 'In Brazil street dwellers have achieved victory in the fight against social exclusion—they can now have bank accounts.'

The third wave
In SA, the third wave of development around transaction banking started around 2001. At that point, the extensive growth that had taken place as employed people opened accounts had slowed. This tapering is reflected in AMPs figures, which show that the number of people with any bank account in 2003 was roughly the same as that in 2001. A negative trend had set in: customers abandoned their accounts (without closing them) and opened new accounts to which to divert their salaries. The phenomenon is known as account churn. Even though over 150 000 new accounts were opened each month in 2001, the number of dormant accounts increased by a third in the same period, with the result that the net number of low-end accounts stagnated from 2001.[18] The opening of new accounts and the dormancy of other accounts obviously add costs to the transaction banking system. This churn was attributed in large part to clients attempting to evade debit orders arranged to meet micro-lending and other commitments.

Despite the difficulties faced by big banks, the third wave was characterised by new entries at the low end. Teba Bank launched its general low-end bank product *Grow with Us* in 2002. Capitec Bank, built out of the consolidation of hundreds of micro-lending outlets, launched its own card-based transaction account in 2003 and today reports more than 18 000 customers. Driven in part by the advent of new technology such as wireless communications, which would reduce the cost of carrying out transactions, a number of other new entrants have begun to look at ways to enter the sector. They represent the early swells of the next wave of development.

The fourth wave?
After a decade of development, we stand on the brink of a fourth wave of innovation. The size and impact of this wave will be determined by the interplay between existing and new players; whether and how new players have access to the National

Payment System; and how the proposed basic bank account is implemented. It is essentially a new class of basic transaction account with restricted functionality and reduced fees (no monthly fee, and the same flat charges for transactions regardless of their bank). It will be offered by all major banks in an effort to meet Charter targets for banking the unbanked.

> Box 2.1: **The basic bank account**
>
> The basic bank account has been designed as the 'first order' bank account which meets the basic transaction and savings needs of the LSM1–5 group, who today are largely unbanked. Its design started following the Nedlac Financial Sector Summit in 2002, and has been undertaken largely by a task team composed of the Big Four banks, coordinated via the Banking Council. This follows experiences with the introduction of a basic bank account by UK banks and similar basic service in the US in recent years.
>
> It is essentially an account standard, rather than a product, under which each participating bank will make available its own branded low-end product. Although not finalised at the time of writing, the core features of the account which have been made public include the following:
> - Unlimited electronic transfers into the account (from employers or government as grant payer);
> - Cash withdrawals at any Saswitch ATM for a fixed fee, regardless of ATM;
> - One free monthly deposit, initially only at a point of presence of the originating bank;
> - No monthly fee;
> - A moderate minimum-balance-based interest rate structure; and
> - Discouragement of large account balances to prevent downward switching of more affluent customers.
>
> While the account will be introduced as a magstripe card-based product initially, the banks intend to allow for innovation in product offering and migration in line with the EMV smart-card debit standard and Home Affairs National Identification System (HANIS) card.

People's use of technology and attitudes towards it
Technology will undoubtedly play an important role in the fourth wave, as it has in the past. Expanded access to transaction banking in the '90s was driven largely by the roll-out of simple technology—the widespread issuing of magstripe ATM cards—and the phasing out of higher-cost manual methods of banking, such as transacting at counters with savings books.

How do banking consumers perceive this move to newer technology? The answer is that many do perceive it as a 'push' by the banks: according to FinScope 2003, 40% of SA adults agree that 'banks force you to use new technology'. However, a closer look at the FinScope results suggests that it is not technology per se that is the problem but rather how it is applied. Two-thirds of people, rich as well as poor, prefer face-to-face service to an ATM (see Table 2.3). There seems to be an antipathy to ATMs, which are seen as faceless, confusing machines. As many as a third of the elderly claim to avoid banking machines as much as possible.

However, almost three-quarters of poorer people (and 83% of richer people) say they are prepared to learn new technology. This is especially true among the young, who are the banking market of the future. The rapid uptake of cellphones across the population also indicates an ability to learn new technology if the benefits are substantial enough.

Table 2.3: **People's responses to new technology**

% are the percentage of each column category agreeing with the statement in each row

	LSM1–5	LSM6–10	Elderly (65+)	Young (18–24)	Black	White
Would rather deal face to face than with a machine	65,9%	63,9%	70,7%	58%	63,7%	61,3%
Avoid banking machines such as ATMs as much as possible	20%	13%	33%	10%	18,9%	14,1%
Prepared to learn to use new technology	72,6%	83,1%	45,4%	80,1%	75,5%	82%

Source: FinScope (2003, Q7b.7; Q26.21; Q7b.14).

Attitudes to banks
If banks are to succeed in bringing unbanked people into the banking system, these new clients must be prepared to trust them with their money. During the past decade, eight banks have been liquidated. Only state guarantees or direct intervention have prevented the loss of retail depositors' money. The country's largest retail bank failure to date, Saambou, affected several hundred thousand transaction-banking clients who at first had no access and then, for a while, only restricted access to their accounts. Even though no depositor lost money in the end, the message sent was that smaller banks are risky. This has consolidated the position of the large retail banks as being 'too large to fail'.

Meanwhile, plans for a deposit insurance scheme, which were developed several years ago, gather dust with the policy-makers. In the absence of a well-publicised national deposit insurance scheme, it will be very difficult for a new smaller bank to gain enough trust to become a major player in the retail deposit-taking business.

Despite the failures, the level of trust in the banks as a whole is surprisingly high. An overwhelming majority of people—rich, poor, black, white, young and old—would choose a bank as a place to keep a large sum of money, in preference to other options. In fact, Table 2.4 shows that poor people are more likely than rich to use a bank for this purpose. Hardly anyone (except 6% of the elderly) would use the proverbial 'money under the mattress' option. Furthermore, poorer people and black adults are less likely than richer people and white adults to agree with the statement that banks take advantage of poor people. Is this a case of reality and perception diverging?

It does not appear that trust in banks—large banks at least—will be an impediment to rolling out access. This gives SA an enormous advantage over countries where hyperinflation or mismanagement have caused serial bank failures—with serious consequences for public trust in the banking system.

Table 2.4: **Attitudes towards banks**

% are the percentage of each column who agree with or follow the row description

	LSM1–5	LSM6–10	Elderly (65+)	Young (18–24)	Black	White
Method to keep large sum of money—BANK	77,3%	64,3%	64,3%	74,7%	75,5%	82%
Method to keep large sum of money—MATTRESS	2,1%	1,1%	6,1%	1,9%	1,8%	1,8%
Banks take advantage of poor people—AGREE	24,3%	29,6%	29,2%	21,2%	24,4%	32,5%

Source: FinScope (2003, Q1, 7b.18).

The Financial Sector Charter and transactions access definitions

Among other access objectives, the Charter commits the banking sector to substantially increasing effective access to first-order retail financial services among poorer (LSM1–5) people, through appropriate and affordable physical and electronic infrastructure. Given the importance of transaction banking to the extension of other financial services, this area of Charter targets deserves special attention.

As Chapter 1 highlighted, defining access is not easy. Traditional definitions have focused on the geographic aspects only—such as measuring bank branches or even ATMs per 1 000 people. But, in an age when new technology is changing the definition of points of presence for banking services, geographic issues alone are not enough to measure access. Affordability and product features need to be considered as well. The Charter describes the transaction banking target for 2008 as effective access for 80% of people in LSM1–5. For achieving this, a bank will earn four of the 18 points allocated for the provision of financial services. Each of the access dimensions will be considered in turn.

Box 2.2: Charter target and current usage

	2008 target	2003 actual usage
% of LSM1–5 Effective access to transaction accounts	80%	32%

Source: Financial Sector Charter (2003, 8.3.1); FinScope (2003).

Geographic

Geographic measures of access are the traditional ones, and they are the easiest to monitor. Measurement is usually in terms of number of people per branch or ATM, or both, in a region (see Table 2.5). On these measures and if ATMs are included, SA compares quite well with countries in its upper-middle-income peer group, such as Mexico or even Malaysia. The monitoring of 'rural versus urban' ratios in developing countries led to policies that compelled banks to open, and keep open, rural branches, if they wished to develop an urban presence.

Table 2.5: Traditional geographic comparisons of access

Country	People/branch	People/branches and ATMs
Brazil	10 600	2 100
Mexico	10 300	3 500
Malaysia	10 700	4 100
SA	14 200	3 500
India	15 800	14 200
Nigeria	43 300	41 900
Kenya	135 600	85 100

Source: KPMG (2004).

However, these ratios do not take into account the impact of distance on bank clients. FinScope 2003 probed this area further. A majority of currently banked customers rely on public transport to get to the bank. However, given the nature of SA's urban system and the largely urban profile of the banked, almost all banked customers take less than an hour, most of them less than half an hour, to get to their bank. For the banked, distance per se is not an issue, although there is a cost associated with the use of transport.

Across the population as a whole (see Table 2.6) most rich people and almost half of urban people agree with the vague statement 'There is a bank nearby', where 'nearby' is subjectively defined. However, it is not true at all for rural people; nor for most black people. Hence, the geographic component of access remains an issue. But the problem of access is not going to be solved by building more bank branches or even installing more ATMs. The solution may lie elsewhere. Half the population, including 41% of unbanked people, are ten minutes or less from a grocery store. Since the store already handles cash, the way to create wider access appears to lie in harnessing and extending existing POS networks. This is starting to happen with FNB's widespread distribution of mini ATMs, which are in effect POS devices rather than traditional ATMs.

While transaction banking relies crucially on being able to access cash, it is also much more than this. Support is required, for instance when someone needs to replace a lost ATM card or query a failed payment. In these situations, distance from points of effective, helpful service matters: especially for the poor, since the time taken to address these issues may make the difference between being able to buy food and going hungry.

Table 2.6: **Banks and distance**

% agreeing with statement	LSM1–5	LSM6–10	Urban	Rural	Black	White
'There is a bank nearby'	16,4%	67,5%	48,7%	6,1%	21%	91%

Source: FinScope (2003, Q35a).

Affordability

Any definition of effective access must include a measure of affordability. However, bank account charges are complex and generally menu-driven across a wide range of possible transactions—which makes comparisons difficult. Moreover, there is the question of what would be a suitable benchmark of affordability relative to income.

Meaningful price comparisons, across products, require a banking version of the 'unit pricing' provided on grocery-store price labels. This involves identifying the typical 'transaction profile' of an average consumer in a particular segment, and costing the bundle of transactions—from cash withdrawals and deposits to statement requests. Fortunately, accurate data is available in SA on the transaction profile among low-end account users. This allows a comparison of the current average monthly costs across the main low-end offerings, which vary from as little as R13 a month to over R40. Weighted by number of current users across the products, the SA norm emerges: a typical low-end banked customer is paying around R34 a month for the services used. This is around 2% of the typical consumer's monthly salary.

Is this expensive or cheap for low-end customers, by international standards? The question turns out to be much harder to answer. A recent KPMG report, for FinMark Trust, which sought to compare the cost of banking across selected developing countries, found no credible transaction profile in these other markets. Hence, they had to apply the SA transaction profile to the costs of the services offered at the low end; i.e. this would be the average cost if clients in the country had a similar transaction profile to those in SA. It is clearly a large assumption but it does allow comparisons to be made. KPMG was unable to assemble weighted national averages, and relied on the published charges of selected leading banks in each country. These charges were converted at prevailing exchange rates—which may not reflect low-end purchasing parity. The results (see Table 2.7) must therefore be treated with some caution.

Table 2.7: **Costs of low-end transaction banking compared**

Country	Monthly cost (R)	Average blue-collar salary	% cost of banking
Brazil	R10,30	R1 320	0,8%
SA	R32,00	R2 000	1,6%
Mexico	R118,00	R4 416	2,7%
Malaysia	R9,55	R2 871	0,3%
India	R252,75	R1 548	16,3%
Kenya	R1 047,5	R1 691	32,4%

Source: KPMG (2004).

Clearly, the results for India and Kenya reflect the fact that SA's electronic transaction profile is still very expensive there, and this type of account is certainly not targeted at the low end of the market. On balance, Table 2.7 suggests that the average SA cost-to-salary ratio is not excessive by international norms. This is little cause for comfort, however. If banking is to move beyond the current, blue-collar worker profile in SA, fees—and therefore costs—need to be brought as low as possible.

Product features
In addition to geography and affordability, account opening and maintenance requirements also determine effective access. They are summarised in Table 2.8. In short, SA banks' requirements do not appear excessive relative to other developing

countries, although more accounts do require a minimum balance. In SA, the Financial Intelligence Centre Act (FICA) required third-party verification of physical address on all new bank accounts as from 30 June 2003 (and eventually will require the same on all existing accounts). This requirement, however desirable from a 'know your client' perspective, is totally unworkable for a low-income environment where addresses are not formal, hence cannot be verified short of site inspection. Although there is a low-end exemption, it is currently cumbersome to implement and monitor. To date, it has not been enforced by banks at the low end; and it now appears that requirement will be waived in favour of a more risk-based approach which recognises that low-end bank accounts, with limited transaction volumes, are not likely to be used by serious money launderers.

Table 2.8: Account-opening requirements compared

Country	SA	Brazil	Mexico	Nigeria	Kenya	Malaysia	India
Account opening							
Payslip required	3/10	Y	Y	Y	Y	Y	Y
Letter of reference	0/10	N	Y	Y	Y	Y	Y
Proof of residence	10/10	Y	Y	Y	N	N	Y
ID document	10/10	Y	Y	Y	Y	Y	Y
Minimum balance to open	10/10	N/A	N/A	N/A	N/A	NA	N/A
Account maintenance							
Monthly charge	7/10	N/A	N/A	N/A	N/A	N/A	N/A

Note for debit card-based products only
Source: KPMG (2004, p.23); SA: Genesis Analytics (2004).

The future: forces for change

This chapter has documented the forces that have widened access to transaction banking in SA over the past decade. Broader transaction access has created a platform for the expansion of access to other financial services, such as insurance or credit. There are several forces that will determine whether the transaction banking platform will widen further in the decade ahead.

Legislative obstacles and solutions

There are currently two major developments in the legislative and regulatory arena, which may have opposite effects on access and could perhaps cancel each other out.

The first includes new consumer protection regulation, which increases the cost of basic banking. It also includes legislation flowing from new international pressure to combat money laundering (known as AML) and terrorist financing (CTF). Domestically, the Financial Advisory and Intermediary Services (FAIS) Act seeks to protect consumers from unscrupulous or incompetent financial advisors. The Financial Intelligence Centre Act (FICA) addresses international AML and CTF concerns. Both are well-intentioned pieces of legislation with clear objectives. But both are likely to have perverse consequences because they increase the cost of compliance, and therefore of access, at the low end of the market. A paper by Genesis for FinMark Trust explores these obstacles comprehensively.[19] There is a strong public policy case for a well-crafted umbrella exemption for a class of low-end transaction accounts.

The second, countervailing development is the opening up of legislative space for new entrants to banking, and therefore to the National Payment System. The Dedicated Banks Bill, still in its drafting phase, allows for a new tier of restricted commercial banks. They will be allowed to take deposits and facilitate payments, but they will be limited in their ability to do high-end banking business, such as foreign-exchange or capital-market trading. Because these restrictions on business reduce the risk, this tier would have lower capital requirements than first-tier banks (currently it costs at least R250m to start a bank); and less intensive supervision. This tier should fit the needs of specialised low-end players, such as PostBank, Ithala and Teba Bank, some of which presently function under exemptions to the main Banks Act.

However, more important, it could also allow the entry of new-generation players, such as cellphone operators or retailers, to specific niches in the payment transaction arena. After all, cellphone companies are among the largest transaction switchers in the country today, using the currency of airtime; and retailers are the largest specialist cash handlers (with the ability to take and disburse money through a nationwide network) as part of their existing business.

In addition, following on from the Nedlac Declaration (see Box 1.1 on p.9), a form of Co-operative Banks Act is planned, which would create a new hierarchy of mutually owned banks. At the top of this hierarchy is the Mutual Banks Act, already on the statute books; at the bottom are the thousands of stokvels which are exempt from the Banks Act. The proposed new legislation would create a middle tier, which would allow informal groups such as stokvels and burial societies to formalise and become limited mutual banks. However, the resources needed to start serious co-operative banking, combined with the strong competition from established trusted brands and new entrants, will be a serious challenge to co-operative banking, which is unlikely to become a major force in the next decade.

Collaboration versus competition
New entrants at the low end of the market face additional competition from the proposed basic bank account (BBA) developed by the big banks. The BBA model is to some extent based on competitive models of accounts used for grant benefi-

ciaries, one of the largest groups of the currently unbanked. Basic account features will be standardised under one umbrella brand, but co-branded by the issuing bank. In many ways this is an attractive feature that will allow national marketing of these accounts to the unbanked. The elimination of monthly fixed charges is also significant in allowing a client to keep an account even if inactive.

However, some of the proposed restrictions, such as not allowing electronic payments from accounts, will limit the value proposition to clients since this undercuts the core purposes of a transaction account—to transfer funds safely and cost-effectively, or to pay insurance premiums or loan instalments easily. Even without this constraint, unless there is much wider geographic access to points of presence for cash back, it is unlikely that the BBA will prove an attractive proposition to the hard-core 'never banked'. After all, it is one thing to receive a grant payment into an account, rather than queuing to receive cash; but it is another to have to get to an ATM or branch to access the money, especially in a rural area. It is more likely that BBA may win back some of the previously banked, and even cannibalise some of banks' existing clients from higher-cost platforms—the banks' worst fear.

In many ways, the BBA is a hybrid competitive–collaborative model: it sets product features and pricing collaboratively while allowing individual bank brands to offer and service it. It also risks combining the worst of both worlds. It will be neither truly competitive, which reduces the incentives to individual banks to market it well, nor truly collaborative, so that getting agreement on changing product features in response to experience may be slow and cumbersome. A further consequence may be to crowd out innovation and new entry in the sector by defining 'reserve' prices for low-end banking which make it unattractive to those who truly wish to do this business.

The features of the BBA, due for launch by late 2004, are not yet final. The more the model becomes a broad umbrella framework to allow for evolution and innovation by different banks offering it, the more likely it will be to increase the percentage of the banked materially in the next decade.

Technology issues

The deployment of appropriate technology will reduce the cost of transacting in the next decade. Perhaps the most significant technological change of the past decade, at a household level, has been the roll-out of cellphones—from almost none in 1994 to well over 15m accounts today. In the next decade, it is likely that the effects of ubiquitous mobile deployment and cheaper bandwidth will have a substantial impact on issues of financial access. Almost as many people have cellphones as have bank accounts; and they will increasingly use them as transacting tools for more than simply buying airtime. Cellphone banking is still cumbersome and is currently used by very few people. But its ease and functionality are likely to increase.

In fact, World Bank analysts have suggested that mobile commerce, and electronic finance generally, are close to take-off in developing countries, as connectivity levels and reliability increase.[20] They predict that this trend will allow developing countries to leapfrog in the development of their financial systems. For SA, 2006 is projected as take-off year for on-line banking. Already, mobile commerce platform operator Simplus reports over two million mobile commerce transactions a year, worth R1,2bn. These are mainly used to recharge airtime on GSM payphones through a Mastercard product. However, Simplus plans to extend this platform in 2004 to allow for prepaid electricity purchase. As the functionality increases, so the likelihood of takeoff grows.[21]

Table 2.9: **Cellphone vs landline access and usage**

% are the percentage of each column group described by the feature named in the row

	Total	LSM1–5	LSM6–10	Elderly (65+)	Young (18–25)	Banked	Unbanked
Access to cellphone	10,04m	23%	63%	23%	46%	53%	20,5%
Telkom phone at home	5,02m	6%	43%	40%	15%	27%	9,7%

Source: FinScope (2003, Q29).

The significance of cellphones is that they are a channel of access to on-line banking for a much larger group of people than will ever have computers and Internet access. A fifth to a quarter of 'never banked' people already have cellphones, as shown in Table 2.9. Penetration is much higher among the young, of whom a much higher proportion is unbanked. 'Business models for the delivery of banking services, via cellphone, will use the smart card (SIM card) functionality built into the cellphone for financial transactions,' says a recent Genesis Analytics report (2004a). 'Cellphone users will therefore be able to make electronic fund transfers and conduct other non-cash financial transactions from their cellphones. Cash transactions can be undertaken on a person-to-person (P2P) basis …'

This P2P functionality is a major part of the appeal of cellphone banking. Already, products that allow P2P transfer of airtime minutes are available from the cellular networks. But the Banks Act restricts them from cashing out the airtime in currency because it would amount to banking. However, the functionality exists. And with the change in banking law, which will enable direct access of new types of banks to the National Payment System, cellular operators may easily become real competitors in the payment space.

Point of Sale devices

Even under the most optimistic network projections, not everyone will have a cellphone by 2014. And, even among those who do, there will still be a need for cash. Hence, the expansion of the POS network—those places where a customer can use his or her debit card to pay for a transaction or to get cash back—is critical. Today POS devices are relatively expensive for the merchant to rent (over R300 a month), and require a fixed phone line to the bank to get electronic authorisation. However, a new generation of wireless POS devices is being deployed. These have multiple functionality (including airtime sales) and therefore generate more revenue for the merchant, at lower cost. This new technology will allow devices to be deployed much more widely. It is conceivable that even highly accessible corner spaza shops in township areas could be connected in years to come.

Today, retail POS devices provide cash back only on a limited basis—for example, through Pick 'n Pay tills for GoBanking/Nedbank customers. Negotiations have been under way for a while in the banking sector to create a generalised cashback system, where any debit card client could withdraw cash at any merchant. The constraint is more a business than a technology issue, since it involves agreeing on a fee-sharing arrangement between banks and retailers. Agreement is likely by the end of 2004. Once this happens, the points of cash access will expand from some 2 700 branches and 9 000 ATMs, to include close to 100 000 on-line POS devices.

Already, FNB is rolling out its mini ATMs, which are essentially POS devices, to a wide new range of merchants. Cell network operator MTN launched its Mobile Credit product in 2003, essentially allowing credit card authorisation via a cellphone rather than a point of sale, at half the monthly cost.

At the same time, both the government and the private sector have invested heavily in systems and infrastructure to promote the usage of smart card technology. HANIS (Home Affairs National Identification System) is likely to move to the implementation stage within the next 24 months. The EMV (Europay, Mastercard, Visa) project, on the other hand, is already in an advanced stage of implementation. This private-sector-driven project aims to ensure inter-operability between chip cards and terminals, globally, regardless of the manufacturer, the financial institution, or the infrastructure the card is used on.

The way forward

The past decade has seen great progress in extending access to transaction banking. In the decade ahead, new technology and new laws hold out the prospect of continued progress. If these changes are to benefit people other than those who are already banked, through lower fees and more convenient service, there must be a quantum leap in the concept of what a bank account is and what it offers.

For many low-income people, a bank account is simply a point where salary is received and from which it can be withdrawn via ATMs. If the value proposition of a bank account is expanded to include widespread ability to transfer electronically and transact with other people, then rapid uptake is possible. Network effects would drive further acceleration. As with cellphones: the more people who have accounts, the more useful the accounts are. This uptake would be demand-driven, as it has been with cellphones. Approaches that are supply-driven, such as the move to salary payment accounts, will no longer ensure that the unbanked are reached. Even in the area of grant payments, it is not clear that beneficiaries will opt for the bank accounts on offer.

Because of the network effects, basic collaboration is necessary to ensure that customers can transact across banks and the ATM network. But a clear lesson of the past decade is that competitive forces make the most impact; when one player demonstrates a viable model, others follow. Collaborative approaches in this sector have not had a good track record, as other chapters will show. Provided the legislative environment allows suitable new parties access, the next wave of development in transaction banking is unlikely to be led by existing banks. Big banks are likely to follow and replicate successful models—with cost structures that make it possible to achieve effective access—over time. This form of competition, from those who are not even Charter signatories, may create a favourable environment for reaching Charter targets of 80% effective access, in the fullest sense of the definition, by 2008.

Government has a key role to play in facilitating and ensuring the interoperability of payment systems, to get the most benefit out of network effects. Government's leverage comes through its control over the payment stream of a critical mass of unbanked clients—social grant recipients. This could determine the adoption of one approach or standard over another, such as in the HANIS national identification card environment.

The impact of all these changes on access to transaction banking is uncertain. One thing is certain, however: that the high levels of innovation seen in the transactions and payments environment will continue well into the coming decade.

Endnotes

1 FinScope (2003, Q.22–25).
2 FinScope (2003, Q.60.2).
3 Visa (2003).
4 AMPS (1984).
5 FinScope (2003, Q.31.3).
6 Deloitte (2003).
7 FinScope (2003, Q2b, 8a, 9a).
8 For more information on this 18-month-long project, see SALDRU website: www.saldru.org.za.
9 Wimaladharma et al. (2004).

10 Genesis Analytics (2003f).
11 Western Union SA's franchisee was closed down in 2001 after six years of operation (Genesis Analytics, 2003d, pp.50–51).
12 FinScope (2003 Q.28).
13 Genesis Analytics (2003a, p.iv).
14 Khuzwayo (2003).
15 Paulson & McAndrews (1998).
16 Seward (2002).
17 Interviews with Caixa officials, October 2003.
18 Deloitte (2003).
19 Genesis Analytics (2003g).
20 Claessens et al. (2001).
21 *Intelligence* (January 2004).

| CASE STUDY

Standard Bank's E Plan: the first wave

In the early 1990s, most major banks were seeking viable ways to enter the mass market. 'There was no successful low-income model at the time,' says Standard Bank director (mass markets) Lincoln Mali. 'But bankers recognised that other segments of the market were overtraded and everyone was looking for new revenue streams.'

Lincoln Mali

Standard Bank was the first to make a determined and sustained attempt to enter the mass market. It established a subsidiary, E Bank, in 1994, under former Perm MD Bob Tucker. E Bank offered an electronic transaction and saving product, E Plan, through special service sites. The role of a supportive environment was considered critical, so an important element of the proposition was that E Bank branch sites were conveniently located for mass-market customers and designed for people unfamiliar with traditional banking. There were no tellers, but accounts could be opened and cards issued instantly. Screens on ATM terminals at the outlets were tailored to the product, which made them very simple to navigate.

Assistance was available from staff, people recruited on the basis of their ability to communicate. 'Because they had to handle only one product they didn't have to learn 22 volumes of rules and regulations that made up the "Standing Instructions to Officers",' says Mali. 'We could place emphasis on people skills and select those who were able to assist and educate clients in their own languages and who came from the very communities we wanted to serve.'

E Plan was a fully functional offering from the beginning and combined transactions and savings in one account, through a dual 'purse' facility. 'When we started, the minimum account balance was R10 and interest rates were linked to the six-month-term deposit rate, which was a very good rate for funds that were not on fixed deposit,' says Mali.

Money in the cash 'purse' could be withdrawn on demand, at any ATM countrywide, and the account could also be used as an electronic payment mechanism and to transfer funds to other accounts when required. Money in the savings 'purse' could, however, only be withdrawn through the intervention of a consultant.

Other benefits were included in the account. 'E Plan offered a R1000 death benefit to next-of-kin, which was revolutionary at the time. That was good value because it would have cost customers more to buy the benefit from an insurer. And we could buy it in bulk so it was reasonably inexpensive for us,' says Mali.

In 1996, when E Bank had 69 outlets and 400 000 customers, Standard Bank decided to incorporate the subsidiary into the parent company, under the parent brand. This was, among other reasons, because the E Bank brand was so popular it had become 'a positioning challenge' for the mother brand in that market sector.

The incorporation involved certain trade-offs. It gave E Bank customers the convenience of a vastly expanded network of outlets. They could open accounts at designated branches and, at a price, conduct over-the-counter transactions. For the bank, the pooling of the parent's 650 000 low-income clients with the newly absorbed E Bank clients brought the client base close to one million, creating economies of scale. The incorporation exposed clients to the more detailed requirements of conventional banking such as a more complicated account-opening process, but this created the opportunity to cross-sell products. However, a major challenge was the loss of simplicity. The specially tailored screens had to be sacrificed and E Bank customers had to contend with the more complex interface of the standardised ATM screen. Staff was recruited more broadly from the branch network, which led to a loss of the carefully nurtured E Bank culture and the specialised people-orientated skills in the E Bank outlets.

Once the original outlets were rebranded to become AutoBank E outlets, new sites were rolled out. 'By 2000, there were 110, equally divided between rural and urban areas,' says Mali.

However, the bank was still on a learning curve. While it attracted a steady stream of new clients, much of the growth was offset by account closures. 'We had accounts with zero balances or no activity. And, though we were getting 60 000 to 70 000 new accounts a month, we were closing a substantial number through our dormancy processes,' says Mali.

Standard's Charles Chemel, who took over E Plan after the incorporation into Standard Bank, made the controversial decision in 1998 to start charging a R2,50 monthly management fee, in addition to the normal transaction fees. 'This brought additional revenue and immediately changed the economics of the product,' says Chemel. 'It proved that low-income business could be profitable. This was particularly important when the volume of transactions per account was low, though less so when transactions increased. The management fee also moved no-transaction, low-balance accounts to a zero balance more quickly, accelerating the elimination of the dormant accounts. The advantage to the bank was that the "figures" presented a more realistic picture of their active account base.'

'Because our business is low-margin, the challenge is to encourage customers to use their accounts more,' says Mali. He says that the bank has been successful in getting people to make ATM withdrawals but less so in getting them to make ATM deposits or to use the payment mechanisms such as cellphone top-ups and Maestro purchases. From both the bank's and the client's viewpoint, an account should be used at least four times a month, to make it worthwhile, according to Mali.

The original E Plan product structure has remained core to the bank's customer proposition but certain features were changed over time, as the bank became more familiar with the growing needs of its customers. For instance, the death benefit was enhanced in 1998 to a two-tier benefit, based on how the account was used by the holder. Next-of-kin can now get quick access to funds of up to R2 700 for funeral arrangements. 'This probably pays for about 60% of basic funeral costs,' says Mali.

Between 1998 and 2003, the number of E Plan accounts more than doubled, says Mali. Balances grew 123% and total revenue by 133%. Of Standard Bank's seven million customers today, 2,9m are on E Plan. If businesses are excluded from the total, E Plan accounts represent 65% of the bank's transactional client base. And its active E Plan base is growing at about 13% a year. Though E Plan was designed for the low-income market, it caters for anyone who wants a simple bank account. 'While we have a few high-value accounts, if you take out those accounts with R10 000 or more, the average balance is R630,' says Mali.

There are now 149 AutoBank E outlets offering an extended product range. Mali says ATM volumes currently exceed 8 500 transactions per machine per month in AutoBank E outlets. And more than 90% of all E Plan transactions are electronic.

Mali says the way forward for Standard Bank is to recognise that the mass market is not 'a homogeneous entity but one that is multidimensional. By understanding the various subsectors better we can develop more appropriate products and services for them.'

In 1998, the World Bank published a paper on the experiences of E Plan,[1] written by Jo Ann Paulson of the World Bank and James McAndrews of the US Federal Reserve Bank of Philadelphia and New York.

'We chose to document the E Plan programme because it demonstrates how a commercial bank used market information to bundle services for low income clients,' the paper said.

> The most notable feature of E Plan, and perhaps its most important lesson in providing basic banking services, has been the focus on demand enhancement. By rethinking the needs of the basic banking customer, i.e. the demand side, a new product emerged that has proven to be valuable to the low income consumer, while providing a way to lower the costs of offering the service. The experiment has shown that even low-balance customers can be profitable for banks. That lesson should be transferable to other experiments in providing basic financial services for the poor.

E Plan is an example of successful innovation. Once this pioneering initiative had proved that the low-income market could be profitable, other institutions showed a greater interest in that market and made more focused attempts to enter it. The range of low-end transaction accounts available today is proof of the demonstration effect of E Plan—the first wave.■

Endnote

1   Paulson & McAndrews (1998).

CASE STUDY: Sekulula

Social grant payments: 'It's easy now'

Gerry Rees, chief director of Social Security in the Gauteng provincial government, recalls touring pension pay points when he took over Gauteng operations in 1996 and seeing 'planks placed on top of piles of bank notes to stop the wind blowing them away'. This ramshackle front end of the delivery system mirrored the chaos behind the scenes.

Procedures were time-consuming and costly. Cash-in-transit vans were an easy target for armed robbery. On site, the pay-out process was haphazard and vulnerable to theft by dispensing officials. And inaccurate records and poor financial management undermined attempts to calculate cash needs at each pay point correctly. So pensioners who had queued for many hours were often exposed to the final frustration of getting to the paymaster, only to find that the kitty was bare.

In 1996, a central register of recipients was established nationally, and provinces took responsibility for delivering the grants. Since then, the system for paying pensions and other social grants has been transformed. Though not perfect, national pension payout initiatives have benefited in many provinces from the deployment of state-of-the-art technology and innovative thinking. In the mid-to-late 1990s, management tenders to undertake payouts were outsourced to private-sector firms, the largest of which were Cash Paymaster Services (CPS) (now owned by smart-card company Aplitec and, indirectly through Aplitec, by major banking group Nedcor) and Absa subsidiary AllPay.

'In Gauteng, the social grant project was put out to tender in 1996,' says Rees. The Gauteng tender board chose CPS, an early entrant to the business of disbursing cash to pay points. CPS biometrically enrolled the 270 000 beneficiaries who collected money at the cash pay points. 'Over three years the situation improved dramatically,' says Rees. 'Pay points were within 10 km of bus and taxi routes. The number of pay days had been increased to relieve pressure on pay points. There was an appointment method which cut queuing, and CPS introduced other elements that generally improved services for beneficiaries.'

When the CPS contract expired at the end of 1999 the project was again put out to tender. 'The tender specifications were different because they included taking over payments carried out by the Post Office,' says Rees. 'Absa and its subsidiary AllPay won the tender. One of its advantages was that the biometric fingerprint verification system was encrypted on a smart card.' Also encrypted on the smart card were the beneficiary's photograph and personal data.

AllPay MD Dirk Kotze explains:

> When a recipient enrols in our system, we capture his or her personal data, a photograph and four fingerprints. We choose the fingers where the

minutiae—the unique reference points—are clearest, and these images are stored on a microchip. When the beneficiary gets to the pay unit, he gives his card to the paymaster, who pushes it into the card reader. The system selects the finger the beneficiary must present; the finger is put on a fingerprint reader where the minutiae are verified. Recognition triggers a cash payment, which is dispensed, along with a receipt that shows the place, date and time of payment. If there are no problems, the transaction from card-in to money-out takes 20 seconds.

The information collected at the pay point is uploaded to AllPay's website so AllPay and Gauteng managers can draw on it. The cost to government of the entire operation is R24 per pensioner a month.

Grant payouts are clearly a growth industry. 'When AllPay took over we had 360 000 beneficiaries,' says Rees. 'Today we have over one million. We have gone from 2 000 new applications a month to 20 000.' At the same time, child support grants, introduced in 1998/9, are burgeoning, with numbers of beneficiaries paid via AllPay growing from 93 000 at the end of March 2001, to about 410 000 by the end of March 2004.

'We realised we must find a way to meet this challenge, and the Sekulula card was born,' says Rees. Sekulula, which roughly translates as 'it's easy now', was launched in August 2003. It is a fully fledged banking product, designed primarily to support payment of the 533 000 recipients of the child support grant. But it has improved service to the 250 000 pensioners and 160 000 people drawing disability payments as well. Beneficiaries are given the option of receiving a cash payment or opening a Sekulula bank account at no cost. Clients can access their funds 24 hours a day, seven days a week, at an ATM or POS device.

'No minimum balance is needed and people are entitled to two free ATM withdrawals each month or, alternatively, two POS transactions free a month, if the vendor is on the Absa banking network,' says Kotze. 'It is possible to make a purchase and draw cash from the vendor in one transaction.'

The finger is put on a fingerprint reader

Cash pay points are more 'user friendly'
Photos: Roland Pearson

By the end of July 2004, Sekulula had grown to 160 000 account holders. By June it was taking up an average of 30 000 new users a month. 'AllPay's target is 250 000 Sekulula account users by November 2004', says Kotze.

Kotze says another innovation is a 'remote opening kit or mobile suitcase with an embedded PC, scanner, PIN selector and printer. We can take that suitcase anywhere and it will allow a person to apply to open an account and file all the information the bank needs. A beneficiary immediately qualifies for the bank account and we can issue a debit card on site and, the next day, the beneficiary can access the money.' The remote opening of accounts is outsourced to a BEE company, Bhenka Financial Services.

Sekulula has cut pension pay-out costs for government from R24 at the cash pay point to R15 for a Sekulula bank debit-card-based service.

'Businesses now perceive that beneficiaries are an opportunity,' says Rees. 'If you get the numbers, you can make money out of serving them.' The pay points are an invaluable point of contact with the recipients of social security and social welfare, which will assist banks in expanding their distribution network to meet the Charter targets. And the technology evolved to meet social needs has the potential to further extend financial penetration to low-income families.

First National Bank (FNB) is involved in a similar initiative in the Eastern Cape. It pays 75 000 social grant recipients through its Social Grant Payment product, which is based on two cards. 'One operates at branch level, and has been tailor-made for those who are unfamiliar with or unable to safely operate a PIN-based account,' says FNB Self Service Channel CEO Mike Arnold. 'And the other is an ATM card for those customers who feel comfortable with an ATM.' The first two customer-initiated withdrawals are free and the client does not need an opening balance. Government pays FNB R14,50 a client. Arnold says FNB has installed 234 mini ATMs in retail outlets in the Eastern Cape, to expand its representation in remote rural areas.

Innovative solutions to social grant payments are a useful point of departure for banks attempting to meet their Financial Sector Charter targets. In 2004, more than eight million people receive a monthly grant from government nationally. Of the eight million, fewer than 1,5m receive their grants directly into their bank account. Most of the rest are paid out in cash, at some 8000 pay points across the country—a fertile field for banks hoping to grow their customer base.

A new dispensation is at hand. Under the Social Security Act, which came into force on 1 April 2004, responsibility for all social payments is to pass to the SA Social Security Agency, funded and controlled at national level. It will rationalise the range of different services in each province. The payment approach it adopts will have a critical impact on inter-operability standards for bank cards. About 18% of social grant beneficiaries now receive their grants through a bank account; the department targets at least 50% by 2008.

The private sector's basic bank account (described in Chapter 2) will be adapted to accommodate grant payments.

Roland Pearson is a consultant who currently advises the Department of Social Development at national level on social grant payment strategies. He says the Sekulula project could offer lessons for various types of government-to-person transactions in other emerging markets. 'It is a good example of using leapfrogging technologies to promote social development.' ■

CASE STUDY
Teba Bank: mining the rural areas

Jenny Hoffmann

Teba Bank is a recent entrant to banking, but it has a long history. Teba Ltd, the recruitment arm of the mining industry, founded in 1912, set up the Teba Savings Fund in 1976. It acted as paymaster to the gold and platinum mines, paying mine pensioners and dependants in rural areas and transferring miners' deferred pay to other parts of southern Africa. In 1983 it became a separate company, finally evolving into a bank, registered by the SA Reserve Bank in 2000. In the same year, it added 10 new rural branches to its mining outlets. Its sole shareholder is a trust, jointly controlled by employers in the mining industry (through the Chamber of Mines) and mining employees (through the National Union of Mineworkers).

Teba Bank has a developmental mandate and operates principally in the rural areas and small towns of southern Africa. About 80% of its clients are in the LSM1–5 band, earning about R770 to R2 195, says CE Jenny Hoffmann. Teba Bank mainly serves low-income employees in the mining industry and their dependants. However, it is expanding into markets outside the mining industry, focusing on small towns and rural areas where the need is greatest. 'Three-quarters of our clients are still from the mining industry, but we have about 100 000 clients who are outside it,' says Hoffmann.

Because of its origins as a payment mechanism, Teba Bank has a relatively large deposit base (R1,25bn in February 2004), but the credit side of the balance sheet is small (R195m). 'We invest our depositors' money largely in the money market and the margins are small,' says Hoffmann, 'so there is a need to expand the credit book and fee income earned from services.'

Teba Bank has an important competitive advantage in the mass market. 'We are a more efficient payment agent than banks. Our system was designed to pay a lot of people, and we process at least one transaction every three minutes,' says Hoffmann. 'We also have many years of experience in difficult environments where telephone lines and electricity are unreliable, distances are large and security is a big issue.'

The basic mineworker product is a savings account, from which clients can withdraw their salaries. There is no fee for the withdrawal because the cost is covered by the mine's payroll fee. The account has an ATM facility and transaction charges are 'at cost plus a very small margin', says Hoffmann. However, only about 25% of miners use ATM cards. 'For reasons of convenience and security, many miners prefer to withdraw at our branches in the small towns, even if it means paying R12,50 for over-the-counter transactions,' says Hoffmann. 'However, transaction fees are only half as much at ATMs and we are now putting them into small towns to encourage greater usage. Most of our growth is among non-mining clients, who are more receptive to technology than our traditional clients and therefore we expect the use of cards to increase significantly in future. In fact, we see this greater comfort with the technology as a major opportunity to affordably service the low-income market.'

In 2001, Teba modified its original mineworker product to create the 'Grow with Us' account, intended for customers outside the mining industry, where the account holder rather than the employer covers the costs. 'Initially, we charged a small monthly management fee and a fee for withdrawals. This account offered a higher rate of interest than the mineworker product. However, it was clear that the monthly fee was very unpopular with our clients. After six months, we did research and decided to rather increase the withdrawal fee and scrap the monthly fee,' says Hoffmann.

In 2002, the Teba Bank Funeral Plan was launched, initially for mine workers. 'It will be extended to the rest of the market when Teba is able to electronically deduct premiums,' says Hoffmann. 'Teba has issued 1 500 debit cards, in a series of pilots to test acceptance and the technology. The cards allow customers all the usual functions of a debit card and a transaction account, including debit orders, as well as access to an interest-earning savings account. Income is derived from fees charged for transactions.'

After the expansion of its distribution network, Teba bank has 100 branches, four full agencies, 45 payment agencies and 37 Saswitch-linked ATMs. Placing of branches is important and so is the immediate environment. 'At our rural branches we try to provide a grassy *boma*[1] area, with benches and toilets, as many of our clients have travelled a long way to reach the bank,' says Hoffman.

Hoffmann says Teba intends to expand into under-served areas, through wireless POS devices, which are now affordable to merchants who would not previously have been able to use them.

> These devices differ from most current machines in various ways. They are connected to the cellular network, which has a far greater reach than landlines. And it is extremely cost-effective. Finally, the devices have the functionality of a mini branch and offer revenue-generating opportunities for merchants. All merchants will be able to accept debit and credit cards, sell airtime and prepaid electricity, as well as offer cash-back services. The best of these merchants will be selected as agents for the bank and will be able to offer a variety of services to customers, such as opening accounts, taking deposits, replacing lost or damaged cards. The bank's strategy is to work with partner organisations who will, with adequate training and monitoring, be able to carry some of the

administrative and oversight burden, although the bank is itself always ultimately responsible for risk.

Marketing is crucial because there is a great psychological barrier to entry among potential clients. 'Our competition is usually the informal sector rather than banks,' says Hoffmann. 'We advertise on radio and we send out a task force of people who speak the language of the potential customers. The task force goes into the communities, to agricultural shows, to taxi ranks, to traditional chiefs. Marketing in this context is more about building relationships and trust; and an important part of the message is by word of mouth. People trust their neighbours. The thrust of our marketing exercise is usually educational, explaining the benefits of using appropriately designed and priced banking products.'

The significant change in client profile in the past four years, with the 20% of clients now outside the mining industry in small-town and rural areas, is a pointer to Teba's growth potential, says Hoffmann.∎

Endnote

1 Protected grassy area.

Chapter 3

Savings

Savings initiatives. *The parties have agreed on activities to promote a savings culture, mobilise our people around the need to increase savings and improve the savings facilities available to all our people.*
Nedlac Financial Sector Summit Declaration (2002)

Introduction

One area in which there has been no progress in the first decade of democracy is increasing household savings. In fact, the ratio of household savings to GDP is lower in 2004 than it was in 1994. This is partly a result of the changes in the political dispensation: improved economic prospects and greater access to credit has increased black South African's propensity and ability to borrow over the decade (see Chapter 4), reducing net savings. And a significant redistribution of wealth to poorer families ensures that more money is spent and less saved in the population as a whole (see **The macro picture** on p.200).

However, the decline in household savings in SA long predates democracy: the ratio of savings to GDP had already declined from an average of 9,1% in the 1960s to 4,2% over the 1990s. Since 1998, it has stabilised somewhat at about 3%. Gross household savings, as a percentage of household disposable income, have also shown a long-term downward trend: from an average of about 10% in the first half of the 1960s, to below 2% after 2000.[1] Possible reasons for this development, and potential solutions, were debated at a special workshop convened by the National Treasury in December 2003.

Andrew Bradley, founder chairperson of the South African Savings Institute, has one explanation for the decline: 'We have a culture of debt, rather than savings.'[2] However, when questions about attitudes to debt and savings are put to South Africans of all races, the overwhelming majority agree that taking loans should be avoided; and almost half report trying to save regularly. Perhaps the spirit is willing but the flesh is weak with respect to the discipline of saving. Or perhaps saving is just too difficult or unrewarding, especially for people with only small amounts to invest.

To address these issues, this chapter focuses on savings patterns at the retail level. Who is saving? And which instruments are they using? The savings instruments considered are not limited to formal products, such as retirement funds and bank savings accounts. Informal means of saving, such as membership of rotating savings schemes, commonly known in SA as 'stokvels', play a major part in the savings behaviour, especially, of relatively poorer South Africans, and deserve attention. Though only 10% of LSM1–5 people report personally belonging to a stokvel,[3] these member-based savings organisations represent an important point of entry into the savings and investment arena.

However, formal access has been improved in part by the expansion of transaction bank accounts described in the previous chapter. Standard Bank's E Plan (see p.46), for instance, offers a savings purse, as do other banks, as part of their mass market offering. However, low interest rates and monthly management fees have been a disincentive to accumulating funds in these accounts.

Given the government's declared policy objective of raising the savings rate, a key question underlying this chapter is: if appropriate savings instruments were more accessible, would households save more? A commonly held view is that poor people cannot afford to save. This implies that poverty is the main constraint on savings, rather than accessibility of instruments. However, an increasing body of research shows that, globally, the reverse is often true: poor people are often too poor not to save; and the safety, cost and accessibility of the instruments they use make a big difference to their lives. This chapter will review the evidence on this.

On a definitional note: macro economists make a clear distinction between savings and investment but, at the household decision-making level, the two words are often used interchangeably. This is true even though some may speak, for example, of a bank *savings* account but of an offshore *investment*. In the research reported in this chapter, the definition of savings and investment is as broad as possible, attempting to capture all ways in which people in SA put aside money from present consumption for some future purpose.

There is also an overlap between savings and insurance products in the minds of many people. The two categories are clearly conceptually distinct: insurance provides cover against a defined risk or set of risks, whereas savings accumulate regardless of the occurrence of a risk event. The popular confusion is generated, in part, by the fact that insurance companies offer both types of products; and some products such as life assurance combine both elements.

The blurring of the concepts of savings and insurance extends to informal products too—for example, members regard burial societies as a means of saving towards a funeral and some of the results reported in this chapter reflect this view of savings. However, since burial societies only pay out on a defined risk event (death), they are more properly a form of insurance, and will be addressed in Chapter 7. Stokvels, or rotating savings groups, belong squarely in this chapter, however, and will be discussed in detail here (see **Village banks** on p.196 and **Stokvels** on p.193).

Who saves and how?

10-year view
The absolute number of people using the conventional savings instruments, tracked by AMPS over the past decade, has not increased (see Figure 3.1). In fact,

the proportion of SA adults with a bank savings account, the largest individually used product in this category by far, has declined slightly over the decade—from some 38% to 34%. Unfortunately, no similar reliable trended figures are available for informal savings instruments, but this category will be discussed in more detail later in the chapter.

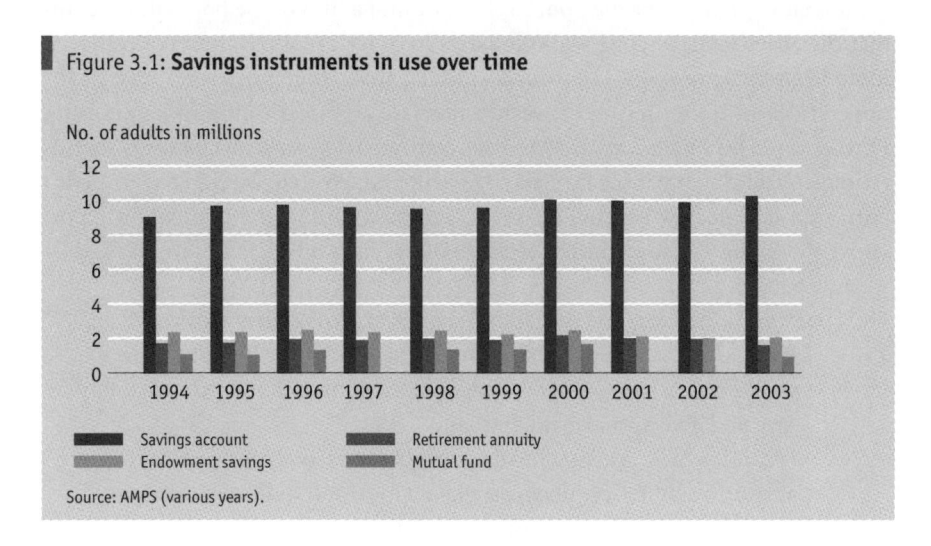

Figure 3.1: **Savings instruments in use over time**

No. of adults in millions

- Savings account
- Endowment savings
- Retirement annuity
- Mutual fund

Source: AMPS (various years).

So who is saving?
FinScope (2003) enables us to take a much closer look at who is saving and the attitudes behind this. Table 3.1 shows quite widespread understanding of the core principle of saving—the majority of adults, rich and poor, believe that regular sav-

Table 3.1: **Savings attitudes**

Statement:	Total adults agreeing with statement	Banked agreeing	Never banked agreeing	LSM1–5 agreeing	LSM6–10 agreeing
If you save and invest regularly, eventually small amounts will add up	17,9m (67% of adults)	11m (80% of banked)	4,7m (49% of never banked)	10,5m (60% of LSM1–5)	7,5m (78% of LSM6–10)
You try to save regularly	11,6m (43%)	9,8m (71%)	1,3m (14%)	5,6m (32%)	6m (63%)
You are saving for something specific	5,8m (21%)	4,9m (36%)	0,6m (6%)	2,2m (13%)	3,5m (37%)

Source: FinScope (2003, Q7b.5; Q26.1; Q26.11).

ing even of small amounts leads to the accumulation of lump sums. However, when it comes to saving regularly in practice, patterns diverge sharply between banked (almost three-quarters are trying to save regularly) and unbanked (only one in seven is); and between rich (almost two-thirds are saving regularly) and poor (only one in three is).

It is clearly harder for the poor to save. Around a fifth of the population report that they have actually gone without basics in order to save. But these people are more likely to be in LSM6–10, which indicates that, while this group may be the upper third of SA in terms of wealth, they are not all wealthy by any means. Furthermore, they are more likely to have contractual savings mechanisms such as retirement funding or insurance arrangements, which they would have to maintain, even if cash flow became strained. Around a fifth of the population report currently saving for something specific—but almost all of these are banked or wealthy people.

FinScope questioned respondents about savings instruments in two ways:
- First, which instruments they were *actually* using, where the answers would reflect constraints on their present situation in terms of ability to save and access to instruments; and
- Second, which instruments they *would* use to save. In this case the answer would reflect unconstrained choice and indicate underlying attitudes towards different means of savings.

Table 3.2 shows the ranking of actual main savings instrument choices across major segments—the banked and unbanked; and the relatively poor and relatively wealthy.

Table 3.2: **Ranking of actual savings instruments in use**

Overall	Banked	Unbanked	LSM1–5	LSM6–10
1. Savings account at bank	1. Savings account at bank	1. Burial society	1. Savings account at bank	1. Savings account at bank
2. Burial society	2. Burial society	2. Stokvel	2. Burial society	2. Insurance policies
3. Retirement fund (pension/provident fund)	3. Retirement fund	3. Buying or making goods to sell	3. Stokvel membership	3. Retirement fund
4. Insurance policies	4. Insurance policies	4. Investment in cattle/livestock	4. Retirement fund	4. Burial societies
5. Stokvel membership	5. Stokvel membership	5. Improving your home	5. PostBank savings	5. Home improvement

Source: FinScope (2003, Q13, Q19.4,5).

Table 3.2 shows remarkable similarity in the top five savings instruments in use. Even among banked and relatively wealthy people, informal mechanisms such as stokvels feature high on the list. And, even among the poor, formal products such as savings accounts at banks, PostBank and retirement funds rank high.

Home improvement is an important means of saving and investing for banked and richer people who own their own homes. It is just off the list in the number six slot nationally. The bank savings account is by far the most popular instrument—used by almost 11m people versus eight million for the next contender, burial societies. The choices of the unbanked stand out starkly. Without access to formal products, their choices are limited. Investment in their own businesses and in livestock feature high on their list, although the numbers reporting this are small. However, a nationwide survey instrument like FinScope or AMPS is not calibrated to pick up the wide range of unconventional savings instruments at the low end. This is why the Financial Diaries project described later is so important.

When the question about savings was asked hypothetically ('If you had to invest your money and had money to invest, where would you consider investing it?'), the savings preferences shown in Table 3.3 emerge. This question removes the weighting in reported current usage towards the patterns of the banked and richer people who currently save. It shows more about underlying attitudes across the population. Note that retirement funds were not offered as a choice in this question, and do not appear below.

Again, bank savings accounts emerge as by far the most popular means of saving. This is surprising in many ways. The University of Cape Town (UCT) Unilever Institute of Strategic Marketing (see **Stokvels**, p.193) points out that the poor have not been the prime target market for the provision of financial services: 'Those with very little, have very little left to deposit and nothing at all to spare for bank charges. Nor can they maintain the minimum balance requirements of conventional bank accounts.'[4]

Home improvement also makes the top five across all groups. Life assurance features in the top ten of all groups, and the top two of the wealthier groups.

However, what is interesting about the rankings in the hypothetical table, compared with the actual patterns shown in Table 3.2, is that a range of new options emerges in the top ten. These relate to enterprise investment such as starting a new business, investing in your own business and buying or making goods to sell. Together, they feature at least once in the top five choices of all the groups. Are we a nation of frustrated entrepreneurs, perhaps? Chapter 5, on small, medium and micro enterprises, highlights research that suggests not.

Furthermore, burial societies remain important in the hypothetical top ten—while stokvels are just edged out of this rank. For wealthier people, these mechanisms tend to be less well regarded than property investment—in investment property or holiday homes—and conventional investments such as unit trusts or

Table 3.3: **Hypothetical savings instruments**

Overall	Banked	Unbanked	LSM1–5	LSM6–10
1. Savings account at bank	1. Savings account at bank	1. Savings account at bank	1. Savings account at bank	1. Savings account at bank
2. Starting a business	2. Insurance policies	2. Starting a business	2. Starting a business	2. Insurance policies
3. Improving your home	3. Starting a business	3. Burial societies	3. Burial societies	3. Improving your home
4. Burial societies	4. Improving your home	4. Improving your home	4. Improving your home	4. Starting a business
5. Insurance policies	5. Burial societies	5. Post Office savings account	5. Post Office savings account	5. Unit trusts
6. Investment in own business	6. Unit trusts	6. Buying or making goods to sell	6. Life assurance	6. Investment in another house/property
7. Buying or making goods to sell	7. Investment in own business	7. Life insurance	7. Buying or making goods to sell	7. Investment in own business
8. Post Office savings account	8. Investment in another house/property	8. Stokvels	8. Stokvels	8. Shares on stock exchange
9. Investment in another house/property	9. Shares on stock exchange	9. Investment in own business	9. Investment in own business	9. Burial society
10. Unit trusts	10. Buying or making goods to sell	10. Investment in cattle or livestock	10. Investment in cattle or livestock	10. Investment in a holiday/second home

Sources: FinScope (2003, D14a).

shares. For poorer people, investment in cattle or livestock still makes the top ten list, although only just; and a Post Office savings account features prominently on their list.

Having considered actual and hypothetical patterns of savings, it is worth considering the overlap between intended and actual usage. What is particularly interesting is whether there is a connection between savings and access to appropriate instruments. Of the 11,6m adults who report trying to save regularly, 85% are banked. But, since the banked tend to be wealthier, this does not imply causality between being banked and a savings ethic. In fact, most of those who say they save regularly have some form of contractual savings mechanism that removes the choice of whether or not to save. This may be in the form of retirement fund contributions, which are usually payroll-deducted, or informal contributions to burial societies and stokvels, where peer pressure enforces regular contribution.

The regular savers are not only the rich, however: half of those who say they try to save regularly are poor; and a third of the poorer LSM1–5 group try to save. In contrast, only 14% of the never banked (who are mainly in LSM1–5) say that they try to save regularly. In other words, being unbanked correlates with weaker efforts and lower ability to save than is the case across the poorer group generally. The causality may not be proven but the correlation is indicative: people with access to banking facilities are more likely to try to save regularly even if they are poor.

Box 3.1: Charter target and current usage

% of LSM1–5 with effective access to:	2008 target	2003 actual usage
bank savings products	80%	28%
life assurance industry products	*	
formal collective investment savings products	1%+ 250 000	Negligible

where the definition of savings products is 'first-order basic and secure means of accumulating funds over time (e.g. savings accounts, contractual savings products such as endowment policies, collective investments and community-based savings schemes)'

*Not yet decided in Charter or at time of writing
Source: Financial Services Charter 8.3.1 and 2.27.2; FinScope (2003, Q13.7,16).

Achieving the Charter targets for bank savings products, reported in Box 3.1, certainly will mean expanding access to suitable products. Even the more formal unit trust industry has a target for LSM1–5 access; although small at effectively 2,5% of the number of people in LSM1–5 currently, it is nonetheless a big increase on the tiny number of users of these products today.

Informal savings: stokvels and savings clubs

Informal savings mechanisms touch the lives of many South Africans. Indeed, communal saving arrangements are common among low-income people in most parts of the world as a way to provide for special items or occasions, or simply as cover against a rainy day. For this reason, it is worth taking a closer look at one of the common forms of informal savings groups—known variously as the 'stokvel' or *umgalelo* or *gooi-gooi* in SA.

While the focus here is on stokvels as savings mechanisms, there is some overlap in intent between stokvels and burial societies: a quarter of stokvel members say that they give 'to help when there is a death in the family',[5] among other reasons for belonging to a stokvel. However, burial societies are focused on payment of funeral and other expenses associated with death (see Chapter 7).

As the **Financial Diaries** case study (see p.73) relates, stokvels arrange regular meetings, typically monthly, at which members contribute a fixed sum of money to a common pool. Members access the pool in turn, at which point they receive a usefully large lump sum of money. In less-developed societies, the money is literally pooled at a meeting and physically passed on to the eligible member. But, in SA today, three-quarters of stokvel members say that their stokvels save the money in a group bank savings account; and a further 14% use an individual member's bank account.[6] Informal savings, pooled through stokvels, are largely channelled into the formal banking system.

Despite the link to formal banks, stokvels rely on trust among members. Members trust that other members will contribute as required; that they will not steal group money; and that they will remain members even after receiving their payout so that the rotation continues. 'Those not familiar with stokvels and burial societies often express surprise at the informal mode of operation of these schemes and the fact that they have been able to function successfully for so long with so little formalised control,' says the Unilever Institute report based on extensive focus group meetings with stokvels during 2003.[7]

> Next, they are incredulous to hear that the mechanism that maintained this smooth operation was nothing other than trust. In modern business practice, trust is not relied on much; enforceable contracts are. What they miss is that, if you have no choice, trust becomes paramount and taking it seriously becomes a social imperative. Trust is the other side of the *ubuntu* coin. The word *ubuntu* is probably best translated into English as common humanity. But it can never be given the same content, the same loaded meaning, that it has accumulated by being practised widely over centuries. The concept is much broader than helping others. It is being an integral part of your community with certain responsibilities.[8]

Levels of trust are often higher in small rural communities or in close-knit urban groups, but cannot always be counted on in a more diverse or complex environment. Table 3.4 shows that half the population says that it does not trust informal groups like stokvels. The perception is more pronounced among the wealthier than the poorer; among the young rather than the old; and among whites rather than blacks. Interestingly, even among members of stokvels, almost a third reveal mistrust. This may show a generalised mistrust rather than a statement about their own stokvel; or it may point to a grudge factor, that certain people are forced to rely on stokvel mechanisms in the absence of alternatives even though they do not trust them.

Table 3.4: **Attitudes to informal associations**

	LSM1–5	LSM6–10	Elderly (65+)	Young (18–25)	Black	White	Stokvel member	Burial society member
I don't trust informal associations like savings clubs —AGREE	45%	65%	45%	60%	45%	76%	30%	43%

Source: FinScope (2003, Q.7b.14)

Trust is, of course, shaped by experience. To get a sense of how sound these mechanisms are, FinScope 2003 probed the extent to which stokvel members had experienced a variety of negative events on a precoded list. Some 43% of respondents reported that they had experienced one or more negative incidents, ranging from members not paying contributions (the most commonly reported), to the loss of money through theft and fraud by a committee member (reported by some 5% of members).[9] The point, perhaps, is that informal associations carry risk like any financial mechanism. While informal savings associations are an important means of disciplined saving for many people, the benefits of these community-based mechanisms, relative to the risks, should not be overstated. And, equally, formal mechanisms should not be denigrated because they are not community-based. Their risk profile may be lower for the poor in many cases.

How many people save using stokvels? And who are they? There has been much hype over the past decade about the size of the stokvel sector. It has been generated in part by industry bodies, sometimes keen to promote the muscle of a widespread grassroots movement to commercial product providers. In addition, the numbers of stokvels and burial societies are often conflated, which causes further confusion. There are now two recent independent surveys, which have asked carefully worded questions about stokvel membership. The 2002 Futurefact survey reported that there are 3,5m stokvel members;[10] while FinScope (2003) found 2,5m members. The truth may well lie between these two numbers, and future FinScope surveys should converge towards a fully reliable number. Overall, around one in seven black South Africans claims to be a member of one or more groups.

Despite their different numbers, both Futurefact and FinScope agree on the profile of a typical stokvel member. She is female (60%), black (96%), urban

(65%) and relatively poor (73% are LSM1–5).[11] However, 80% of stokvel members have their own bank accounts, implying that the stokvel is a complement, rather than a substitute, for an individual bank account; and indeed that stokvel members are more active managers of their money.

The average stokvel member contributes R181 a month, with a wide spread around the mean.[12] This means that R5,4bn a year (R5,6bn according to Futurefact) flows through stokvels; and almost all of this passes through accounts in the banking system—indeed, less than 10% of stokvel members report that the group money is kept by a person rather than in a bank account. Various initiatives have been attempted to aggregate and channel this funding, as the case study on the **People's Benefit Scheme** on p.70 shows.

The Appendix (see p.196) on **Village banks,** which have been operating in SA over the past ten years or so, highlights a savings-and-loan mechanism which has been successful in other countries. Village banks are a hybrid mechanism. Group-based, like stokvels, they aim to serve a geographic community, typically a rural town or village without a bank branch. They are larger than stokvels and require more formally developed governance and administration mechanisms. This makes them expensive to run, and outside donor support is needed to get them started. But there is some evidence of village bank membership in a rural community being associated with higher savings rates.[13]

Proposed new banking legislation may open the space for stokvels and other informal deposit-taking bodies to expand and become limited co-operative banks. Those which reach sufficient critical mass could even become full mutual banks— the top of the co-operative banking hierarchy in SA today. This status has been out of reach of almost all, due to high capital and supervisory requirements. Despite the enabling legislation and generous amounts of donor assistance, co-operative or village banks will face harsh competition from the new-generation commercial entrants to banking mentioned in Chapter 2.

Savings and the poor

Stuart Rutherford, a pioneer provider of financial services for the poor in Asia, has pioneered the methodologies behind much recent international research on savings patterns among the poor. In his seminal book, *The Poor and Their Money*,[14] he documents the mechanisms used by poor people in their day-to-day struggle to survive. He shows how important it is to their survival strategies to accumulate usefully large lump sums of money. They are put to many uses: to cover an unexpected illness; to fund a business or a household purchase; to finance life cycle events such as weddings; or to pay for children's education. While the amounts involved may be small, and would not show up in macroeconomic savings aggregates, Rutherford suggests that the poor are often too poor not to save.

The ways in which poor people save are often not picked up in conventional research. Rutherford shows that there is often little difference—at least in cash flow terms—between 'savings up' (accumulating regular small sums towards a larger lump sum in future) and 'savings down' (borrowing the money upfront and repaying it in small regular amounts); though, clearly, the cost of credit will mean either that the upfront lump sum is smaller, or that the regular 'savings down' credit repayment goes on for longer. Having access to secure mechanisms for savings up and down is important to the welfare of poor people, and Rutherford has highlighted how they use a wide variety of informal mechanisms for this purpose.

To track the use of such mechanisms, Rutherford pioneered the methodology of the so-called Financial Diaries of the Poor in Bangladesh.[15] The cash flows of a sample of poor and near-poor households and their use of financial instruments were monitored bi-monthly for a year. The exercise created detailed 'financial diaries' for each household. An analysis of the diaries provides a fascinating in-depth view of what poor households are using on the ground—something a national survey is unable to pick up with sufficient clarity.

Rutherford's Bangladesh study identified a wide variety of informal mechanisms regularly used by poor people who hardly touch the formal financial system. These range from extensive borrowing from and lending to neighbours, to money-guarding (entrusting spare cash to a neighbour) and burying money in the ground. His conclusion is that poor people are active money managers since, in the absence of elaborate safety nets, their day-to-day livelihood often depends on their ability to access sums of money quickly.

Rutherford's approach to understanding the poor and their money has been applied in urban and rural India[16] and in SA. MicroSave-Africa consultants Moyo et al. report on the variety of formal and informal mechanisms used by people in KwaZulu-Natal, and the interplay of client choice among them.[17] Their information comes from a series of one-off focus groups. To get a more detailed picture over time, Daryl Collins, a senior economics lecturer at UCT, is managing a major research project co-funded by the Ford Foundation and FinMark Trust. One hundred and sixty households in three poor communities across SA—one rural, one peri-urban and one urban—are visited regularly and questioned (see the case study on p.73 for early vignettes of diary households). The diaries cycle will conclude in December 2004, and should yield fascinating insights in 2005, to complement and extend existing knowledge.[18]

Traditionally, the focus of pro-poor financial development has been heavily skewed towards lending, with relatively little effort going into creating savings opportunities for the poor. However, emphasis has been changing as the micro-finance community gains new insights into the real needs of poor households through research like Rutherford's and, in Africa, that of MicroSave-Africa. Graham Wright, the founder and director of MicroSave, based in Nairobi, has widely promoted the cause of providing safe, appropriate savings products for the poor. He says that savings is an 'emerging issue' that now tops the micro-finance agenda.[19] This shift in perceptions is channelling fresh energy into serving the savings needs of the poor.

But the process is challenging. As Madeline Hirschland says, in a recent *MicroBanking Bulletin* article focused on micro savings:[20]

> Providing manageable, viable services for small depositors—especially rural depositors—requires ingenuity and, in many cases, trade-offs. The costs of providing secure branch or ATM services, that are completely liquid and near enough to be relevant, can be too high to be supported by small balances alone. However, there are many alternatives that reduce cost—such as the group savings account used by stokvels in SA and in other countries like India. Another alternative is found in Ghana, where informal *susu*[21] collectors are served by banks during special evening hours.

The way forward

Increasing the national savings rate calls for a multifaceted strategy. There is no proven link between improved access to savings facilities and higher savings, although there are indications that it may exist. Poverty is undoubtedly a barrier to higher household savings in aggregate. However, the ability to access usefully large lump sums has a material effect on the welfare and vulnerability of the poor. The case for increased access to appropriate savings facilities can rest on this alone.

As the chapter has shown, bank savings accounts are overwhelmingly the most popular formal savings vehicle, largely because of their flexibility and relative accessibility. This is demonstrated by the high current usage, and it accounts for the higher savings target in the Charter (reflected in Box 3.1, p.63) relative to the other savings categories.

The popularity of a bank account in no way diminishes the role played by the informal savings associations, highlighted in this chapter. But these savings associations are insufficient in their reach, often inflexible in their practices, and carry their own risk profile for the poor. They are likely to be used less as personal ties become more diffuse in a mobile, differentiated society. In an urbanising and modernising economy, access to formal savings products, provided by regulated and supervised formal institutions, must be a practical option for the poor if they are to be economically empowered. These products may take a variety of forms to meet different savings objectives and profiles. However, if formal savings instruments are to yield a real return (one that is not consumed by costs), savers must have ready access to transaction accounts from which funds can be transferred cost-effectively and easily.

This essential linkage was illustrated clearly in the recent launch of the latest addition to the list of available savings instruments in SA: the retail government bond. Offering this bond widely is part of government's strategy to encourage household savings, particularly among middle- and lower-income earners. The bond is available in denominations between R1 000 and R1m, for fixed terms of two, three or five years. It pays a good interest rate (9,5% per annum, which is much higher than the interest typically offered on bank savings accounts) and is to be distributed mainly through the Post Office. However, bi-annual interest payments can only be made to those with bank accounts.[22] The take-up of the retail bond will be worth monitoring in years to come; if and when the roll-out of bank accounts gathers steam, it is likely to boost the level of bond sales. In the absence of expanded access to bank accounts, the bond may not make much impact on household savings despite the low-cost, high-return features.

The take-up of the retail bond will be a live experiment which tests whether access to better savings instruments reverses the decline in the household savings rate. And further research findings, such as those from the Financial Diaries project in SA expected in 2005, will advance understanding about the savings choices made by the poor across unconventional instruments.

In 2004, we do know this at least: the poor can and do save. And promoting safe, accessible means of saving will have a material impact on their welfare.

Endnotes

1. Prinsloo (2003).
2. *Financial Mail* (12 September 2003).
3. FinScope (2003).
4. UCT Unilever Institute of Strategic Marketing (2003).
5. FinScope (2003, Q.9b).
6. FinScope (2003, Q.12a).
7. UCT Unilever Institute of Strategic Marketing (2003).
8. UCT Unilever Institute of Strategic Marketing (2003).
9. FinScope (2003, Q.12b).
10. AC Nielsen (2002).
11. FinScope (2003, Q.9a).
12. FinScope (2003, Q.10).
13. Dallimore (2003).
14. Rutherford (2000).
15. Rutherford (2002).
16. Ruthven & Kumar (2002).
17. Moyo et al. (2002).
18. For updates on the SA Diaries project, see website www.uct.ac.za/depts/saldru.
19. Wright (2000).
20. Hirschland (2003).
21. *Susu* is the term for stokvel in Ghana.
22. *Mail & Guardian* (21 to 27 May 2004).

CASE STUDY
People's Benefit Scheme: the missing link

Andrew Lukhele

The People's Benefit Scheme (PBS) was an early attempt to link the formal and informal financial sectors. 'The concept was, and remains, a good idea,' says National Stokvels Association of SA (Nasasa) president Andrew Lukhele. 'But it was probably ahead of its time.'

Like other organisations operating in the informal financial sector, Nasasa was exploring the benefits of linkages with formal banks. With Nasasa CE Stephen Japp, Lukhele devised a way to tap into them. They set up PBS in 1993, in a joint venture with First National Bank (FNB). The scheme was based on a formula which Lukhele hoped would 'energise' stokvel savings; effectively generate a better return than the 3–4% interest paid at the time by banks on small retail deposits, and, in the process, give members access to credit.

The key was to use stokvel savings as collateral for member loans. 'Conventional banks generally look only at proof of income when deciding whether or not a potential borrower is credit-worthy,' says Lukhele. 'This excludes people who aren't formally employed and it seriously limits the market for loans, in an economy where large numbers of people are unable to prove their income.'

Lukhele saw this focus on income as tunnel vision and a strategic gap in the lending market. 'What better collateral can a bank wish for than cash?' he asks. 'Moreover, a savings record is proof of disposable income and of self-discipline. And, in the context of a stokvel, it is proof of group cohesiveness and trust.'

This was the arithmetic behind the scheme, according to Lukhele:

Let's say that stokvel members had R400m deposited in 80 000 accounts. Our members would have been earning about 3% on their savings, at a time when the prime interest rate was over 20%. The banks were earning huge margins. We thought: 'why not take that money and cede it to the bank as collateral?' So we designed a scheme to give our members access to credit. Say a group of 21 ladies wanted to borrow R21 000, we would simply apply two criteria. First we would tell them that the loan would cost the group R2 000 a month over 24 months. If they said they could afford it, we would tell them they would have to prove it by opening a savings account and saving R2 000 a month for six months. So you are testing affordability and cohesiveness because, if a group has got problems with its internal dynamics, it will crumble. The second criteria would be whether the group could raise the collateral for two-thirds of the loan—i.e. R14 000. Well, by then, they would have a little more than R12 000 and would have to find an additional R2 000.

When they had achieved this, the R14 000 was ceded to the bank. The loan was drawn down in the name of the group and every member was jointly and severally liable. The R14 000 was placed either in a 24-month fixed deposit with the bank, where it would have earned about 15%; or in the People's Benefit Income Fund, an authorised unit trust managed by BoE, where it earned about 16%. (It was one of the first money market unit trusts in SA.)

But, though the bank had the R14 000 collateral, it was still exposed to the tune of R7 000. So we created the Nasasa Indemnity Fund Trust, by borrowing R8m from the Development Bank of SA, at 10% interest rate, fixed for five years. The borrowed funds were then invested in the same BoE cash fund at 16% a year. So we had a fund with a debt of R8m, costing 10% in interest; and an asset of R8m earning 15–16%. So we had a net improvement of 5–6% per annum. That allowed us to issue a loan guarantee to the bank for the R7 000 it was exposed for. So there was no risk to the bank on the capital amount.

Japp explains:

The product had an interesting feature. BoE shared the management fee from the cash fund with the indemnity fund, which helped Nasasa issue more guarantees to the bank. And then there was another interesting little twist. Instead of the arrangement being based on the typical bond curve, with most of the initial payments going into interest costs, repayments were structured along a hire-purchase model. That meant the capital amount was reduced in a straight line. And, because we were reinvesting the income on the ceded savings, after eight months there was enough in the savings to repay the outstanding capital on the bond, and the bank didn't need the additional guarantee. That meant, on a 24-month loan, the R7 000 guarantee could be recycled twice.

To help the borrowing groups manage the risk, PBS gave each one a package consisting of a ready reckoner and pre-printed schedules to help the treasurer keep track of the savings, collateral and repayments.

'When a group had finished repaying, it was free to borrow again,' says Lukhele. 'And, because it now had a credit record, the second loan wouldn't have the same onerous conditions. The group only had to put down R7 000, while Nasasa put down a R7 000 guarantee, leaving the bank to take the R7 000 exposure.'

Ingenious as the product was, it failed to attract enough borrowers. What lessons were learned? 'To introduce a leveraged loan element and a wholesale-rate money-market-type fund simultaneously was, in hindsight, a bit ambitious,' says Japp. Lack of marketing spend was another problem. 'It's difficult to measure the success of a scheme when no one knows about it. And Nasasa had neither the capacity to follow through its own initiative, nor the financial muscle to make things happen,' says Japp.

After two years, the joint venture unravelled and the PBS product was discontinued. The cash fund became the BoE Income Fund; the bank savings element was rebranded.

Nasasa is not discouraged by the failure and Lukhele and Japp are preparing to launch a new initiative based on a linkage with the formal sector: a national membership registration and benefits programme. They hope to assemble a formalised national database of stokvel membership.

They say they have learnt the PBS lesson: successful delivery of a hybrid product needs 'a properly developed methodology of targeting the consumer. And it needs proper data bases of registered members/groups. In 2004, it is possible to recreate the PBS on a technology platform, whether it's debit cards, POS banking or cellular technology,' says Japp.

Ideally, developmental projects should be self-sustaining, which means they must become commercially viable over time. But Japp argues they often need a launch pad of donor funding to get off the ground. The logic is simple enough, yet hybrid schemes are often seen as too soft to attract investment capital and as too commercial for donor funding. Up against this hurdle, Nasasa has turned to joint venture capital for this latest initiative. Lukhele says that joint ventures between Nasasa and various commercial organisations will ensure that the scheme can be marketed effectively. And he is convinced it will be commercially sustainable. ∎

CASE STUDY
Financial Diaries: household decisions

Daryl Collins is director of the Financial Diaries project.[1] The Financial Diaries is a year-long household survey that examines financial management in poor households. It is based on fortnightly interviews conducted in three different areas: Langa in Cape Town, Diepsloot in Johannesburg, and Lugangeni, a rural village in the Eastern Cape. The profiles present a picture of the household to place behaviour in context. 'This data set will capture financial-instrument usage across different types of households and track that usage over time,' says Collins. 'Not only will financial flows be captured but also the texture of the decisions that went with those flows. There is a depth of data on a range of issues relating to the use of financial devices.'

Daryl Collins

This case study presents small vignettes of the financial lives of a range of SA households.

Stokvels

Stokvels (as they are known among our Diepsloot respondents) and umgalelos (as they are called in Langa and the Eastern Cape) are extremely well-used and important savings mechanisms. Even households that have access to, and use a variety of, formal financial instruments will also belong to one or two stokvels or umgalelos. They differ in their payout structure, in the number of members, in the amount people contribute and in whether they lend or not (see the Appendix on **Stokvels** on p.193). Below is an example.

Mr Mvambi is a successful undertaker who belongs to a prestigious umgalelo named Lingelihle. This umgalelo has about 40 members and they meet on the first Sunday of every month. Although Mr Mvambi has a hectic schedule, running funerals both in Langa and in Mount Frere, he always makes sure that he is in Langa for the umgalelo. His dedication is not unusual—we have another respondent, in the same umgalelo, who says he'd rather starve than miss a payment. Both men say this is their main form of savings. The umgalelo has been running since 1973. At that time it was only men, because it was started in the Old Flats (an old block of flats) and only men were staying there. It is a Rosca—a rotating savings scheme—where everyone contributes money to one person each month and takes turns in receiving the money.

Mr Mvambi invited us to attend a meeting one Sunday when he was the one to get the pot of money. It was held in the basement of one of the Old Flats and we were invited in only after being cleared by Mr Mvambi. With large amounts of money being handled, you just cannot be too careful. Men and women were sitting separately, with the most prestigious men sitting close to the person getting the money. Mr Mvambi sat in the chair of honour. Several video cameras were recording the events. I wondered if this was for safety or to record the amount of money given, but I soon realised that Mr Mvambi wanted to record the things each person said about him. Slowly, one by one, each person stood and spoke to Mr Mvambi about his character and his place in the community. It was as if it were his birthday. Each person had already made a big deposit into Mr Mvambi's bank account and given the deposit slips to the secretary. In between each speech, the entire crowd joined together in song. This was the first and major round of giving.

In the second round, people would give about R10–R20 and make a short speech about Mr Mvambi. In the third round of fund-raising, they would go up and shake his hand and add R2–R5 to the pile. After the third round, the committee stopped and took stock of how much Mr Mvambi had now been given.

The chairman started chastising the group—the entire sum was only R90 945 and he thought they should give Mr Mvambi R100 000. He said Mr Mvambi always made sure they were taken care of, and that they should take care of him. There was more singing and people stood up and took out their wallets, giving more money and having their donations recorded. Now the sum totalled R91 365. Still, the chairman said, it was not enough; there was another round of giving and now it stood at R91 565. The giving became a frenzy. Suddenly the total was R91 600. One last heroic woman stood up and reached into her wallet for R400 to make the grand total of R92 000. All the while Mr Mvambi sat impassively on his throne.

Now it was time for awards. There were eight award statues of varying sizes standing on the committee's table. The individuals who had contributed the most got an award. The person who received the smallest of those trophies had given R4 050; the one who received the largest had given R13 000. The last order of business was to choose a date for the following month and to let everyone know whose turn it would be. The committee was very organised—they had copied the amounts that this person had given to each of the members the last time it was their turn. The members were expected to give her the same as she had given them, or more. It became clear why everyone was trying to find as much money as possible to give to Mr Mvambi—when it is their turn, he will be obliged to give them as much as they had given him today or more. The meeting ended with a feast. (Mr Mvambi had hosted a braai the night before.)

The value that each of these members puts into the umgalelo is apparent. For Mr Mvambi, with a successful business and ample cash flow, meeting the financial requirements of membership is usually easy. In the previous two months, he had made two contributions of about R3 000 each. Keep in mind that he is a long-time member and tends to give others big gifts. Others, however, do not find it as easy to make the payments—some are unemployed, others live on a pension. Mr Mvambi told me that the committee recently 'pensioned' off three older men, allowing them to take their turn earlier and then stop participating in the umgalelo. He said they each received about R30 000 from their turn in the umgalelo.

What did Mr Mvambi use his R92 000 for? Most of it he used to buy furniture for his house in Mount Frere.

Rural savings

In the rural areas, it is much more difficult to save from incomes that are generally much smaller than those of households in the urban areas. Often savings are accumulated after the sale of a large asset, as in the example below.

Thina* is 36 years old and a widow. She lives in Lugangeni with her three children and her sister's child. The children attend the local school. The house they live in belongs to her sister, who is working in Johannesburg. She used to have her own home in another area of Lugangeni but she sold it and put the money into a PostBank account for her children's tertiary education. Her assets consist of some chickens and a goat, an expensive bedroom suite, some other furniture and a bicycle.

Thina, who has only passed Standard six, is unemployed, but she is not seeking a job at the moment. She relies on a disability grant for herself and periodic remittances from her brother and sister, who both work in Johannesburg. In an average month the household income is about R900. Of that, roughly 35% goes to food and regular expenditure on household products and transport. Thina suffers from what she says is a heart-related disease. She spends quite a bit of her income on doctors and medicines.

Thina was using a total of eight financial instruments: a bank account, a formal burial plan, an informal burial plan, a stokvel, credit at the school, an account at a furniture shop, one-on-one lending and informal individual savings. She had also taken two umgalelo loans but had paid these off.

She has an account at the PostBank with a balance of R16 000. She belongs to an umgalelo, to which she contributes R50 a month. There are ten people participating and they lend out money at 15% a month. At the end of the year, they will split the proceeds. All the money is kept by one of the members in her home. Thina took a R300 loan from an umgalelo to pay school fees in January. She paid it back in March, including R60 in interest. She had taken another loan from a different umgalelo, of R200 for medicines for one of the children, which she paid back that same month. She has two forms of burial insurance—one formal and one informal. The formal one is from a local undertaker. She pays a monthly premium of R20 and, when she dies, they will arrange the funeral and give her family R600 for groceries. She also belongs to an informal burial society in Lugangeni, where the members contribute only when there is a funeral. In

March, she contributed R50 in cash. She also lent R200 to a friend for a funeral in November. She says that they help each other like this. In February she bought a wardrobe from a furniture shop in town. She pays R200 every month and should finish paying for it in a year's time. She said it would have cost her R1 600 if she had paid cash. Every month she travels into town to pay this amount; the transport costs her R10 each way. She also owes a small amount of money to the school. She also keeps money in the house, which she uses for emergencies.

Money guarding

As strange as it seems, some respondents trust others more than they trust themselves or a financial institution. They trust a friend, relative or neighbour to 'guard' their money for them. Stuart Rutherford discusses this concept in *The Poor and Their Money*, using examples from Bangladesh.[2] We found several cases of money guarding in the Financial Diaries study. Here is one.

Stephen* lives with his girlfriend, Bertha,* whose family is a loosely structured household in one of the more established areas of Langa. Bertha's son, Kevin,* and his girlfriend, Sheila,* also live in the house. The members of the household coexist, but with little cooperation.

Bertha knows that Stephen has a casual job, but she is not sure how much he gets paid. Every now and then he helps her out with groceries, so she is not going to complain. However, Sheila took us aside one day and explained exactly where Stephen's money was going.

Bertha owns the house they live in and she gets paid rent by three tenants who live in shacks in the backyard. One of these is an older woman named Louise,* who is also our respondent. Stephen uses Louise as a money guard. He gives her his salary when he gets paid and makes 'withdrawals' when he needs money. The reason (says Sheila) is that he often gets drunk and loses the money. Another motivation for doing this is to hide his income from Bertha, because he does not want her to find out about the girlfriend he spends it on. Since hearing this story from Sheila, we have had some confirmation from Louise and are able to track the deposits and withdrawals that Stephen makes more closely. Louise is nervous about talking about it because Bertha is her friend. We wonder if the reason she looks after the money, despite the personal conflict, is that she earns something from providing this service. ∎

*Names have been changed to preserve the anonymity of the respondents.

Endnotes

1   Collins (2004).
2   Rutherford (2000).

Chapter 4

Micro Lending

Introduction

In the early 1990s, making finance available to micro enterprises was seen as one way of addressing the country's growing unemployment crisis. To support the sector, micro finance was effectively legalised by the last Minister of Trade and Industry of the apartheid era on 31 December 1992 when he signed into law an exemption to the Usury Act. This exemption removed price control on small loans.

The outcome was totally unexpected: the subsequent emergence of commercial micro lending in SA has proved to be one of the most dramatic developments in the landscape of access over the past decade. Few predicted the explosive growth in micro lending, or the degree of commercialisation. Nor did they anticipate that micro lending would be channelled mainly into consumer spending rather than into micro enterprise. Lenders were only too happy to lend, often well in excess of consumers' ability to repay—if indeed lenders even bothered to calculate this. And millions of consumers, who had had little or no access to formal credit before the 1990s, found they had easy access to small loans; in fact credit was now actively marketed to them.

One interpretation of what happened is that SA experienced a consumer credit bubble in the late 1990s as a result of micro lending, which was bound to burst. The evidence for a general credit bubble is in fact limited (see **Was there a credit bubble in the late 1990s?** on p.203). However, the sudden withdrawal in 2000 of payroll deduction (Persal) facilities for micro lending to civil servants had a dramatic effect with far-reaching fall-out. Following the loss of depositor confidence triggered by bad debts in its micro-lending business after the Persal decision, Saambou Bank—the sixth-biggest retail bank—failed in 2002. It was SA's largest banking failure to date and the shock waves almost brought down the country's fifth largest retail bank, BoE, which was profitable at the time. For better or for worse, the impact of micro lending has therefore gone far beyond simply providing expanded credit access to retail consumers. It affects the financial system as a whole.

Because of the attention it has attracted, the development of micro credit in SA is given this chapter of its own. The title of this chapter requires some clarification, since the phrase 'micro lending' has been used in different ways over time. Here, micro lending or micro credit refers to small or micro loans, usually beneath the ceiling of R10 000 to which the Usury Act exemption applies, but which can be made for any purpose—from finance for productive enterprise to the purchase of goods. It therefore includes, but is not the same thing as, credit for micro enterprise—which to some purists is the only true 'micro credit'. In reality, micro lending in SA belongs in the realm of consumer credit used for a variety of purposes that are part of a household livelihood strategy. It is a subset of the broad category of micro finance—which encompasses all forms of financial services offered at the low end of the market, such as micro savings and micro insurance. In this chapter, the focus is on this subset only. Other chapters address other aspects of micro finance such as micro insurance or micro savings.

However, on the micro-credit side alone, there are clear linkages to the chapters that immediately follow. Micro credit has played an important part in housing—financing mainly incremental housing. It has not yet played as important a role in financing informal micro entrepreneurs as it was originally intended to do. The global micro-credit movement, which expanded greatly in profile and scale during the 1990s, was born of the insight that informal micro entrepreneurs could and would repay small loans taken to fund their micro businesses. But in SA, lending to self-employed people for their micro enterprises has been marginal in its overall penetration and its impact. The salaried worker was, and remains, the mainstay client of the micro-loan industry. The specific difficulties of financing micro and small enterprises are considered in the next chapter, on small, medium and micro enterprises (SMMEs). However, the broader issue of why SA did not follow the commoner global pattern of micro lending will be considered in this chapter.

A key theme of this chapter is the evolution of consumer credit regulation in response to the way in which the market developed. From no regulation, to a hybrid form of regulation under the Micro Finance Regulatory Council (MFRC) (see the case study on p.93), micro lending is now likely to be integrated into the broader consumer credit market under proposals tabled by the Department of Trade and Industry and released in 2004.

History of SA micro lending

There are unfortunately no accurate trended numbers on the use of micro loans over the decade. Household surveys such as FinScope appear to pick up mainstream consumer credit categories such as mortgages or credit cards quite accurately. However, there appears to be a stigma associated with the taking of micro loans which results in under-counting. AMPS figures for the category 'personal' or 'other loans' are well below the number of clients of the largest micro lender alone. And we do not yet have accurate supply-side figures that eliminate double counting of clients across lenders. The National Loans Register should provide this picture in future.

The history of micro credit in SA must therefore be told in more general terms. Certainly, it fits well the standard industry growth curve shown in Figure 4.1. This analytical tool shows that any market sector goes through four stylised phases. In each phase the industry structure, as measured by the number of firms, changes. The phases are:
- **The pioneer phase**, when a few early entrants launch and test their products and start to succeed

- **The breakout phase**, when the success of the pioneers is noticed, leading to rapid entry of new firms and expansion of the market
- A **consolidation phase**, when a shakeout of firms occurs, due to increased competition or external factors such as regulation
- A **maturity phase**, when the number of firms in the industry and its norms and rules are settled.

In general terms, the number of micro-lending borrowers over the decade has followed a similar trajectory: from very low usage in 1994 when there was limited supply, to a peak in the heyday of the late 1990s, followed by some fall-off since then.

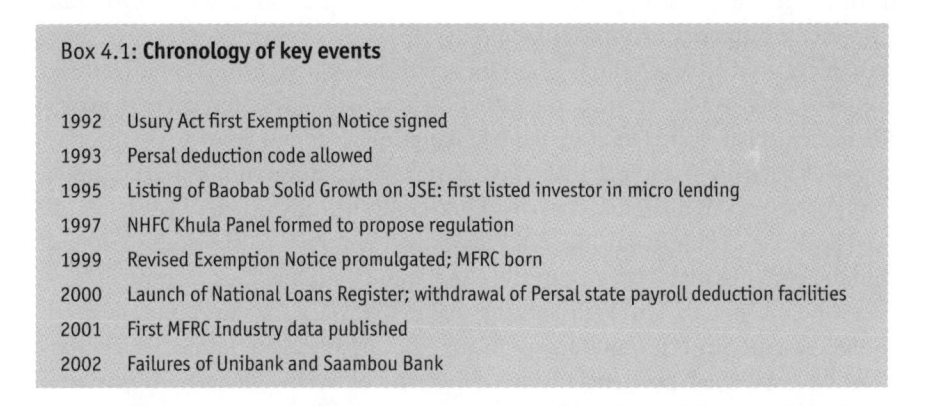

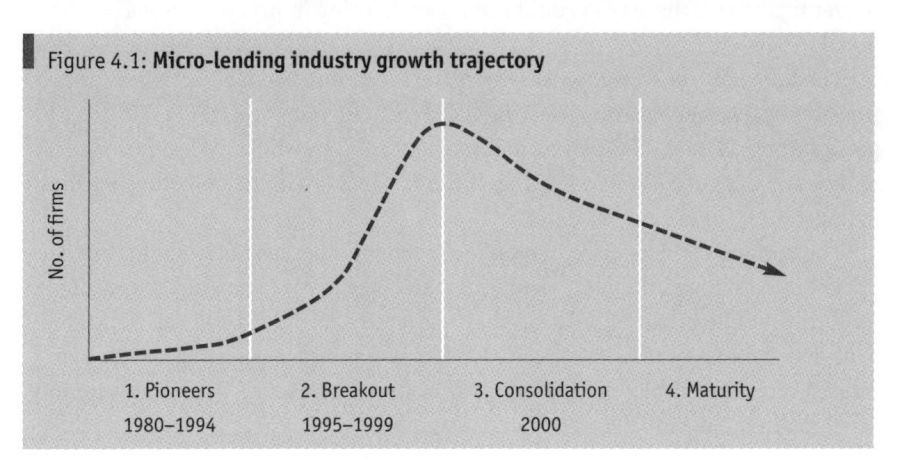

Box 4.1: **Chronology of key events**

1992	Usury Act first Exemption Notice signed
1993	Persal deduction code allowed
1995	Listing of Baobab Solid Growth on JSE: first listed investor in micro lending
1997	NHFC Khula Panel formed to propose regulation
1999	Revised Exemption Notice promulgated; MFRC born
2000	Launch of National Loans Register; withdrawal of Persal state payroll deduction facilities
2001	First MFRC Industry data published
2002	Failures of Unibank and Saambou Bank

Figure 4.1: **Micro-lending industry growth trajectory**

1. Pioneers 1980–1994
2. Breakout 1995–1999
3. Consolidation 2000
4. Maturity

Pioneers

The pioneers in modern SA micro finance date back to the 1980s—excluding the *mashonisa* or informal loan sharks who have presumably been with us in some shape or other for much longer. Several key institutions were created in those decades, most of which are still around in some form today. Significantly, this early group comprised both not-for-profit lenders and commercial lenders.

Among the best-known lending NGOs from this era are Get Ahead Foundation (formed in 1983—now part of Marang Financial Services); Group Credit Company (GCC) (1989—became CashBank, which was absorbed into BoE, which in its turn was absorbed into Nedcor—see the case study on p.143); and the Small Enterprise Foundation (SEF) (started in 1991).

One of the original larger-scale commercial lenders was Credit Indemnity. It was formed even earlier, in 1978, and by 1994 already had nine branches. Louhen Financial Services, the original card-and-PIN franchise lender, started in what is now Limpopo Province in 1989. King Finance, the pioneer of commercial payroll-deducted lending, started a little later, in 1993 (see the case study on **African Contractor Finance Corporation** on p.114).

Different profit motivations apart, these pioneers started for different reasons. For some, such as SEF, a taste of the gathering international excitement over micro finance, especially from Grameen Bank in Bangladesh, led to a desire to try the new approach back home. Others, such as GCC, started as natural corollaries of significant policy work done in the 1980s by think-tanks such as the Urban Foundation.

The Urban Foundation made the case that, contrary to classical apartheid thinking, urbanisation was unstoppable and, more than that, was a positive force for economic growth. This logic naturally led to the policy conclusions of the need for micro-enterprise promotion to absorb the urban labour force, which was growing faster than the demand for labour; and alternative housing forms and shelter finance for those who could not access housing in urban areas via conventional means.

The Independent Development Trust (IDT), an independent but state-funded trust, set up a financing arm called the IDT Finance Company (IDTFC) in 1991 to promote both. The IDTFC played an important role as a wholesale funder, or apex, in the early days of SA micro lending. It funded 11 start-up retail lending entities, mainly NGOs, in 1992–1993.

The commercial lenders emerged independently because they sensed market opportunity arising from the aspirations and needs of a growing, increasingly upwardly mobile urban population that was largely excluded from the traditional bank-based credit system. These early lenders functioned outside the law, charging interest rates above the ceiling prescribed in the Usury Act of 1968, but were too small to attract any official attention or sanction.

The selling of goods, such as furniture, to poorer people on credit long pre-dated this era. This was possible for retailers within Usury Act rate limits, for two reasons. There was a durable good to repossess if the borrower defaulted, reducing the risk. And the retailer could compensate for the inadequate interest margin on lending with a higher margin on the sale of the good, even in the case of non-durables like clothing, as well as adding other fees and finance charges. However, retail lending was undertaken initially by individual trading stores on a monthly 'on account' basis, until large chains such as Ellerines and Edcon pioneered the mass marketing of retail credit.

This pioneering era piloted and established the two collection technologies that were to be at the heart of the developments in the following decade:

- **Cash lending:** increasing numbers of employees had debit-card-based bank accounts, into which their salaries were paid to reduce the risk associated with cash payment. But these same employees were not considered creditworthy enough for credit cards or other conventional bank credit products. Starting with the Louhen group in 1989, cash lenders retained a borrower's debit card and PIN number, which allowed them to withdraw the instalment due as early as possible on payday—a primitive cession on the borrower's account.
- **Payroll deduction:** the salary system for civil servants (Persal) first granted access codes to lenders, for deduction of instalments on non-mortgage housing loans to civil servants, in 1993. This little-noticed administrative action opened the door to rapid growth in unsecured lending to salaried employees, since the payroll deduction removed willingness-to-pay risk issues and reduced collection costs. Larger private-sector employers were soon willing to do likewise, in response to a growing clamour by employees for access to these usefully large lump sums.

Breakout: 1995–1999

Breakout or take-off, in the commercialisation of SA micro lending, can be dated to around 1995. An essential precondition to take-off was the 1992 exemption to the Usury Act. The exemption effectively removed price control on all small (under R6 000), shorter-term (less than 36 months) loans. Although some lenders had traded in contravention of the Act prior to this, the exemption legalised their situation, increasing the flows of formal capital they could attract. Another precondition for take-off was the public success of the early pioneers, which attracted further entrants to the sector and further capital to fuel the growth of the existing firms.

The most widely publicised success story was that of the stock-exchange-listed venture capital fund, Baobab Solid Growth Ltd, one of the earliest and largest formal investors in the sector. As a listed entity, Baobab had to disclose the extent and source of its earnings, and its soaring profits demonstrated to the market that there were super-returns to be made in the sector. At its height in 1998, Baobab, renamed Theta Group, traded on historic price: earning multiples well over 90, much higher even than the then-inflated market as a whole. The market success of Theta, which made multi-millionaires out of the founders of some of the original (now commercialised) NGO lenders, led to a frenzy of new listings of micro lenders on the JSE Securities Exchange in 1997/8 (see the case study on p.96 on **African Bank**, the largest micro lender, which is the outcome of the consolidation of the early Baobab investments).

Investor perceptions that micro lending to the emerging market offered a new wave of profitable growth for banks ensured that no SA retail bank was without a declared micro-lending strategy by the end of the decade. By 1999, banks dominated the longer-term lending market, with its larger funding requirement. The big banks' strategies varied considerably—from lending directly (Saambou, First National Bank), to entering joint ventures with a micro lender (Standard) or wholesale funding of an associate or subsidiary under a different brand (Absa—Unibank; Nedcor—Peoples). Micro lending had arrived in the credit mainstream of South Africa's financial system.

One of the first formal analyses of micro lending, by the University of Stellenbosch's Professor PG du Plessis in 1997,[1] estimated there were 3 500 formal micro lenders—an increase of 192% over 1995. Turnover for the industry had almost trebled from R3,6bn in 1995 to R10,1bn over the same period. The same study also estimated that there were 2 000 semi-formal micro lenders and some 25 000 informal micro lenders, 'dramatically more than was estimated in 1995'. Most of this growth occurred in 'cash loans', the short-term end of the market where small, one-branch lenders predominated. There was no state support given to this sector; in fact, there was considerable official uneasiness, both over the high interest rates charged, averaging 30% a month, and the retention of bank card and PIN, which was prone to abuse.

Apart from growth in the cash side, the term-lending or 'salary-deducted' market grew rapidly too. State-owned institutions helped create new lending capacity by financing new entrants. Among the most active were the wholesale housing funder, National Housing Finance Corporation (NHFC) (see Chapter 6); and the wholesale funder to SMME lenders, Khula Enterprise Finance (see pp. 215–17).

Consolidation: 2000 onwards
The rapid growth recorded by major payroll lenders and cash lenders could not be sustained and, by the end of 1999, consolidation of the industry had started.

While it seemed to some, in the heady mid-1990s, that the iron law of finite market size had been suspended, the law started to bite by the end of the decade. The reality was that, for methodologies relying on payroll deduction or production of payslip as proof of income, the total market was, and is, limited to formal employment. This was around 6,6m people, by narrow measure, or 8,4m if agricultural and domestic workers were included (although they would tend not to have payslips).

Much of this market had already been tapped—one way or another. According to the best available rough estimate, there were already around 2,5m regular micro-loan customers in 2001.[2] And, in the mainstream banked market, there were 3,5m or so people who generally had mortgages, credit cards and overdrafts and therefore had no need to access micro loans. So there was little scope left for finding new customers among the seven million or so people who fitted the narrowly defined description of 'formally employed'.

Growth in the industry was no longer extensive but intensive; in other words institutions increasingly competed for the existing market. This meant downward pressure on interest rates and a lowering of credit standards. Some of the increased risk was unintentional: as clients became more credit-active, accessing various lenders, it was much harder for lenders to assess a borrower's overall capacity to pay.

But market size was not the only constraint. Other factors were at work. First was the implementation of new regulations for micro lending, in the form of a revised Usury Act Exemption Notice, promulgated in 1999. This was the culmination of a long period of uncertainty as to the state's intent, especially in the face of rising public concern over the exploitation of low-income borrowers by highly profitable micro lenders. Most significantly, the new exemption notice provided for the creation of regulatory bodies for micro finance with the power to supervise and regulate under the exemption. In fact only one such body, the Micro Finance Regulatory Council (MFRC), was ultimately recognised by the Minister of Trade and Industry under the exemption, and it has become the *de facto* sole regulator of micro lending in SA (see the case study on p.93).

Ironically, this action resulted in the so-called 'exempt' sector of the consumer credit market being regulated more heavily than the sector which (in theory at least) fully complied with the Usury Act. The arrival of regulation, together with the costs and formalities of registration and compliance, served to drive some lenders out of the market.

Another important consequence of the 1999 revised Exemption Notice was that the card-and-PIN collection methodology was outlawed, with significant consequences for the cash-lending industry. However, in the absence of alternative collection methodologies, a number of smaller lenders continued to rely on this mechanism until recently, though it was illegal.

The term-lenders were not left unscathed. The second major action of government that contributed to consolidation was the peremptory withdrawal of payroll deduction facilities for civil servants on unsecured loans (and insurance policies) in June 2000. Overnight, large and small micro lenders were left groping for collection alternatives; some of the new collection systems that were hastily developed proved to be unstable.

The impact of these two factors is reflected in the first formal micro-loan industry statistics, released by the MFRC for the period ending 30 November 2000, based on returns from lenders. Whereas Du Plessis had estimated the formal micro-lending industry at 3 500 firms in 1997, the MFRC registered only 1 334 lenders in 2000.

Of course, tracking unregistered (and therefore illegal) lenders remained a problem, although these would not have been included in Du Plessis's formal estimates either. Today, almost all large lending groups are registered and hence subject to regulation. But, based on area surveys in certain towns, the MFRC estimates that unregistered lenders make about 4% of micro loans by volume.[3]

A separate survey of 657 unregistered township-based lenders (*mashonisa*[4]), undertaken for the Micro Lenders Association (MLA) in three provinces in 2001, found they were mainly micro businesses: two-thirds were making fewer than 20 loans a month; and almost two-thirds lent as a sideline to other activities, including formal employment.[5]

The consolidation process is also reflected in the experience of various apex lenders involved in financing micro finance organisations (MFOs). The wholesale Rural Housing Loan Fund, which had supported and funded eight start-ups between 1996 and 1999, has only three of these effectively operational today. The rest have failed or are undergoing consolidation into larger, more viable entities. Khula, which has funded 32 MFOs in total, today has only 14 (40%) operational. By way of comparison, the IDTFC, the earlier era apex, funded 11 retail lenders, of which only four lasted longer than the first three years. Of these four, one failed subsequently, while two are being wound up today.

However, the retail lender formed from the failed shells of some of the original start-ups, today known as African Bank, went on to become spectacularly successful in developing and changing the term-lending market, which it still dominates. One in 11 turned out to be a 'superstar': such are the odds in social venture-capital-type financing.

While the onset of the consolidation phase can be dated back to 1999, some of the most spectacular failures occurred only several years later as mounting arrears fed through to the bottom line. In particular, mismanagement of micro-lending exposure resulted in the sizeable failure of Absa subsidiary, Unibank, in January 2002. This contributed to a climate in which SA's largest bank failure ever, that of Saambou Bank, was triggered in February 2002. The scale and impact of these failures brought widespread negative publicity for the sector. *The Economist* newspaper carried an article in February 2002 entitled 'Never a micro lender be'. Many leaped to the defence of micro lending and laid the blame for the failures on the absence of basic banking disciplines, such as the separation of sales and credit assessment. But the industry had been tainted.

Less publicised than the stories of Saambou or Unibank is that of Provident SA. Its story is relevant and important because it was located in the small, self-employed lending sector and it was not directly affected by the regulatory changes discussed above, such as the changes in the collection methodologies. Using the home-based credit approach, developed by its UK parent Provident Financial but adapted to SA, its operation experienced rapid growth from inception in 1998. It reached 100 000 clients, mainly rural women, of whom 95% used the funding for their micro enterprises.[6] However, collection experience was poor, bad debt levels became unacceptably high and fraud was widespread. The loss-making operation was closed in late 2001.

The consolidation process has continued to this day. However, the MFRC industry statistics do not reflect declining firm numbers: despite a slight dip in 2002/3, the total number of registered firms has increased from the 1 344 first registered, to 1 476 in February 2004. Clearly there are still new registrations taking place, particularly as the MFRC's net became more effective and was cast wider. So it is possible that the initial number in 2000 was an undercount.

However, a process of ongoing concentration underlies this apparent stability of firm numbers. The MFRC found that the percentage of the industry book, held by the 50 largest firms, soared from 52%, when the reporting started, to 95% in 2003. Some of this may be due to the absorption of subsidiaries into parent companies. But the underlying factor has been an overall decline in profitability measured relative to book size, which has driven firms out. Of a random sample of 30 lenders reporting in 2000, drawn by MFRC in 2003, one-third had gone out of business by 2003. And, of those that were still in business and for which financial reports were available, profitability measured by return on assets had declined by half, on average.

Micro credit in SA today

In 2004, just over a decade after the start of legalised formal micro lending, the micro-lending sector has not yet moved into the mature-industry phase. For one thing, a mature industry requires a stable regulatory framework, which does not yet exist. However, if the new Consumer Credit Bill published in 2004 by the DTI, following a review of consumer credit legislation made by an expert panel, becomes law, this may be in sight.

The DTI has published the Credit Law Review on its website.[7] The recommendations provide for the modernisation of SA's disparate and obsolete credit legislation, incorporating the Credit Agreements Act and Usury Act in a single Consumer Credit Act. A single statutory regulator would be established, which would take over the functions of MFRC but would also oversee the rest of the credit sector—at present hardly regulated at all. The report emphasises the importance of improved disclosure of lending terms, since 58% of people agree that 'when buying on credit, it usually ends up being more expensive than [I] thought'.[8] It also proposes that the focus of consumer protection should be on the enforcement of reckless lending prohibitions rather than on usury rate ceilings. This has become a global trend since rate ceilings are often unenforceable and have negative effects on credit-constrained sectors such as housing and SMEs.[9]

The growth of the micro-lending sector over the past decade is in many ways an object lesson in unintended consequences. Had government realised what the effect of price decontrol would be, it is doubtful that it would have allowed the exemption to the Usury Act. However, once the genie was out of the bottle, private interests drove very rapid expansion in access to credit; and the state spent much of the remainder of the decade trying to limit the fall-out. Similarly, had the

National Treasury foreseen that the withdrawal of the Persal deduction facility would bring the banking system to the brink of collapse two years later, it probably would have approached the payroll deduction issue differently.

Nonetheless, it is possible to look back over the decade with a sense that considerable progress has been made in certain areas at least, as Table 4.1 shows.

Table 4.1: **A decade of progress**

	1994	2004
Legal operation of micro lenders	Yes—recently promulgated exemption but with no consumer protection elements	Yes—under exemption with consumer protection via MFRC rules and enforcement
Regulation of micro lending	None	Yes—by MFRC
Size of the sector	Unknown, although small	Detailed industry statistics available
State support	Limited—to foundation of NGO MFIs through IDTFC	Plethora of overlapping apexes and policies

The most recent available MFRC industry statistics, for the quarter to 29 February 2004, reflect a micro-credit sector paying out over R4bn per quarter, in around three million individual loans. The average size of outstanding loans is R3 000, less than 12% of SA GDP per capita in 2003, compared to global microfinance industry norms of 115%.[10] Table 4.2 shows the breakdown of the industry by main type of lender.

Table 4.2: **Micro-loan sector by institutional type**

Institutional type	Motivation	Number registered	% of new loan disbursement	% of outstanding loans
Banks	For profit	8	37%	50%
Retailers and cash lenders	For profit*	1358	60%	48%
Trusts	Unknown/mixed	63	1%	0.2%
NGOs (Section 21 and Co-ops)	Not for profit	47	2%	1.8%

*This category is defined by MFRC as public and private companies and CCs, and may include some that do not have a profit-distributing motive, but these are likely to be the tiny minority.
Source: MFRC Quarterly Statistics for quarter ended 29 February 2004.

Most of the lending, by the first two categories in Table 4.2, is to formally employed borrowers. Because of the many different types of consumer credit and the many different types of lender, it is difficult to estimate the number of individuals with access to credit. However, the country's largest credit bureau, TransUnion ITC, has 16,5m unique individuals listed in its database as 'credit active'. This is around 57% of the adult population, which is the number reflected on the landscape of access. But it probably underestimates the total, since not all lenders, especially smaller or informal ones, use credit bureaus. Of the total, as many as two million have had judgments against their names for bad debt, and would therefore be denied access to formal credit.

Consumer loans are often considered to be 'bad' in that they displace productive credit for enterprise or provident credit for housing. However, it is important not to underestimate the extent to which so-called 'consumer loans' are used by formally employed borrowers to finance the informal business activities of family members. ECI uses existing surveys, mainly of payroll lenders, to suggest that 2–4% of micro loans are used to finance micro enterprises.[11] Furthermore, 15–30% of micro loans are used for incremental housing, and 20–30% for financing education.

Ted Baumann, SA-based expert on community-based development and microfinance programmes, has provided an overview of one niche within the sector.[12] He uses the 'hardest core' definition of micro lending as 'micro credit offered by pro-poor, not for profit lenders, using social intermediation methodologies'. In 2002, he could identify only ten micro-finance organisations (MFOs) that qualified, of which two were now defunct umbrella bodies for financial services cooperatives or village banks. However, in some cases, underlying co-operatives continue to function. The total client base of this sub-sector was around 120 000, with one Accumulating Savings and Credit Association (ASCA)-type network alone contributing 80 000 clients. The number of end-user clients had barely increased to 123 600 when he repeated the survey in 2003. These small numbers mean that recorded credit to micro enterprises barely touches the micro-enterprise sector of SA. Sustainable lending for micro enterprise remains the frontier issue for micro credit in SA into the next decade, which will be discussed further in the next chapter.

How and why SA's story differs from that of international micro credit

What has become the global micro-credit movement originated more than two decades ago and many miles away from SA. Mohammed Yunus started the Grameen Bank, the most significant pioneer, in Jobra, Bangladesh, in 1976. By the mid-1980s Grameen had begun to attract widespread attention for its radical philosophy that the poor could be creditworthy.

On the other side of the world, in Bolivia, the NGO Prodem made its first loans in 1987. Prodem followed a solidarity-group lending model, which had been developed by Acción in other Latin American countries in the 1980s,[13] in which borrowers assumed responsibility for each other's repayments. The impact of this group lending model was felt in the early days of SA micro finance through the input of international experts such as consultant Hank Jackelen (who was also involved in the Community Bank) and even Prodem's charismatic founder, Pancho Otero. Prodem commercialised part of its operations to become BancoSol in 1992, leading the next phase of commercialisation of NGO lenders.

Both of these organisations, in particular, had had a remarkable demonstration effect by the mid-1990s, making policy-makers, regulators and donors aware of the possibilities of micro credit. In SA, the influence of Grameen and Prodem-type initiatives had helped persuade the somewhat reluctant authorities to pass the Usury Exemption Notice; and even to persuade bank regulators to exempt forms of informal banking enterprise such as stokvels and promulgate the Mutual Banks Act. The global micro-credit movement gathered momentum in donor and recipient countries alike.

The climax of this phase of the global micro-lending movement came at the Micro Credit Summit in February 1997. Attended by 2 900 people from 137 countries, it attracted royalty and politicians to support the cause of micro finance. The cause was embodied in a declaration in which signatories aimed to reach 100m people with micro finance by 2005 (from 13,5m borrowers in 1997). Its essence was a belief that even the poorest were not beyond the reach of the benefits of micro credit; and the flavour of the summit was heavily NGO- and donor-dominated.

The international micro-credit movement has developed considerably since 1997. It has become more commercial and more focused on an appropriate range of services for low-income people, of which micro credit is one part. To many, it is not even the most important part any more, compared with savings or insurance: hence the increasing use of the broader category 'micro finance'.

The best bellwether of this new thinking is perhaps contained in the objectives and vision of the latest phase of the World Bank-affiliated programme, the Consultative Group to Assist the Poorest (CGAP). It reflects (and shapes) the thinking of leading donor agencies and has the broadest reach and influence of any micro-finance support-and-development agency. CGAP has itself evolved though two prior phases (1994–1998 and 1998–2002), and has recently entered its third phase to 2008 under a newly published strategy. The Phase 3 Strategy Document states:

> The overarching goal of CGAP, in this vision, is to support the development of financial systems that work for the poor. This approach requires that we remove the walls—real and imaginary—which separate the micro finance community from the much broader world of financial systems, markets and

development ... This vision embraces institutions that are motivated to provide sustainable financial services to the poor because it makes economic sense as well as those driven by the objectives of poverty alleviation and/or job creation.[14]

Achieving this vision means increasing appropriate financial services for the poor through a diverse range of appropriate institutions. CGAP estimates that a billion people are within reach of micro finance. Meanwhile, the State of Micro Credit Summit Campaign 2002 recorded that programmes reporting to the summit had 55m customers, en route to the 2005 goal of 100m.

Against the background of the international mobilisation around microenterprise credit and services to self-employed people, the question is why this form of micro credit has not yet taken off in SA. As discussed earlier, it directly touches the lives of, at most, a few hundred thousand borrowers today.

SA's situation is not dissimilar to the position of certain other larger countries with relatively developed financial systems, such as Brazil. A World Bank report on access to financial services in Brazil found just 175 000 micro-finance clients in 2002, although the number had increased rapidly in the preceding four years.[15] This suggests that micro credit generally thrives in the presence of both a less-developed financial sector and less-developed manufacturing and distribution sectors, which open productive opportunities to small entrepreneurs. In larger, more developed economies, despite their large informally employed sectors, there is perhaps less space for small entrepreneurs and for unorthodox finance.

More specifically, SA micro credit differs from the global norm for the following reasons:

- **SA's special initial circumstances:** in the apartheid era, the credit needs of a large group of moderate-income salaried people had been ignored by the banking sector. The arrival of democracy increased the demand for credit from this group; and, with the comfort of high margins for risk, this group constituted an 'easy' market to reach with available formal instruments— payrolls, ATM cards and debit orders. There was little drive for lenders to embark on the harder task of moving outside of the formal world. However, now that the demand from the formally employed has been all but saturated, the focus cannot but move to the informally employed.
- **MFO sustainability problems:** there are still no large sustainable MFOs which lend only or mainly to self-employed people in SA. The recipe for sustainability, which would unlock faster growth, has been hard to find. One of the main reasons for this is the enduring dualism of the SA economy, which means that the salaries of MFO loan officers are high relative to loan sizes. Baumann has compared key ratios of a small group of pro-poor SA MFOs with *Micro Banking Bulletin* averages for their peer group of equivalent size and geography.[16] He finds that the staff expense for SA

MFOs is the highest of all expense types, relative to African peers: SA MFOs pay loan officers high salaries, relative to their average loan size. However, they do not seem to get the benefits in terms of higher loan officer productivity relative to their peers. This is because any formal salary in SA is high, relative to the income of poor self-employed client groups. Individual MFOs can do little about this structural feature, other than attempt to increase staff productivity over time. However, micro lending's high cost structure means it is difficult to sustain MFOs that target informally employed client groups.

- **Funding horizons:** one of the features of the past decade seems to be the impatience of 'patient' capital, whether from donors or state-funded apexes. They have little tolerance for the slow, painstaking business of institution building. Many of today's most successful international MFOs were substantially donor-funded and took a number of years to reach sustainability. To some extent, the impatience in SA may have been "a spin-off both of the increasing global pressure for MFOs to become sustainable faster, and of the political demands for state-funded apexes to show quick results. Impatience was not limited to donor and government circles: private investors, including big banks, saw commercial micro lending as a new El Dorado in the late 1990s and sought to earn immediate returns while the going was good. But institution building is a process. And the creation of a stable long-term policy environment, stretching return horizons, is essential for that process.

The way forward

For all these reasons, micro credit in SA, in its first decade of formal development, has been focused on the easier market—the salaried consumer market. As long as the perception, at least, of rich pickings was there, private entrepreneurs largely met the unleashed credit demand with their own money. The role of the state was confined to opening up the regulatory space, albeit unintentionally, and providing some start-up funding in the early 1990s from state development finance institutions. These helped create some positive models in the payroll-deducted environment. In the high-growth environment of micro credit, there have been abuses—by both lenders and borrowers. There have certainly been unintended consequences. A large number of salaried people may have burned their fingers on micro credit, but there is no evidence of a generalised consumer credit bubble overall.

Profitable, sustainable micro credit for the self-employed or informally employed remains the next frontier of development. After the development path of the past 10 years, the returns from consumer finance are no longer as rich, or at least not as rich for as many. Will the drive for new markets force micro lenders to move on to service the self-employed in the next decade?

There is clearly strong political commitment to this goal: Box 4.2 shows the statement of support from all parties for 'developmental' micro credit made in the Nedlac Summit Declaration. The government's *Ten Year Review* also speaks of micro credit as a key part of poverty alleviation strategies. Ten years ago, this would have been unimaginable. However, the Declaration also reflects ongoing ambivalence in certain circles, at least towards micro lenders, referring to the 'negative effects of usurious practices'.

Box 4.2: Excerpt from the Nedlac Financial Sector Summit Declaration

3.6 The parties also agree that all the constituencies should seek to support financial co-operatives and micro-credit providers. After the Summit, they will engage on a concrete support programme.

3.7 In the absence of realistic alternatives, many wage-earners have had to resort to micro-lenders when they need credit. In too many instances, the result has been an accumulation of excessive debt at a high price. Following the summit, the parties will propose appropriate regulation for micro-lenders to minimise the negative effects of usurious practices.

There are two to three million people in the self-employed or informally employed market who are generally unable to access formal credit today. Although many of these people are relatively poor, and can therefore afford only small loans, there is still a substantial market for formal credit providers. Despite this opportunity, it is still not certain that supply will extend to cover the self-employed in the next ten years.

Several pieces must fall into place. First, successful models must be found that can be reproduced at scale. Profitability will be essential, since the availability of donor funding for micro finance is likely to be restricted in the next decade; and the focus of state attention is (rightly) on the social grant system. Given the cost factors that impede sustainability, successful solutions are likely to involve economies of scale. These models will depend to a large extent on the availability of reliable low-cost information on borrowers via credit bureaus or the National Loans Register; and on the spread of bank accounts among potential borrowers. Having a bank account not only makes electronic repayment possible, reducing the cost to the lender, but it also monetises the transaction history of an informal business so that the bank statement provides an easy independent source of income verification.

Since the 'easy money' in micro lending has already been made, the next generation of micro lenders will have to raise funding with a longer-term horizon. This will only take place if the regulatory environment is stable and enabling. There has clearly been much progress since the early days when the Minister of

Trade and Industry publicly gave notice of intention to withdraw the exemption notice: legal micro lending is now here to stay. However, the nature and type of credit regulation introduced under the proposed new Consumer Credit Bill will determine whether or not the cost of doing this business legally makes it attractive to private capital and entrepreneurs. If the new environment is clear and enabling, the forces of competition and new technology—which are driving areas such as transaction banking—are likely to drive successful new micro-lending solutions. If the legislation turns out to be onerous and uncertain, then progress will be slow.

If the framework is enabling, the next decade may mean the end of micro finance as we have come to know it. Globally, micro credit is becoming integrated into the mainstream of consumer credit. The more micro credit expands and demonstrates its viability, the more the distinctiveness of micro finance, as a sector, will fade; and the more the central issue will become simply the appropriateness and depth of financial services across the market.

Some of these services will qualify as what today is called micro finance and some will not. But the issue of qualification itself will be largely redundant. To be sure, the poor will be with us beyond this decade, even beyond the most ambitious overachievement of the 2015 Millennium Development Goals to reduce poverty substantially. But the big achievement of micro finance in the decade ahead may be to make itself redundant as a separate category of financial service. Just as today we do not speak of 'micro retailing', but rather the retailing of various products at various prices to a wide range of consumers, the label 'micro finance' may not exist at all ten years from now.

Endnotes

1   Du Plessis (1998).
2   Porteous (2001).
3   See MFRC (2002).
4   Informal money-lenders, often with the reputation of being loan sharks.
5   Micro Lenders Association (2002).
6   Cadogan (2002).
7   Available from www.dti.gov.za/ccrdlawreview/ccrd.htm.
8   FinScope (2003, Q46.22).
9   See, for example, *The Economist* (29 August 2002).
10 *MicroBanking Bulletin* (2002).
11 ECI (2003b).
12 Baumann (2002; 2004).
13 Rhyne (2001).
14 CGAP (2003, p.5).
15 Kumar (2003, p.17).
16 Baumann (2003).

CASE STUDY
The Micro Finance Regulatory Council: policing the frontiers

Money lending outside the banking sector has always been an emotive issue. But it is particularly so in the micro-lending industry, where the loan recipients are poor households, with limited savings opportunities and little access to conventional finance. And it is a strongly politicised issue in SA, where blacks had little access to credit until 12 years ago. So, on the one hand there is an urgent need to extend access to credit among the poor black population; and, on the other, there are fears that their economic vulnerability and their lack of experience as borrowers leave them open to abuse. So regulation requires a fine balance between preserving the precious stream of micro finance, and protecting its consumers, which now number more than two million.

The Micro Finance Regulatory Council (MFRC)—a Section 21 company—is funded by members and governed by a board of directors, representing stakeholder groups in the industry: government, consumers and lenders (through various industry associations). Its mandate goes beyond consumer protection. It embraces the development of the sector: 'to promote the sustainable growth of the micro-lending industry, [and] to serve unserved credit needs while ensuring that consumer rights are protected'.

It has no statutory powers, although it is increasingly perceived as an arm of the state department responsible, the Department of Trade and Industry (DTI). But it has a special standing as a regulatory body, deriving its authority from the revised Exemption Notice to the Usury Act—which requires all micro lenders who want to benefit from unregulated interest rates to register with an approved regulatory body. In theory, under the Exemption Notice, SA could have multiple regulatory bodies but only the MFRC has been approved.

Gabriel Davel, who provided consulting support to the original promoters of the MFRC, was appointed CE in February 2000. A chartered accountant with a passion for development finance, he capped an honours degree in accounting and economics from a local university with a master's degree in development studies from the Institute of Social Studies in The Hague. In 1995, he spent time with what was then Deloitte & Touche, in its financial institutions team, and subsequently became a partner. His consulting experience with Deloitte extends to other countries in Africa, including Uganda, Namibia, Botswana, Kenya, Zambia and Sierra Leone.

When the spirit of Grameen banking reached SA in the early 1990s, Davel was one of the first people to practise its principles. He introduced Grameen-based policies (which had inspired early micro finance in the 1980s) when he was asked to become financial director of the Small Enterprise Foundation, one of the early pioneers of micro-enterprise finance in SA, in 1993.

As micro-lending regulator, he has created a regulatory model with little international precedent to guide him. The MFRC is unusual, possibly unique, in that it is a stand-alone organisation as opposed to a unit within a central bank or national treasury—the usual status for micro-lending regulators internationally.

Davel's immediate job was to bring stability to an industry that was on a rollercoaster ride, as the chapter shows. The Exemption to the Usury Act was introduced in 1992—to deregulate the industry. It removed the cap on interest rates for loans below a stipulated minimum, heralding an explosion of micro lending (as this chapter details) along with evidence of reckless lending and gross abuse by micro lenders. The Act was amended in 1999—to re-regulate the industry, setting up the MFRC to 'supervise the operations of institutions, lending under its unrestricted interest rate window'.[1] The objectives were to protect consumers and regularise micro lending in a growing market.

The MFRC brought the micro-finance industry regulation, transparency and legitimacy. This new-found respectability attracted major players, though it did not prevent some from becoming victims of their own poor management. By 2002, it was generally recognised that MFRC had made substantial progress in rooting out malpractices and stabilising the industry.

The MFRC's regulatory dispensation is rooted in 'modern, western consumer protection principles', says Davel. Its interventions are based on the precept that regulation works best when it persuades players in the industry to accept responsibility for their own decisions. Davel has implemented this approach through 'truth in lending' guidelines. These oblige micro lenders to disclose the total costs of their loans and the implications of their loan contracts fully. The process helps consumers make informed *borrowing* decisions. The MFRC also introduced 'reckless lending' rules. These put the onus for ensuring that loans are affordable on the lender. In other words, reckless lending rules help the estimated 1 600 micro lenders to make informed *lending* decisions. In addition, the MFRC spends about 20% of its resources on 'borrower awareness initiatives and borrower education each year', says Davel.

Another MFRC initiative has been the National Loans Register (NLR), which allows for sharing of positive, as well as negative, information on clients. Since July 2002, it has been mandatory for registered lenders to submit information to the NLR and to use its resources to check on the credit status of clients. This information is supplemented by an exchange of information with retailers (represented by the Consumer Credit Association). Management of the NLR is outsourced to two major credit bureaus—TransUnion ITC and Experian—which, in turn, outsource parts of the operation to six second-tier credit bureaus.

'The credit records include information on previous enquiries about the consumer, on potential fraud, on court judgments and defaults, and on behavioural data and credit scores,' says Rashid Ahmed, MFRC research and development manager. The NLR now has more than five million records and, since its introduction, it has fielded more than seven million enquiries.

An investigation and prosecution division conducts reckless-lending inspections, checking the credit standing of random samples of borrowers. And it monitors debt administration and debt collection practices.

Micro-finance regulation is activity-based rather than institution-based, says Ahmed. And there is a diverse range of institutions in the field, including listed companies, NGOs, co-operatives and a large number of small cash lenders. 'However, banks (African Bank, Capitec and the Big Four banks) and retailers (like JD Group, Relyant and Lewis) account for 74% of the loan book and 62% of the borrowers.'

The proposed Consumer Credit Bill could see the MFRC absorbed into a new national credit regulator. But the expertise built by MFRC in the toughest end of the R350bn consumer credit industry in SA should not be lost. Davel and his team have earned the respect of the industry, despite the perception that he would like 'to regulate everything that moves'.■

Endnote

1   Wilkinson & Meagher (2001).

CASE STUDY
African Bank Investments Limited: the Henry Ford of micro credit

African Bank Investments Limited (Abil), with 400 branches and 1,5m customers, has established a track record for successfully managing risks that threatened to sink the sector in the early 2000s. And the formula that drives its strategy is simple: good business principles. To CE Leon Kirkinis, this means appropriate pricing, no soft funding and no cross-subsidisation. It also means a clear focus on credit risk. Where banks traditionally make money from taking a range of risks, African Bank insulates itself against all but credit risk. And it manages the credit risk through direct interaction with clients.

Kirkinis's involvement in development finance started in the mid-1980s when he worked on special projects at merchant bank UAL. 'At the time, most special project teams were concentrating on tax-based deals. To me that was not adding value. I wanted to find a way to bridge the dichotomy between our deep and sophisticated financial markets and the development needs of the great majority of the people.'

Kirkinis discovered that the challenge was not to raise capital; it was to find ways to deliver finance to communities. Having persuaded the Independent Development Trust to provide about R45m in seed capital to set up the Independent Development Trust Finance Company (IDTFC), and having raised R120m from institutional investors, he realised that 'the real issue was to find entities that could use the funds productively, making unsecured loans to shack dwellers for housing'.

Funding was channelled through about 15 non-traditional retail lending institutions, the most successful of which was King Finance, whose business model was based on securing payroll deductions for the repayment of unsecured loans. But the process proved hazardous and progress erratic. 'Except for King Finance and the Credit Guarantee Corp, which became CashBank, the institutions started to fail,' says Kirkinis (see **CashBank**, p.143). One by one the failed entities were absorbed by the IDTFC, which converted from wholesaler to retailer and changed its name to Altfin.

'I left UAL in 1993, and set up Theta Securities to mobilise capital for development needs,' says Kirkinis. In 1995, Theta, 'together with JSE-listed private equity fund Baobab Solid Growth, tried a new approach,' says Kirkinis. 'Rather than acting as pure facilitators raising money, we started taking stakes in King and Altfin.'

Shortly afterwards Baobab acquired stakes in Theta, King, Altfin and Unity Financial Services. 'Baobab, which was run by Gordon Schachat, originally had investments in IT and in financial services,' says Kirkinis. 'But it decided to become more focused and disposed of its IT interests, the biggest of which was computer company Mustek—and became a financial services group focused on the moderate-income market.'

In 1997, Theta reversed into Baobab, which became the Theta Group. And in 1998, Theta bought African Bank, which had come a long and convoluted route since its inception as a savings and loan bank in 1975. It was sucked into Theta's trajectory when it emerged from its second curatorship in 1998. 'We needed a banking licence and we loved the brand,' says Kirkinis. 'But we didn't want the assets and bought only the shell.'

The bank has consistently focused on business it knows best—credit risk in the moderate-income market—absorbing the micro-loan book of the failed Saambou Bank in the process. In its first half, to March 2004, it reported 27,4% return on equity, up from 25,9% in the previous year.

Another ingredient in its success is that outlets look more like retail stores than bank branches. 'And the client sits next to the consultant and looks at the screen instead of sitting across the desk, looking at the back of the computer. It's a very high-touch approach as opposed to technology-driven contact.

'Also a big difference between us and a conventional bank is that banks give you a yes-or-no decision about a loan. In our case, you get a loan, but the type of loan depends on your risk profile: the higher the risk, the shorter the repayment period, the smaller the loan and the higher the interest rate,' says Kirkinis.

Managing costs is vital to the process. 'Costs are more than twice the bad-debt charges,' says Kirkinis. 'So you must ensure everything is dealt with in an automated environment and manage only exceptions manually.'

Another element in the formula is insulating against all but credit risk. 'We manage liquidity risk by borrowing longer-term than our asset profile. That gives you time to deal with emerging risks. Our average liability period is 22 months and our average asset period is ten months.' This is in contrast to most other banks, which generally make money on their liabilities as well as on their assets.

African Bank deals with solvency risk by holding 30% capital against the risk-weighted profile of its assets, though banks are only required to hold 10%. This is another buffer against adversity.

African Bank has no interest rate risk because it borrows and lends at fixed interest rates. This too is unlike traditional banks, which make money on taking interest rate risk. By insulating against all but credit risk, African Bank also cuts out opportunities to make profit. So volumes are critical: both to diversify risk and absorb costs.

Micro lenders, internationally, tend not to reach critical mass. 'That means costs are too high. And they aren't diversified enough to make sure there are enough good apples to compensate for the bad apples. That's why, worldwide, they then tend to go for soft money from donors.'

Kirkinis has strong views on soft money: 'Businesses have to survive on their business merit. You may have a social underpinning and a social conscience but the business must stand on strict business principles. The moment you start to cross-subsidise—whether good customers subsidise bad customer or taxpayers' money subsidises borrowers—you create preconditions for failure. We have never accepted any form of grant finance, even in the early days when we had a lot of aid agencies trying to help.'

Nor does he believe in soft money for launching an operation in order to turn it into a viable business venture. 'You must run a business on business principles from day 1,' he says. 'Soft money conceals inefficiencies and you should rather find out inefficiencies upfront, not later on when you have built up volume.'

Mistakes?

We made lots of them. I guess the first was using intermediaries in the days when the IDTFC operated through retailers. The lesson learned was that, if you are going to provide unsecured credit, you have to have a direct relationship with the client. You can't operate through third parties. That was the big difference between ourselves and Saambou and Unibank: they used brokers to originate loans to clients; we have our own distribution network.

Another thing we learnt the hard way is that a payroll deduction doesn't mean you don't have risk. Our risk underwriting processes were not always as good as they should have been. When you get a payroll, you focus as much on the nature of the employer as on the employee. But group schemes blunt your individual credit assessment. We should have been—and we have since become—more focused on individual rather than group risk.

But the biggest school fee we ever paid was in a business called African Contractor Finance Corporation [see pp.114–17]. And I think that's because we allowed our business instinct to be superseded by social instincts. It had all the elements we were looking for: empowering contractors and providing housing. We didn't see a number of problems embedded in the model, such as that the margin in the provision of housing through these schemes is very low. The project goes out to tender and contractors undercut each other trying to get the job. This leaves very little margin for the risk. So we made some big mistakes there.

Kirkinis identifies appropriate pricing as essential to success. 'The key to success is to price for the risk you take. People often think that pricing high for risk is at odds with developmental objectives, particularly NGOs and regulators and government oversight authorities.' This lack of understanding is particularly debilitating when it leads to flawed policy decisions. 'By not allowing markets to discover the price of risk they effectively cut people off from access to credit,' says Kirkinis.

Kirkinis's achievement has been to identify workable micro-lending models and streamline their operations, to maximise the benefits of efficiencies and scale. ■

Small, Medium and Micro Enterprise Finance

Introduction

'Starting a business' is one of the top five hypothetical investments South Africans say they would make (see Chapter 3).[1] And it is tempting to visualise a vibrant culture of get-up-and-go business people setting up a range of small businesses, if not in the main street, then in their own backyards. Yet the Global Entrepreneurship Monitor finds that SA's actual entrepreneurial start-up rate is consistently lower than that of other developing countries. So is SA a nation of armchair entrepreneurs? Or is lack of access to credit a major constraint on small-business development? Certainly some 43% of respondents to the FinScope 2003 survey agree with the statement 'You often think you would like to start your own business but you can't get credit'.[2]

The question has shaped the terrain of the debates within the Small, Medium and Micro Enterprise (SMME) sector over the past decade. As in many developing and developed countries, government in SA is aware of the need to encourage SMMEs because a healthy growing sector will promote job creation and transformation. And there has been a welter of new state initiatives designed to provide a range of technical and financial support for SMMEs at both the retail and wholesale level. But the outcomes are paltry compared with the inputs. Even the diplomatically worded government *Ten Year Review* expresses disappointment: 'The experience with regard to small business creation is reflected in the [government support programmes] having made modest impact ... Small business strategy is currently under review.'[3] What is wrong?

This chapter chronicles the many changes in the sector over the decade. There is certainly much written material available—perhaps the volume of research in a sector is inversely proportional to its material outcomes. But, despite this research, there are large gaps in what is known about the size of the sector, for example, or the demand for financial services.

To complicate matters, the label 'SMME' is a very broad one, made broader by a variety of different definitions in use. These range from complex formal definitions, often used to determine eligibility for state support, to more functional or descriptive ones. To clarify this issue, these terms are defined in the Appendix on p.208. A key distinction is between SMME and SME, where the dropping of the second 'M' means that informal micro enterprise has been excluded, and the focus is on formal small and medium businesses.

However, it goes further and investigates the real problems relating to SMME finance, and asks what we can do about them, as we move into the second decade of freedom. This is a key issue for the Charter, since financing mainly black SMEs is one of the four big targeted investment areas.

Our message, which is also a pervasive theme of this book, is clear: supply-driven finance does not work. This is true for households, as shown in the previous chapter on consumer micro lending, and for small businesses, as shown in this chapter. Certainly, finance alone is not enough to promote small-business growth and development on a large scale. The level and pace of SMME development reflect the opportunities and constraints in society as a whole. So forcing banks to lend is pointless. Unless real opportunities are identified and real constraints lifted, more energy and resources will be wasted trying to push on a piece of string.

The size of the SMME sector and its financing needs

Most literature on SMMEs begins with the rider that figures on SMMEs are either difficult to find or unavailable. As a result, many of the figures in use are based on interpretations of various types of employment figures provided by Statistics South Africa (SSA). However, there are no reliable figures over the decade that allow a meaningful comparison between the number of enterprises in 1994 and the number in 2004.

The SSA Labour Force Survey (LFS) provides the most comprehensive view of employment, but it samples households rather than businesses. A recent LFS survey of non-VAT-registered small and micro enterprises shows that an estimated 2,3m people, of an estimated national population of 44,4m, were running informal businesses. According to the LFS, there were 11,6m employed workers in total in March 2003, and almost two-thirds of these were in the formal sector. The LFS puts the share of employment in the informal sector (excluding subsistence or small-scale agriculture and domestic service) at an estimated 16%.

Many attempts have been made to quantify the number of enterprises in the various size categories from tiny to large, as reflected in Table 5.1 on p.102. The numbers often vary significantly.

The estimated contribution of the SMME sector to GDP and employment also varies considerably, depending on the definition used. For example, if survivalist and micro firms were excluded from the definition, the value added by SMEs was estimated to be around 40% of GDP in 1997, and 35% in 2000.[4] However, if the survivalist and micro categories are included, the number grows to over 50% for both. Both estimates demonstrate the material contribution of SMMEs to the SA economy. The share of SMMEs in national employment may be as high as 50–60%.[5] Falkena et al. suggest that the job-creating capacity of SMEs will become even more significant owing to structural changes in the economy affecting bigger firms.[6]

Ted Baumann focuses on quantifying micro enterprise in the retail trade sector, where it is quite prevalent.[7] He estimates that nearly 40% of sectoral employ-

Table 5.1: **Estimates of the number of enterprises in SA by size category**

Source	Survivalist	Micro	Very small	Small	Medium	Large	Total
Ntsika 1997 totals	184 000	466 100	180 000	58 900	11 322	6 017	906 700
Business Partners	2,3m		600 000		35 000	Not reported	2,9m
Management Sciences Group, 1999	960 740	862 580		445 880			2,3m
Eskom Survey 1999	900 000+ 'in home businesses': total 3m if one includes small/ emergent/established.						N/A
Statistics SA 2000							1 628 797

Source: Falkena et al. (2002)

ment is in micro enterprises, but the contribution of these enterprises to national retail trade output, by value, is only just over 2%. And he says that, overall, micro enterprises provide nearly 20% of SA's jobs but contribute only 5% to GDP.

Despite uncertainty over their accuracy, all these estimates underline the fact that small enterprises play a vital role in employment in SA. And no one disputes that the SMME sector is large or important. The problem is that there is a lack of concrete data that would shed light on market potential and provide information for targeting and marketing strategies. In other words what is needed is micro-level survey data around entrepreneurs' needs, by area or by region. In 2002, FinMark Trust supported the development of an SME lending scheme by one of the large banks, which was launched as a pilot in four selected branch areas. In 2003, the pilot was called off, since the take-up of credit facilities was much lower than expected and too low for viability. One of the key lessons drawn from this pilot was the need for better information by area, on market potential, which would make for better marketing and targeting of bank products to SMEs.

Government support initiatives for SMMEs, 1994–2004

Preparatory work on the SMME sector predated the first democratic election in 1994, and was based on ANC economic planning and the work of some foreign support groups. Official initiatives began with a White Paper on a National Strategy for the Development and Promotion of Small Business in South Africa, presented to the Presidential Small Business Conference in Durban in March 1995. Much of the subsequent history of the sector (see Box 5.1 and the Appendix on

Government support entities on p.212) is about the implementation of this strategy and the creation of a wide range of state initiatives, often with overlapping mandates.

> Box 5.1: **Chronology of key events in SMME development**
>
> 1995   White Paper on Development and Promotion of Small Business
> 1996   National Small Business Act; Khula and Ntsika established
> 1998   National Empowerment Fund (NEF) Act; Preferential Procurement Act
> 2001   BEE Commission; NEF, Umsobomvu established
> 2003   Govt published BEE strategy; Financial Sector Charter signed
> 2004   BEE Act promulgated
>
> Source: Angela Motsa & Associates (2004)

There are a plethora of state institutions crowding this sector. They often have overlapping and confusing mandates, which causes uncertainty. To address the coordination issues, at least among DTI entities, proposals were developed and floated in 2002 to create an Integrated Financial Institution (IFI), which would combine and rationalise the support functions of Khula, the National Empowerment Fund (NEF) and certain DTI departments, at least.[8] However, nothing has yet come of the idea.

As if this were not enough, a new apex-financing body for micro enterprises was announced in the President's speech at the opening of Parliament in 2003. This body was intended to take over the financing (of retail financing institutions (RFIs)) functions of Khula, and provision was made for it to receive some R40m a year. However, almost two years later, the apex has yet to be created.

Finally, after some years of discussion, government made its first integrated and comprehensive attempt to ensure the fairer distribution of wealth, income and skills. The move followed the report of the Black Empowerment Commission (BEC) in 2001. In March 2003, government released *The Strategy Document for Broad-Based Empowerment*, which included strategies based on BEC findings. The Broad-Based Black Empowerment Act was promulgated in January 2004. BEE legislation includes Codes of Good Practice, partnerships with the private sector and the development of sectoral Charters.

Private-sector initiatives—micro enterprise

University of Stellenbosch professor A Schoombee outlines four conventional strategies used by banks to extend finance for micro enterprise in a sustainable way.[9] Most have been tried over the decade.

- The first involves the creation of a specialised micro-finance bank from scratch. This was the approach followed without success by Community Bank, 1994–1996 (see the case study on p.139).
- The second strategy involves the creation of a specialised division within a bank. Standard Bank's Community Banking Project was one of the first examples. In 1993, it set up the Business Growth Plan as a pilot project in four black townships. Loans of between R1 000 and R6 000 were granted to micro entrepreneurs without conventional forms of collateral. Standard succeeded in keeping bad debts below 4% of the portfolio, in part by adopting some proven informal procedures. But the project was terminated at the end of 1996 for the following reasons:
  - Operating costs were high (SA has relatively high wage rates and security costs in areas with a high incidence of violence).
  - Rather than charge full costs and create a perception of a powerful bank charging poor clients excessive rates, the bank lent at very high interest rates. In 2004, no large SA bank makes micro-enterprise loans on any scale, although at least one bank is reportedly about to start (again). However, there are some emerging successful examples of downscaling from Zimbabwe and Kenya, although there are often substantial obstacles to overcome, 'including resistance to the new micro-finance culture from mainstream bank staff'.[10]
- The third strategy is for banks to form linkages with existing micro-finance organisations (MFOs). The banks provide wholesale funding, for on-lending, as well as technical skills. And they cross-sell other bank products, such as transaction accounts, to the clients of the MFO. Nkwe Enterprise Finance, a commercial micro-enterprise start-up, adopted this strategy, although without success. It closed after two years in 2003. Nonetheless, there is evidence of linkages emerging today with some of the larger micro-finance organisations with a track record.
- Finally, an MFO can evolve to become a registered bank, and therefore be allowed to take deposits, as has famously happened with BancoSol in Bolivia. There are two known examples in SA from the past decade, although they both had very limited experience with micro-enterprise finance. CashBank was formed in 1995 from the group-lending experiments of the Group Credit Company, and had a largely housing finance focus. However, it experimented with business loans at one stage (see the case study on p.143). The new African Bank (see the case study on p.96) was formed in 1998, by reversing the micro-lending interests of two of the larger payroll micro lenders and a cash lender into the restructured bank. Other assets were subsequently stripped out, leaving African Bank as the country's largest micro lender. However, only a tiny proportion of its R6bn loan exposure is directly to micro-enterprise finance. Until recently

this business was channelled through franchisee Quattro Trading, which provides guarantees for credit facilities used by some 10 000 informal spaza shops across the country to buy their stock from the wholesaler.

All four strategies have therefore been tried, but with limited or no success to date. Direct micro-enterprise lending today is undertaken by a small group of mainly NGO MFOs, which Ted Baumann has dubbed 'the developmental microfinance sector'. In a survey for FinMark Trust, updated in 2004,[11] he reports that the 11 programmes surveyed had only 123 600 clients among them. Two of the MFOs—Small Enterprise Foundation and Marang Financial Services, which have also been in existence the longest—now have 20 000 or more clients. They are starting to cover their costs with their lending income—a concept known as operational sustainability. Although it has been a slow and costly process, their example is important in making the case that true micro enterprise can be carried out in SA.

Private-sector initiatives—SMEs

The Task Group of the Policy Board for Financial Services and Regulation estimated that SA banks had about R20bn in exposure to formal SMEs in 2001.[12] The finding was part of their investigation into SME financing. The amount was about 5% of banks' total loan exposure. By comparison, the Khula Credit Guarantee Scheme was insignificant, covering less than 1% of the total. The R20bn was owed by some 370 000 SME borrowers, representing 16–40% of the estimated number of enterprises in this category, depending on which statistics are used.

Although the numbers imply an average bank loan size of R54 000 to SMEs, very few of the SMEs borrow more than R50 000. Most of the amount comes from instalment sale finance used to purchase equipment or vehicles, with almost a third in overdraft facilities and 11% in term or revolving loan facilities.

Because of the apparent failure of banks to make much progress in lending to small businesses outside the usury-exempt loan size, the Banking Council launched a new cooperative effort in 1998, in conjunction with the four big banks. The Sizanani-Sizabantu Scheme aimed to support the supply of bank loans worth R10 000–R50 000 to small businesses. Mentoring was a crucial element of the plan to supply loans to small businesses through Sizanani Advisory Services (a not-for-profit company). Funded by interest-free loans contributed by the four big banking groups, and a grant received from the WK Kellogg Foundation, Sizanani provides mentors to help entrepreneurs draw up their business plans, and to assist in advising the business for up to two years. Banks provided loans to these businesses at the prime overdraft rate plus 6%.

The Sizabantu Guarantee Company, financed through Khula, was established to provide guarantees to banks, above the Khula level, to 95% of the value of a loan, for a period of two years. Sizabantu was discontinued in 2002, following advice that it would have to be set up as an insurance company, and Khula has since been providing indemnities of 90%.

Despite assisting some small businesses, the schemes have failed to make any scale impact. There were low levels of uptake because applicants had poor credit records, lacked experience and commitment, and lacked viable business plans.

The introduction of scoring and other techniques that reduce the cost of originating loans has encouraged some banks to target the SME sector as a new growth market. They use specialist SME units and focused marketing to target potential clients. This is a natural and inevitable market development.

The exact role of banks in providing finance to SMMEs in general has been subject to some uncertainty as to whether banks were expected to finance micro enterprise as well as SMEs. The Charter clarifies this issue. The role of the banking industry, in terms of developmental or targeted investments, is restricted to black SMEs, i.e. formal businesses with a reasonable turnover as in Table 5.2 on p.108, and does not extend to micro enterprises. Individual banks, of course, could go further than this. The Charter also contains more extensive commitments to enterprise development (see Box 5.2).

Perhaps most significant for black SME development, however, is not the financing per se but the affirmative procurement provisions in the Charter: 50% of the value of procurement by 2008. This is linked to further forms of enterprise support as in clause 6.3 (see Box 5.2). If these provisions ripple through the formal economy, as financial institutions require their suppliers to comply (clause 6.3.3), new viable business contracting opportunities will open for black SMEs. The provision of working capital, linked to such contracts with large reputable customers, should be easy to undertake. This should apply, above all, to contracts flowing from government's affirmative procurement strategy at all levels, which must far exceed the spend of any one sector in the economy.

However, the experience of African Contractor Finance Corporation (ACFC), an African Bank subsidiary, suggests that this is not the case (see the case study on p.114). ACFC found it almost impossible to get government to provide the cession of subsidies to small contractors, which was necessary security for ACFC loans to these contractors. After an initial take-off, the credit risk on unsecured construction contracts caught up and, with mounting losses, ACFC closed in 2003.

The demand side: SMMEs and their financial-service needs

Now that we have reviewed the many supply-side initiatives—public and private—for financing SMMEs in the past ten years, it is appropriate to end the chapter where any new initiative should start: knowing the demand from the clients—the SMMEs themselves. (See also **Government support entities** on p.212.)

SMME discussion is often so focused on the provision or non-provision of credit that the broader range of SMME financial service needs is overlooked. Even

> **Box 5.2: Charter Commitments to SME development**
>
> 7. Enterprise development
> 7.1 The financial sector commits itself to fostering new, and developing existing BEE accredited companies through the following initiatives:
> 7.1.1 improving the levels of assistance provided to BEE accredited companies in the financial sector and other sectors of the economy through skills transfer, secondment of staff, infrastructure support, and giving technical and administrative support and assistance. Measurable financial support given in this connection will be scored under procurement;
> 7.1.2 supporting the establishment and growth of BEE accredited companies as broking agencies and/or enterprises in the financial sector through which the sector sells its products and services. Measurable financial support given in this connection will be scored under procurement; and
> 7.1.3 joint ventures with, debt financing of, and equity investments in BEE companies, in the financial sector and other sectors of the economy. Measurable financial support given in this connection for a black SME may be scored under Targeted Investments, or, for a BEE company, it may be scored under BEE transactions financing, measured on the basis of rand spend.
> 7.2 The financial sector will ensure that, where appropriate, it refers business opportunities to, and procures financial services from, black owned financial institutions.
> 7.3 The financial sector's support for the development of second- and third-tier financial institutions may take, but shall not be limited to taking, the form of measures set out in paragraphs 7.1.1 and 7.2.
> 6.3 Financial institutions will:
> 6.3.1 provide support to black SMEs to enable them to benefit from targeted procurement programmes. Such support will include programmes designed to assist black SMEs in tendering for financial sector business, setting aside areas of procurement reserved or preferred for black SMEs only;
> 6.3.2 promote early payment for services provided by SMEs;
> 6.3.3 encourage existing suppliers to address BEE and become BEE accredited.

those SMMEs that need finance do not necessarily need debt, as opposed to equity. The financial service needs vary, depending both on the size and status of the SMME, and their stage in the business life-cycle. Table 5.2 on p.108 shows the needs of SMEs across the informal–formal spectrum.

The transaction account remains the financial service anchor for a small business, as for the individual—not only as a means to store money safely or pay accounts, but also as a means of demonstrating cash flow. It can unlock other needed services for SMMEs, such as short-term insurance and credit facilities.

The main focus of debate remains SMME access to finance, however. Global Entrepreneurship Monitor (GEM) reports have confirmed that the overwhelming

Table 5.2: **Financial service requirements of SA SMMEs**

	Informal			Formal		
Needs:	Micro: survivalist[13]	Micro: 0 employees	Micro: with employees	Very small: 0 employees	Small: >0 employees	Medium-sized
1. Transaction account • A safe place to store money • Easy access to money when required • Ability to make 3rd party payments • A means of providing external financial statements	Store needed, but typically only overnight.	Store of value needed.	Start to have payments needs as well —to pay wages, etc.	Need all of these.	Need all of these.	Need all of these.
2. Funding • Equity • Own • External	Typically have none or little of own.	May have some of own capital saved; or else family and friends.	May have some of own capital saved; or else family and friends.	Typically own capital —maybe from bond on house.	Typically owner capital only; but may require expansion capital to grow.	More likely to have external capital providers.
Debt • Liquidity facility • Working capital • Asset finance	Need debt to finance stock.	Probably accesses through informal lenders or formally employed family member.	Probably accesses through informal lenders or formally employed family member.	Liquidity facility (overdraft type) usually required. Rest depends on type of business.	Liquidity facility (overdraft type) usually required. Rest depends on type of business.	Liquidity facility (overdraft type) usually required. Rest depends on type of business.
3. Insurance • Assets • Debtors • Key man/ life assurance/ medical	Typically no assets held for any term. Very vulnerable to sickness and death of owner.	Few business assets to protect. Very vulnerable to sickness and death of owner.	Maybe assets to insure, but unlikely to take unless required by financier.	Maybe office equipment to insure —probably self-insure. Very vulnerable to health and death risk.	Equipment to insure. Still vulnerable to health and death risk.	Equipment to insure. May still be 'key man' risks.

Source: Porteous (2002c).

source of funding for start-up businesses, regardless of race or location, is self-finance from people's own savings. 'Angel' finance from family and friends comes next. André Ligthelm of the Bureau of Market Research reported that 63% of owners in the informal retail sector (spazas[14]) used their own or family savings to get going.[15] A small minority were able to access bank finance initially. This is appropriate, since a high dependence on credit, especially if short-term and at high interest rates, is undesirable for a new business. SSA's Pali Lehohla found that 83% of informal businesses borrowed funds from friends and relatives to start up.[16] Loans from other sources, such as banks and money lenders, were minor sources of finance (roughly 5% each), while NGOs and credit societies were not significant sources of finance (less than 1%). Most recently, the Township Residential Property Markets project (see p.124) revealed that 68–92% of households operating a business from the house had used their own money to fund the business.

Many South Africans show the desire to start a business of their own and say that lack of credit constrains them. Table 5.3 reflects the answer to the FinScope statement reported at the beginning of this chapter: 'You often think you would like to start a business but can't get credit'. Interestingly, the proportions of aspirant entrepreneurs are higher among black people than white, among young than old, among unemployed than employed and among poorer rather than richer, which may underline the predominance of 'necessity' entrepreneurship in SA.

Table 5.3: **Attitudes to starting a business in SA**

	Total agreeing	% of young (18–24)	% of black	% of white	% of full-time employed	% of unemployed
You often think you would like to start a business but can't get credit	11,5m (43%)	44%	47%	29%	42%	51%

Source: FinScope (2003, Q7b.12).

Entrepreneurs often identify lack of financial support as the main constraint facing small businesses in SA. But GEM research shows that this situation is common across the world, especially the developing world. Internationally, study after study reports lack of access to financial services as a constraint. And many respondents go further, to list the underlying reasons such as no collateral and negative credit record.[17] So the SA experience is not unusual. There is a difference between informal and formal entrepreneurs, however. Informal entrepreneurs are more likely to report funding constraints than formal entrepreneurs, probably because they rarely have their own savings or family angel investors to call on.

> Box 5.3: **Global Entrepreneurship Monitor**
>
> The Global Entrepreneurship Monitor is a global initiative benchmarking level of entrepreneurship across 31 countries. It has been run in SA for three years by the UCT Centre for Innovation and Entrepreneurship and comprises 3 500 household interviews annually nationwide. Each year, the report takes on special themes of analysis and commentary. For further information on GEM, visit www.gsb.uct.ac.za/cie.

The 2003 GEM report found evidence of black-owned businesses being cash-constrained, even among formal small and medium businesses. But this was linked to a lack of financial administration, since cash flow difficulties were significantly less in firms that kept cash books, records of accounts receivable and records of inventory, and in firms that practised active debtor management. Implementing these accounting control measures reduced the probability of exhausting overdraft facilities, and significantly increased the probability that a firm would succeed in a loan application for term loan finance.

At the end of the day, successful small-business creation relies most on the scarce factor of production known as entrepreneurship. According to GEM, SA is consistently behind most developing countries in this respect, ranking lowest in all measures of entrepreneurship among developing countries surveyed by two key measures: opportunity entrepreneurship and new-firm activity (see Figure 5.1). This was ascribed to the lower entrepreneurial activity among young men and to the fact that fewer believe they have the skills to start a business. The supply of potential entrepreneurs in an economy is influenced by factors such as culture, education and family support structure. However, the development of

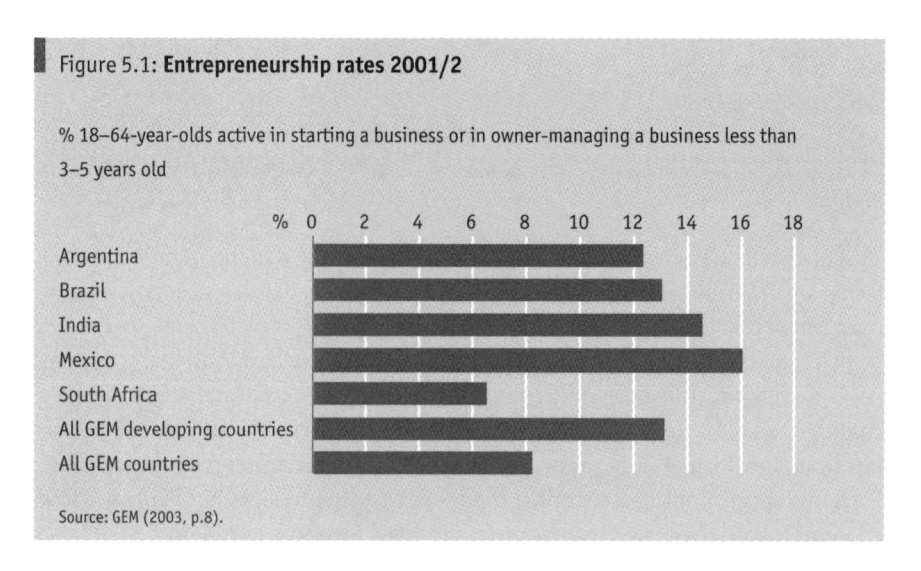

Figure 5.1: **Entrepreneurship rates 2001/2**

% 18–64-year-olds active in starting a business or in owner-managing a business less than 3–5 years old

Country	%
Argentina	12
Brazil	14
India	16
Mexico	17
South Africa	4
All GEM developing countries	14
All GEM countries	8

Source: GEM (2003, p.8).

effective entrepreneurs also depends on the demand for entrepreneurs.

GEM found that SA start-ups had a low success rate; relatively few enterprises survived longer than three months.

The GEM reports have challenged the view that there is a ready pool of potential entrepreneurs in SA who simply need technical and financial support to start successful businesses. Rather, broader strategies are needed with better education as a key factor.

The way forward

There has certainly been much ado in the SMME finance sector over the past decade. And it has not been about nothing. The size and importance of the SMME sector for job creation and growth are beyond question. What is questionable is why there has been so little to show for so much activity. There has been no shortage of analysis but rather a succession of well-meaning, and often well-researched, publications which examine the woes of the sector and make far-reaching proposals. Among those producing detailed proposals are Falkena et al. on behalf of the Policy Board for Financial Services,[18] and the DTI's own working group on SMME Access to Finance, which produced a comprehensive report before going dormant.[19]

There remains a shortage of real data on the size and nature of the sector, by area or region. Development finance consultants Vulindlela have undertaken some recent household surveys by defined area, seeking to establish the number and type of businesses operating from households in the area. They find that between 4,5 households of every 100 (in Soweto) and 20,4 of every hundred (in the more rural Chris Hani district in the Eastern Cape) operate businesses from their home premises.[20] Similarly, in 2004 the Township Residential Property Market project found that between 12% and 20% of metropolitan households in township areas operated a business from their house. Surveys like these make it possible for providers to assess more accurately the potential market for micro-enterprise finance.

There is also a lack of proper impact assessment around the plethora of state programmes. The *Ten Year Review* reports that one is under way which could lead to substantial changes in the structure of state assistance to the SMME sector.[21]

The GEM studies perhaps provide the clearest answer as to why the sector struggles: finance for SMMEs must be demand-driven, not supply-driven. Formal SMEs, which are growing and have adequate records, are unlikely to struggle to get bank finance. What is needed is a supply of opportunity-driven entrepreneurs with the necessary skills and education. In the absence of this supply, the SMME finance terrain is bleak—especially at the micro-enterprise level.

To be sure, finding the capital to start up a business remains an issue, even for opportunity entrepreneurs and especially in disadvantaged communities where family and friends are less able to play an angel investor role. This is why it is so important to unlock the 'dead capital' contained, for example, in housing stock, since new business is often financed in developed countries against the collateral of the owner's house. How to make this happen is in part the subject of the next chapter, on housing finance.

Necessity entrepreneurship, by far the dominant form in disadvantaged communities, is a response to poverty. However, while it is important as a means for survival for a large number of people, it is unlikely to relieve poverty on the scale required in SA and it is unlikely to drive job creation in the economy. At best, micro credit can only be one part of a broader poverty alleviation strategy, which will require state welfare grants to address immediate needs, and investment in human capital (education) over time.

At the end of the first decade of freedom, the micro-enterprise finance sector remains marginal in SA. However, some of the early micro-finance pioneers are now reporting growth and performance levels that bring them close to sustainability. And developments within the broader micro-credit arena, highlighted in the previous chapter, will push commercial micro lenders to find ways to extend loans to informally self-employed people on a profitable basis. Automation of credit-granting processes, together with efficient collection platforms, will facilitate progress.

While there are no easy or quick answers to the SMME funding issue, there are glimmers of light on the horizon. They are generated by underlying market forces—banks seeking new markets—rather than by state facilitation or intervention. If the many state programmes in this area were rationalised and focused, the outlook would be brighter still.

Endnotes

1. This chapter draws on a longer background paper on SMME finance by Angela Motsa & Associates (2004), which can be accessed for more detail.
2. FinScope (2003, Q46.12).
3. Presidency (2003, p.40).
4. Falkena et al. (2002).
5. Ntsika (2001) estimates 50%; Falkena et al. (2002), 62%.
6. Falkena et al. (2002).
7. Baumann (2002).
8. Anicap Venture Partners (2003).
9. Schoombee (2003).
10. Bell et al. (2002, p.1).
11. Baumann (2004).
12. Falkena et al. (2001).
13. This is the category of 'necessity entrepreneurs' as defined in the UCT GEM, as opposed to the other categories, even informal, being mainly or only 'opportunity entrepreneurs'.

14 Micro outlets, often family businesses run from home.
15 Ligthelm (2002).
16 Lehohla (2002).
17 See Angela Motsa & Associates (2004, 2.2 and 2.3).
18 Falkena et al. (2002).
19 Department of Trade and Industry (1998).
20 Vulindlela Development Finance Consultants (2004).
21 Presidency (2003).

CASE STUDY
African Contractor Finance Corporation: hidden pitfalls

'Housing the nation' was a priority for the ANC government when it came to power in 1994. A housing subsidy scheme for first-time home owners had been in place for some years and the ANC government used it vigorously to promote home ownership. To empower small black businesses, and increase employment among people who traditionally worked in the informal sector, the new government channelled the subsidy through small contractors, awarding housing construction contracts on an 'affirmative procurement basis'.

However, small contractors were mostly unable to take advantage of the subsidy, which was paid only on delivery, because they had no infrastructure, no working capital and no access to credit. And even those contractors able to get initial finance were faced with delays when claiming the subsidy on completion of housing projects. This slowed the pace at which they were able to take on new projects.

The first private-sector player to spot an opportunity to supply contractors with finance was pioneer micro lender King Finance. Philip Vermeulen founded King Finance in 1993 with loan funding—on commercial terms—from the Independent Development Trust Finance Company (which financed retail lending for incremental housing in particular) and the Development Bank of SA. He raised equity capital and long-term interest-bearing debenture capital from Metropolitan Life, Sanlam and Norwich Life. By 1998, King was a national organisation with over 60 branches, serving the finance needs of over 20 000 borrowers monthly.

King offered the contractors bridging finance, against a cession of the subsidy claim on the house, and took over administration of the subsidy claims and payments to suppliers, to secure its repayments. 'And the contractors were able to focus on their core activity—building the house, on time, and to the required quality standards and specifications,' says Vermeulen.

King also provided top-up loans to subsidy beneficiaries, who wanted more than the basic structure covered by the subsidy, and granted unsecured, fixed-term loans over a maximum of 48 months, with repayment arranged through payroll deductions. In addition, it granted loans to people who earned more than R3 500 a month, the ceiling for subsidies. The interest rate was prime plus 2%, and King charged an administration fee of R100 per housing unit.

'We started with about 500 houses on two projects in the northern Free State,' says Vermeulen. 'We advanced the contractors enough money, each week, for their labour costs and we directly engaged with the contractors' suppliers, paying on delivery of the materials, giving contractors the ability to negotiate better prices with material suppliers.'

The contractor was entitled to claim payment in three stages: on completion of the foundations, of the superstructure, and of the roof. 'By taking cession, King would step into the shoes of the contractor and obtain the subsidy payments, then pay the suppliers and ultimately pay the profit out to the contractor,' says Vermeulen. 'At the time, the profit allocated to the contractor was about R1 500 per house.'

Control of the process on the ground was in the hands of an engineering company, which would manage the logistics of the material supplier and whose responsibility it was to monitor the work on the ground and certify progress—a necessary step in the claims process.

There was no shortage of demand. 'The provincial housing board pushed a huge amount of work to these contractors,' says Vermeulen, who started providing contractor finance at the beginning of 1998. However, not only did the contractors have difficulty accessing finance but they also lacked administrative and logistical expertise. 'Interacting with all the stakeholders required a very hands-on approach. It was like having a patient permanently in a hospital intensive-care unit,' says Vermeulen.

Early in 1999, King Finance was wholly taken over by African Bank, which expanded King's contractor finance activities nationally. 'The revolving loan book grew from the R20m–R30m at the start of 1999 to about R200m in 2002,' says Johan de Ridder, an executive director of African Bank Investments Limited (Abil).

'It was a good scheme but it relied very much on the contractor being able to perform adequately; on ACFC being able to track construction progress and quality on the ground effectively; and on the housing boards performing on their obligations when the ceded draw-downs fall due,' says De Ridder. 'If any of these processes break down you have a mess.'

In 2000, African Bank transferred the operation to African Contractor Finance Corporation (ACFC), a subsidiary of the Abil nursery fund, Theta Investments. By 2001, ACFC was involved in close to 350 projects, having advanced R600m that year. Abil reported that around 70% of ACFC's business was housing, originating mostly from provincial housing projects. The remaining 30% involved public works projects.

However, Abil's 2001 annual report conceded that, though the concept was sound and demand for the product was strong, the business model had not been perfected, and provisions for doubtful debts amounted to about R20m or 10% of the outstanding book. ACFC was aggressively overhauled. And, in January 2003, in the face of further mounting bad debt, ACFC terminated lending and efforts were refocused on recovering the outstanding book of about R200m.

'We have to acknowledge that part of the problem was the inexperience of the ACFC management team at the time,' says De Ridder. 'ACFC, the contractor and the housing board and Public Works all made mistakes. But unfortunately the party that paid the price was ACFC, who ultimately took the risk and carried the financial exposure.'

De Ridder says that a fundamental flaw was that contractors were not selected on their ability to deliver against expected standards. 'If the contractor is not delivering within budget and on time, you can't make the draw-downs. We found the contractors were inexperienced and didn't make deadlines, which drove up fixed costs. Or they didn't perform adequately and claims would be submitted and the housing board would reject the quality of the house and we would not be paid. We were forced to take more and more responsibility for mentoring the contractors but we couldn't charge for that and it's an expensive process, severely complicated by the national scale of the operation.'

In many cases ACFC had to step into the contractor's shoes. 'At the end of 2002 we must have intervened on 100 projects where we organised contractors to complete the project, so we could lodge a claim and recoup some of those losses,' says De Ridder.

Problems relating to performance accumulated, and eventually ACFC found that the housing board was refusing to pay out for the last batch of houses on a contract because it was not happy with the quality of those delivered earlier. 'We were not just taking the financial risk, but also the delivery risk. We would advance the finance, but if anything in the admin process wasn't 100% correct, we got punished. We would be told only at the time of payment that there was some or other shortfall and we wouldn't be paid,' says De Ridder.

Then a new issue emerged: government became averse to paying out to cessionaries. 'Government wanted to make contractors financially independent and give them a chance to build up a financial profile. We couldn't find a model that would give us enough security and ensure we wouldn't make major losses. And, eventually, in 2002, we said, without securing the income we can't continue.'

Demand for finance remains, and De Ridder believes it is difficult today for small contractors, without their own capital and a successful track record, to access commercial finance. 'We have a multitude of people coming to us for working capital.'

One of the lessons learned from the venture 'is that the cost of the mentoring process must be accounted for,' says De Ridder. 'You can't take an inexperienced operator without investing in his technical competence. Another key lesson is that a programme like this needs a solid partnership between the contractor's employer (the housing board or Public Works Department), the agency monitoring the quality and progress of construction, and the provider of financial support.'

The heart of the matter is that most small contractors need finance; and the only security they can offer is a cession of the proceeds of the work contract. 'If these cessions are not recognised and honoured by the employer, and if the claims are not supported by actual delivery of the required quality on the ground, the process breaks down,' says De Ridder.■

CASE STUDY
Rural Finance Facility: democratic management

Chris Hock founded Rural Finance Facility (RFF) as an NGO in 1991. When the developmental micro lender was liquidated ten years later, it had 'disbursed 30 000 loans worth over R200m, and helped shape the family of development finance institutions, set up by the first democratic government,' says Hock. It had been active in both the micro-enterprise and incremental housing loan markets.

RFF spent two years 'investigating appropriate interventions in the micro-enterprise market and providing financial advice to community water programmes,' says Hock. Lending started in 1993, with a wholesale facility from the Independent Development Trust (IDT). RFF operated nationally, providing unsecured working capital to rural women, mainly for the informal retail trade. Rural Housing Finance (RHF) started as the housing finance division of RFF, but grew, by 1998, into a separate, wholly owned subsidiary, operating in urban areas but often financing rural housing. Both companies relied on only one loan product. RFF provided a Grameen-style group loan for micro enterprises. RHF provided an incremental building loan for lower-income, formally employed workers, against the security of retirement savings; repayments were by way of payroll deduction.

'We competed purely on service, as we could never match the banks on price,' says Hock. 'Our cost structure was higher, due to a smaller client base and our more expensive working capital.'

Housing loans grew rapidly and, by 1998, the RHF had 6 000 clients and a housing loan portfolio worth R50m. 'Though not profitable, the business was sound,' says Hock. 'We had zero loan losses and RHF's performance helped smooth out the more risky and experimental micro-enterprise lending,' says Hock. 'By comparison, RFF was high-cost, high-risk business but also high-impact in terms of job enhancement.'

RFF never reached critical mass, says Hock. Though it had 10 000 clients, the loan portfolio outstanding was only R7m. By 1999 the RFF loan book 'was floundering on weak oversight by branch managers, and repayment rates began to fall with on-time repayment dropping from 90% to below 40%'. Relations with funders—micro-finance wholesaler Khula and Dutch green bank Triodos—were deteriorating.

However, a turn-around strategy was devised with the help of external advisers. 'We reviewed operating systems, improved operating procedures, retrained field staff, developed a standard operational procedure manual and introduced performance contracts. In 2000, a new operations manager was appointed. Her first step was to freeze loan disbursements on the part of loan officers whose on-time repayments were below 80%. The freeze exposed some loan officer fraud: ghost clients and rolling loans (new loans were disbursed to keep bad loans' repayments going). 'The guilty staff members were dismissed and the fraud was vigorously prosecuted,' says Hock.

At about that time, RHF started experiencing funding problems. Though it had become profitable by 1999, profits were not enough to reassure its major funder, the National Housing Finance Corporation (NHFC). 'The NHFC expected us to earn the fat margins its micro-lending clients were making. But our loans were closer to lower-margin mortgage loans than to micro loans,' says Hock. In mid-2000, NHFC refused to renew its facility because RHF was 'too risky and not profitable enough'. Instead, it offered an interim funding arrangement, investing R10m in convertible preference shares at 24% a year, in September 2002. But when the R10m was disbursed, no more was forthcoming. RHF chairman Isaac Shongwe asked Hock to resign, and NHFC called in its facility. Shortly after, the board put RHF into liquidation and the loan book was sold at a substantial premium. At the same time, RFF was merged with micro lender Get Ahead. 'The fact that both operations are still going vindicates what we did,' says Hock.

RFF and RHF finally failed because the development financiers withdrew their credit lines. 'But perhaps we were to blame for taking too optimistic a view of the balance between profits and development impact,' says Hock. 'RFF grew out of the NGO movement and carried within it many of the blind spots of the movement and the time,' says Hock. 'I used to think we were pioneering and uniquely pro-poor. Now I believe we were also inefficient. People don't examine failure carefully enough.'

What went wrong? 'A combination of things, and it's difficult to decide which was most important.' Hock identifies internal weaknesses. 'Balancing flexibility and formality is not easy in a rapidly growing organisation. RHF outgrew its governance structure two years before its demise. At that point, it should have implemented a formal board policy for member selection, training, performance assessment and strategic planning.'

RHF did not stay close enough to funders. 'We were aware of problems but were reluctant to criticise because of our dependency on the funder. If we had given better feedback and listened more carefully, we might have avoided the loss of trust which bedevilled all subsequent exchanges.'

RHF timed its technological investment badly. 'We should not have embarked on a major IT project without having secured the capital needed to achieve the growth on which the project benefits depended.'

Another weakness in both operations lay with people management. 'We valued teamwork and used a participative approach. But we overdid it. The high tide was probably when I tried to get our sales staff to set their own salaries. I called a sales team meeting and set out the link between output and earnings. Most of my team opted for top salaries not linked to performance. We did not implement their suggestion.'

A key lesson, he says, is: 'Democratic management's lack of formal hierarchy leads to informal hierarchy, which is unaccountable and therefore does not learn easily from its mistakes.' ∎

Chapter 6

Housing Finance

Introduction

Most South Africans claim to own their home.[1] And Census 2001 found that 72% of households in formal dwellings do own their home. Although the precise legal forms of tenure differ across informal and rural housing categories, the perception of home ownership in the nation as a whole is high.

The government's housing programme has contributed to this, delivering over two million subsidies to first-time home buyers, over the decade to 2004, and transferring an additional half a million rented houses to the occupants. An estimated six million people have received housing as a result of these initiatives. And R48bn in housing assets has been transferred to poorer citizens—one of the largest direct wealth redistribution programmes by the government to date.[2] Government therefore claims that housing is one of the areas where delivery has been successful in the first decade of freedom. The provision of private housing finance, rather than the delivery of fully subsidised houses, has been notably less successful.

To be sure, housing finance in SA has come a long way since 1994. As with the SMME finance sector (see Chapter 5), a host of new government programmes and entities has been created. But the central dilemma—how to make housing finance accessible—remains as it was in 1994. Then, banks had almost stopped mortgage lending for home purchase in township areas because of mounting arrears and the difficulties of perfecting mortgage security. This arose because, in the event of repossession, a bank could not sell the house to recoup the outstanding loan; there was no secondary market in most areas. Moreover, some households resisted eviction. And, even if they were successfully removed, someone else (even the security guard appointed to look after the house) would illegally occupy it. Another problem was that the courts were unable to handle the volume of repossession cases in some areas, and sheriffs were scared to implement eviction orders. So banks resorted to a process of area-based exclusion of mortgage finance, and the term 'redlining', familiar in the US, entered the SA lexicon.

Today, while lending has resumed, to a certain extent and in some areas where conditions have improved, there is still a widespread feeling in political circles that banks have not 'come to the party'. Banks, in turn, feel that unrealistic expectations exist at a political level, given the realities in township areas. However, substantial commitments have again been made recently, under the Charter, to finance affordable housing; but it will require a public–private partnership to mitigate potentially higher risks.

In SA, innovations such as securitisation have brought down the cost of mortgages in the past five years. And mortgage markets work well, in general, for suburban home buyers who wish to borrow R100 000 or more. The proportion of mortgage finance to GDP, at around 18%, is higher than that of wealthier economies such as Korea or Greece and well above emerging economies such as Mexico (6%) or Brazil (7%).[3]

At the other end of the scale, micro lending has developed substantially (see Chapter 4), making loans below R10 000 accessible for home improvements and alterations—at least to formally employed people.

However, the cost of buying a new starter house, depending on area and quality of construction, is likely to be anywhere from R60 000 to R100 000, given construction and land costs of around R2000/m² in urban areas. And the income profile of most South Africans means that they cannot afford more.

The question for housing policy is how to provide access to decent housing for all citizens, as required in the new Constitution, given the high levels of poverty. The capital subsidy programme for the poorest has been one approach. But this is available only to first-time home buyers earning less than R3 500 a month. The scheme was designed on the assumption that those earning more than R1 500 per month would access top-up finance to supplement the reduced subsidy, but this has not happened in practice.

Specifically, then, the problem is how to provide appropriate finance to the more than 25% of households which:

- Earn more than R1 500 a month, at which point they can, theoretically, afford credit and are therefore potential home buyers, but less than R7 500, from which income level normal mortgage finance would typically be available; and
- Can afford more than R10 000 in credit but less than R100 000.

Plugging this R10 000–R100 000 'credit gap' is the central problem of SA housing finance today. This chapter will describe the evolution of housing finance over the decade and discuss the causes of the credit gap.

Home ownership and housing markets, 1994–2004

Eighty-one percent of SA adults say that they own their houses (see Table 6.1). The balance—around one in five people—rent their houses, especially in urban areas. Since the claimed ownership in rural areas and among the poor is even higher—85–90%—this answer clearly covers a multitude of tenure types in addition to conventional freehold ownership. By way of indirect comparison, in the US, 67% of households own their home—although this is only freehold ownership. However, the perception of ownership in SA, with all the benefits of security and household stability, is high. This perception generates one of SA's most popular means of savings and investment (see Chapter 3): not surprisingly, 92% of home improvement is undertaken by people who say they own their homes.

In this diverse area, there are few accurately trended data series available with which to measure changes over the decade accurately. However, the 1996 and 2001 censuses provide at least two snapshots of home ownership levels. They show an increase both in the overall level of home ownership and in the proportion of formal housing in overall home ownership—which has increased from 56% to 72%. This indicates that a higher proportion of households have become owners of formal houses over the period, probably largely as a result of the housing subsidy programme. According to the 2001 census, half a million more black households became owners of formal housing during the period. Most black formal home owners continue to live in townships, which will receive special attention in this chapter.

There is a diversity of housing types in SA: three-quarters of people live in brick houses; and most rental housing is built of brick.

Table 6.1: **Home ownership and types of home in SA**

% are the percentages of each column which fall into the row category.

	Total	LSM1–5	LSM6–10	Metro	Rural	Never banked
Own	81%	85%	74%	75%	90%	85%
Rent	19%	15%	26%	25%	10%	15%
Mortgage (current)	6%	0,5%	16%	10%	0,4%	0
Type of dwelling						
Brick house	56%					
Traditional dwelling	15%					
Informal dwelling not in backyard	12%					
Flat/maisonette/ townhouse	8%					
Backyard room/shack	8%					
Other	1%					

Source: Own/rent/mortgage: FinScope (2003, Q48,49).
Type of dwelling: Statistics South Africa (2003b).

Although the rate of home ownership is high, only 10% of people say that they bought their home using mortgage finance. This includes current and past mortgage borrowers, and almost all who have are in the middle- to upper-income ranges (LSM6–10). The penetration of mortgage finance is much lower than other forms of retail credit. This is a symptom of a fundamental flaw in the evolution of housing markets, especially in areas that were designated black townships under apartheid. Mortgage finance is critically dependent on the existence of a secondary housing market. It is only through a secondary market that the value of a house, as security, can be easily established and, in the event of default, realised through sale. But the secondary market in township property is in its very early stages of development.

A recent major research project called the Workings of Township Residential Property Markets investigated the extent to which the secondary market has developed in townships.[4] It categorised township areas into four distinct segments:

- **Privately developed:** unsubsidised formal housing developed by the private sector.
- **Old township stock:** formal housing units built as rental accommodation for black South Africans by government, mainly between 1948 and 1960.
- **RDP housing and site-and-service:** which could be formal free-standing basic units (RDP houses), or site-and-service schemes, where a site is provided and, in some cases, funding for the development of a dwelling.
- **Informal:** dwellings erected by occupants, without the permission of the land owner, using non-conventional building materials.

The study found very limited evidence of a secondary market across all these segments in 2003/4. Of more than 2000 township households in four metropolitan areas investigated as part of the study, only one in eight said that they had bought or sold property in the secondary market (i.e. excluding buying or receiving new houses) in the past eight years. The majority of these had only transacted in housing once in their lifetimes, as household heads. A very small minority had had two previous homes. The rate of secondary-market transactions, at around 10%, is about a third of the expected average turnover of 30% in a 'normal' suburban market, or indeed of suburbs with comparable socio-economic features.[5]

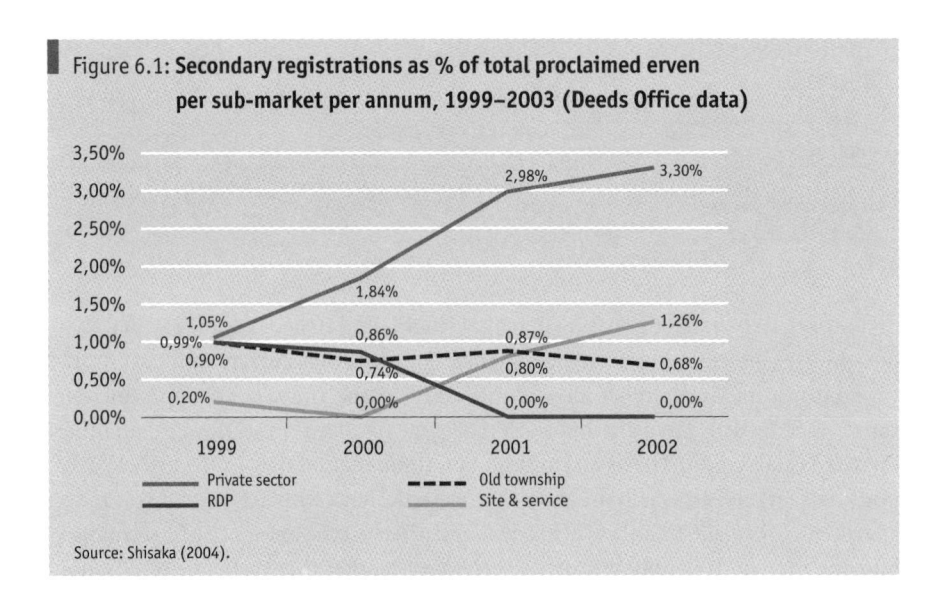

Figure 6.1: **Secondary registrations as % of total proclaimed erven per sub-market per annum, 1999–2003 (Deeds Office data)**

	1999	2000	2001	2002
Private sector	1,05%	1,84%	2,98%	3,30%
Old township	0,99%	0,86%	0,87%	—
RDP	0,90%	0,74%	0,80%	0,68%
Site & service	0,20%	0,00%	0,00%	1,26% / 0,00%

Source: Shisaka (2004).

Figure 6.1 tracks the change in registered transfers of properties in each segment in the years 1999–2002. It seems that the private-sector and site-and-service markets are becoming more active, though the percentage change is off a very low base; while the 'old township' market has remained largely stagnant. Registered transactions in RDP housing stock declined to zero because the Housing Amendment Act of 2001 made it illegal to sell state-subsidised properties for eight years following occupation; however, informal transfers may be taking place.

Government policy and interventions, 1994–2004

Relative to some other social delivery areas, government housing policy started with a bang in 1994. A housing summit was convened by the new Minister, Joe Slovo, at Botshabelo, at which all the role players in the housing process—government, civil society, banks and so on—signed the National Housing Accord. This built on considerable earlier work done by the National Housing Forum.

The context of the summit was one of rising crisis. After the removal of apartheid-era property ownership restrictions in the 1980s, some banks had been relatively quick to provide mortgages to black clients. An estimated R10bn had been lent in this market by 1994. But some R2bn of this, representing almost 49 000 mortgage loans, was non-performing.[6] The reasons varied from bond boycotts connected to political mobilisation (though these were the minority) to lack of understanding about mortgage finance and problems with the quality of construction. And, most importantly, default was due to economic pressures in the early 1990s that led both to loss of employment and to high interest rates that squeezed new home owners on variable rate mortgages.[7]

The Housing White Paper, issued in 1994, framed government policy for the decade although policy emphasis has changed over time. It contained three main thrusts:

- **Stabilising the housing environment:** in part through the Masakhane campaign to encourage payment of rates and services.
- **Mobilising credit:** a Record of Understanding (RoU) was signed with banks, to stabilise expectations and risks around mortgage lending. The RoU led, among other things, to the introduction of the Mortgage Indemnity Fund (MIF) as a transitional mechanism to cover banks against so-called non-commercial risks of mortgage lending in township areas until 1998. In addition, a range of other housing finance entities, at a wholesale and guarantee level, were established to mobilise new finance for housing.
- **A housing subsidy programme:** the introduction of a credit-linked housing subsidy, which was expected to stimulate demand for housing credit among those who could afford it.

> Box 6.1: **Chronology of key events**
>
> 1992　National Housing Forum formed
> 1994　Record of Understanding signed at Botshabelo Housing Summit
> 1995　Mortgage Indemnity Fund (MIF) started; Nurcha, NHBRC and Servcon formed
> 1996　National Housing Finance Corporation and Rural Housing Loan Fund established
> 1997　Housing Act promulgated
> 1998　'New Deal' signed between banks and government; Thubelisha Homes formed to undertake rightsizing of defaulting mortgagees
> 1998　Presidential Job Summit Housing Project agreed; MIF closes down as planned
> 1999　Gateway Home Loans pilot launched
> 2000　Home Loan and Mortgage Disclosure Act promulgated
> 2001　Gateway pilot ends
> 2002　Community Reinvestment Bill tabled in Cabinet

The White Paper led to the frenzied creation of new institutions: by 1999, nine new national housing institutions had been established. Table 6.2 summarises them and their functions in terms of the policy thrusts and strategies.

Table 6.2: **Institutions established in terms of SA housing policy**

Strategy	Policy initiative	Institution	Mandate/focus
First policy thrust: Stabilise the housing environment			
Stimulate existing supply of housing finance	Record of Understanding	Mortgage Indemnity Fund	Provide banks with guarantees against political risk in approved areas.
		National Home Builders Registration Council	Provide a five-year structural warranty on all housing.
		Servcon Housing Solutions	Take over and manage PIPs and non-performing loans from the banks.
		Masakhane Campaign	Encourage a resumption of rates and services payments in support of normalising the lending environment in former township areas.
	New Deal	Thubelisha Homes	Procure or develop housing stock appropriate for Servcon's rightsizing programme.

Strategy	Policy initiative	Institution	Mandate/focus
	Second policy thrust: Mobilise credit		
Diversify supply of housing finance	Non-bank housing loans	NHFC	Wholesale financing of retail housing lenders.
	Lending for rural housing	RHLF	Wholesale finance of retail housing lenders in rural areas.
	Securitisation	Gateway Home Loans	Securitise mortgage loans to low-income earners.
	Social (rental) housing	Social Housing Foundation	Provide capacity support to emerging social housing institutions.
	Guarantees	Nurcha	Provide guarantees and other support to encourage low-income housing delivery.
	Third policy thrust: Housing subsidy programme		
Stimulate demand for housing finance	Credit- and non-credit-linked subsidies targeted at projects, individuals, and consolidation initiatives in both urban and rural areas.	Provincial housing departments	Promote and facilitate the provision of adequate housing (Housing Act, 1997).
	Institutional subsidies for providers of rental accommodation. Relocation subsidies for beneficiaries willing to vacate repossessed properties.	Local authorities	Take all reasonable and necessary steps to ensure that the right to have access to adequate housing is realised on a progressive basis (Housing Act, 1997).

Source: Rust (2004, p.6).

Of these, the national housing development financial institution, the National Housing Finance Corporation (NHFC), was the largest in terms of funding provided. Government has invested some R2bn in the NHFC and its various funds, which NHFC has made available in the form of long-term debt facilities, largely to retail lenders and housing associations.

NHFC finance played an important role in the growth of incremental housing lending, which was mainly payroll-deducted. Most of the housing impact achieved has been through micro loans for housing; and growth in numbers has slowed since 2001 (see Figure 6.2).

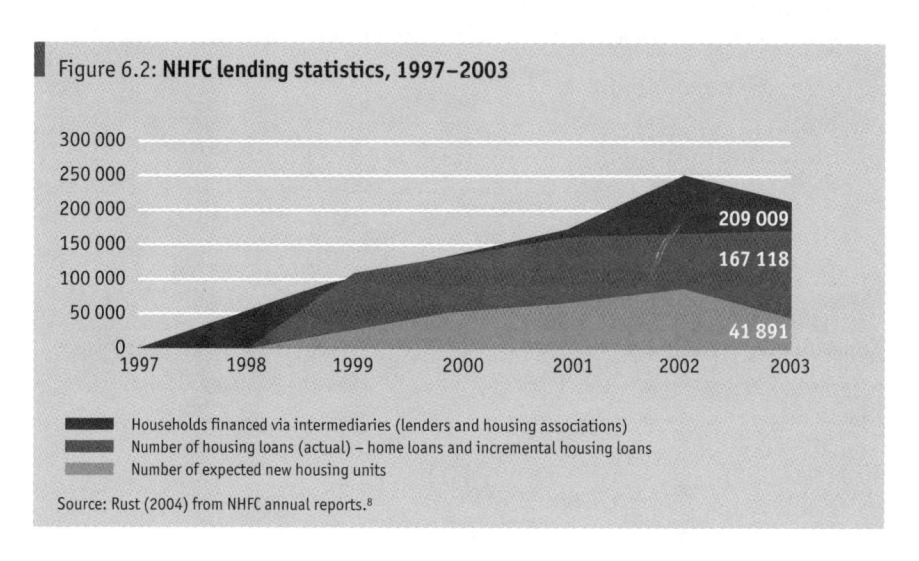

Figure 6.2: **NHFC lending statistics, 1997–2003**

[Area chart showing three series from 1997 to 2003, with 2003 values: 209 009, 167 118, and 41 891]

■ Households financed via intermediaries (lenders and housing associations)
■ Number of housing loans (actual) – home loans and incremental housing loans
■ Number of expected new housing units

Source: Rust (2004) from NHFC annual reports.[8]

Underlying this slow-down (see Table 6.3) has been a decline in the retail lending client base of NHFC, together with its sister Rural Housing Loan Fund (RHLF), originally started under the NHFC umbrella but independent since 2002. Rising numbers of incremental housing lenders are in distress and there has been considerable consolidation in micro lending (see Chapter 4), resulting in a very limited retail network.

Table 6.3: **Current status of RHLF and NHFC lender clients**

	RHLF clients		NHFC clients			
			Incremental		Home loans	
Year	2002	2003	2002	2003	2002	2003
No. of lenders	9	8	8	11	5	5
Lenders in distress	6	6	2	4	2	2
Lenders who left RHLF/NHFC	1	3	3	0	0	1
Expected consolidation	0	6 to 2	0	3 to 1	0	0
New clients	0	3	0	3	0	1

Source: Rust (2003).

In this respect, NHFC is trapped in a vicious circle like its sister development finance institution, Khula. On the one hand, it is unable to deploy the funds it has. In 2003, NHFC's actual 'advances outstanding' to housing intermediaries were R550m, on a total balance sheet of over R2,4bn (of which all but R100m was originally provided by government in capital or accumulated reserves).[9] This was less than 25% of assets, little changed from 2002. The remainder is invested in tradable securities and on deposit with the same large banks that are often accused of not lending. On the other hand, it is unable to meet the needs of those entities that could absorb large amounts of funding. NHFC's exposure limit of R100m per client means that it is unable to respond to the needs of even mid-sized entities (such as CashBank in its day), which require far more to be viable. The limit is partly self-imposed and partly prudentially related to the size of its balance sheet.

As a way to engage the banks and address the credit gap, NHFC launched Gateway Home Loans in 1999. It was started as a two-year pilot initiative to test both a new non-mortgage loan as well as the possibilities of funding through securitisation (see the case study on p.147). After failing to reach the target in terms of volumes of loans purchased, the pilot ended in 2001, with Gateway absorbed into NHFC.

Over the decade, relations between government and banks in this sector were extremely volatile. From an initial high, at the signing of the RoU in 1994, they swung to a low point in 1998 when recriminations were flying over the alleged non-delivery of banks under the RoU. For their part, banks argued that they had not seen the anticipated improvement in the lending environment in many areas. And, where losses were incurred under the RoU lending programme, they did not receive all the cover promised in the RoU. The reality was that, despite the over-ambitious expectations of both banks and government of the RoU, it did result in more than R10bn in new mortgage lending in areas where lending had ceased. Unfortunately, this new lending did not long outlast the closure of the Mortgage Indemnity Fund (MIF) in 1998.

It was in 1999 that government dusted off earlier plans for legislative mechanisms to place pressure on banks. These followed the American legislative approach. First, a Home Loan and Mortgage Disclosure Act was passed in 2000 to ensure better information about lending on an area basis. Armed with this information, government and others could at least apply moral pressure to banks that were redlining certain districts. However, nearly five years later, the regulations to the Act, which would give it effect, have yet to be promulgated and the effectiveness of this approach has therefore not been tested. Then, in 2002, the Department of Housing tabled a Community Reinvestment Bill, which would require all home lenders to reach certain prescribed targets for low-income lending, or face a fine. However, this bill never reached Parliament. The Charter process in 2003 resulted in new commitments, which allowed government to withdraw the Bill for the time being in favour of the more consensual Charter target approach.

In early 2004, intense high-level meetings between government and banks over how to implement Charter undertakings in this sector signalled a renewed thaw in the relationship. Financial institutions committed themselves to originating affordable housing loans, as part of the targeted investment goal. But they said that the extent of lending would be contingent on new public–private risk-sharing mechanisms.

The environment in which lenders are expected to lend remains difficult in many areas, however. In 2002, Servcon MD Denis Creighton described the situation in many historically disadvantaged townships as 'the housing swamp'. Servcon acted as an agency managing bank 'properties in possession' in township areas, for most of the decade. Despite these and other initiatives to stabilise the market,[10] Creighton's 2002 list of problems mirrored the underlying issues in 1994: poverty and unemployment; lack of education; construction defects; breakdown of law and order; and local authorities' failure to maintain service standards and to control arrears on rates and service charges.

The problems that bogged down housing delivery were deeply rooted and intertwined. Most go well beyond the narrow competence of housing finance. As long as they remain, the environment will remain hostile to housing finance in the areas affected; and indeed, there could be retrogression. Between 1997 and 2002, about 32 000 new properties had fallen into default in the township areas, of which Servcon had 'normalised' about 11 000.[11] Most of these defaults were tied to socio-economic issues such as rising interest rates and retrenchments.

While housing finance policy has essentially remained constant, the emphasis has changed over the first decade. One shift relates to rental housing. Initially neglected in favour of ownership as a tenure form, rental became a major focus after the Job Summit of 1998. It was to be provided through social housing associations on a European model. A second shift relates to the target group. Initially, households with incomes in the higher subsidy bands (R1 500–R3 500) were considered the prime market for intervention and support of housing finance. However, in part because of wage inflation and in part because of rising political pressures of an emerging middle class, the definition has been widened at the upper end. The Charter definition of low-income housing (see Box 6.2) extends the monthly income of households to R7 500.

Housing finance products available today
Despite the 'swamp' in some areas, there is a much wider range of home finance product options available in 2004 than in 1994. In 2004, due to ongoing innovation, the end-user finance product range includes:[12]
- **Mortgage bonds:** targeted primarily at the middle-to-higher income households, these generally range from R100 000 upwards. Penny Hawkins of financial and economic research company Feasibility estimates that 55% of the value of the entire consumer credit market in SA comprises

> **Box 6.2: Charter definition and commitment to low-cost housing**
>
> Definition:
> 2.34.3 low-income housing for households with a stable income in excess of R1,500 per month and less than R7,500 per month. This income band will be increased in line with the CPIX on the 1st of January each year commencing on 1 January 2004.
>
> Commitment:
> 8.3.2 in accordance with the arrangements concluded with Government and the DFIs in terms of paragraph 9.1.3, to originate the low-income housing loans, agricultural development loans, and loans to black SMEs, necessary to achieve the desired breakdown of targeted investment.
>
> Source: Financial Sector Charter (2003).

mortgage credit.[13] However, only 14% of mortgage loans by value (R27bn), or 20% by number, were estimated to be at the lower end (households earning R4 000 or less a month) of the market.[14] The Banking Council contends that banks provided around R18,4bn in 350 000 new mortgage loans of less than R150 000 between 1994 and 2004. However, in the absence of an active secondary market in which the lender can be sure that the value of the mortgage is realisable on foreclosure, fewer lenders are seeing a mortgage as a viable option in the low-income market.

- **Instalment sales:** targeted primarily at middle-income households, these support housing products between R45 000 and R80 000. The instalment sale product allows title to remain with the financier, until a defined repayment threshold (usually 50%) has been reached. Then the borrower has the right to take transfer. This option is often used in sectional-title arrangements in the inner city or on housing projects, where the borrower 'rents' the property until transfer is effected. However, this product requires the existence of a sufficiently strong landlord or management agent, who can manage the stock before transfer. While several such institutions emerged in the late 1990s, most were facing financial difficulties by the early part of this decade.
- **Secured housing loans:** targeted primarily at the formally employed borrower with a middle-to-lower income, these loans are normally secured against the borrower's pension or provident fund benefits. Often the loan size is enhanced by additional securities such as credit insurance provided by the likes of Home Loan Guarantee Company (see the case study on p.163). Loan size is typically R10 000–R20 000.
- **(Micro) housing loans:** targeted primarily at the home improvements market for lower-to-middle income earning households, they are generally

between R2 000 and R10 000—though some (offered by NGOs) extend lower and some extend higher (to accommodate the RDP top-up market for households not eligible for the full subsidy). While many of these loans are disbursed as cash, a significant proportion of them are offered by building materials suppliers and are used to buy building materials in-store.
- **Institutional loans:** targeted at housing institutions offering housing—generally within the R80 000–R120 000 range—for rent. Institutional loans are wholesale loans to cover the long-term financing of a number of units in a development. Originally, the NHFC was the only institution offering such finance. More recently, however, Absa Bank has made two loans for successive projects to the Johannesburg Housing Company—a social housing institution operating successfully in inner-city Johannesburg, with some 2 000 units under management. However, as with the instalment sale product, most institutions that were established in the 1990s to provide rental housing faced financial difficulties in the early part of the next decade.

Despite this apparent diversity of options, effective access to housing finance remains constrained for most lower-income people and for people who wish to buy in certain areas. The credit gap remains and, indeed, has widened. The central question of housing finance in SA today may be paraphrased as: 'How can you turn a monthly instalment of R500 into a housing finance package worth R50 000 on a sustainable basis?' The instalment relates to what is affordable to many people; the package relates to the minimum price of a basic small house in many urban areas.

The credit gap

FinMark founder David Porteous and Rand Water GM Keith Naicker have provided a full analysis of the factors causing the credit gap.[15] In essence, it results from a mismatch between what home buyers can afford to repay and what available homes they are willing to buy. The gap will only close if buyer incomes rise faster than housing costs, increasing affordability; and as more houses and housing options become available at a wider range of prices. This is why the development of the secondary housing market in township areas is so important; it should allow prices of houses to clear against demand over time.

In the current 'swamp', however, there are few transactions; and, in part because there are so few transactions, there is more risk associated with lending against houses. And the restriction of finance availability further debilitates effective demand. A vicious cycle sets in, which is very hard to break.

Given a maximum affordable loan instalment size and a minimum 'complete house' price, set by availability of stock and construction costs, the only flexible parameters in the housing loan equation are:

- How much can be borrowed relative to property price (i.e. how much of the buyer's own equity is needed)
- The term of the loan
- The interest rate.

Box 6.3: The economics of micro finance for housing

Ms X is a teacher in Kimberley. She takes home R1 316 per month. In 1992 she took a R25 000, 20-year mortgage loan at 15% per annum on average with a R330 per month instalment from a large bank, to build a house. She elected to pay R380 per month (29% of her take-home pay) to pay off the loan faster and save on interest charges. Seven years later, by 1999, she had repaid 40% of the capital amount, and still owed R15 048. She had also paid R21 968 in interest charges.

Ms Y is also a teacher in Kimberley, with the same monthly take-home pay of R1 316. Rather than taking out a mortgage loan, Ms Y chose to take out five successive micro loans of R5 000 each. These loans were repayable over 18 months at an interest rate of 40%. She also chose to pay R380 per month (29% of her take home pay) to repay these loans. By 1999, she had repaid all five micro loans and owed nothing more. She had paid R6 920 in interest (31,5% of what Ms X paid on the R25 000 bond, and only 27,7% cumulatively on the R25 000 capital she had borrowed).

	Mortgage	Micro loan (unsecured)
Loan size in 1992	R25 000	5 × R5000 – successively
Term	20 years	18 months per loan
Average interest	15%	40%
Monthly instalment	R330	
Amount paid	R380	R380
By 1999		
Amount of capital repaid	R9 951	R25 000
Amount of capital still owing	R15 048 (60%)	R0
Total paid in interest	R21 968	R6920

Today Ms Y owns a bond-free house and continues to improve it every year, borrowing small amounts. She did the construction work with the help of her son and spent capital on materials and specialists such as an electrician and a plumber. Her house today is 20% bigger than the house Ms X built for R25 000, in 1992, through a contractor.

Source: De Ridder (2004).

In the affordable housing market, borrowers are constrained in their ability to contribute their own savings. Also, stretching the loan term may reduce the instalment, but this is not necessarily advantageous, as Johan de Ridder, former CE of the NHFC, shows (see Box 6.3). The only remaining variable is the interest rate. This is made up of four components, two of which—inflation and real interest rate—are determined by macroeconomic conditions and economic-policy prescriptions. They are not directly influenced by housing. The other determinants are cost and risk.

In the absence of an active secondary market, it is hard for lenders to price for risk. Although geographic risk data for the industry as a whole is still very inadequate, Table 6.4 (based on 2001 data) shows that there is some justification for the perception of high risk in low-income areas. The average loss suffered by lenders in suburban areas is around 25% of the outstanding balance, but the experience in many low-income areas has been more in the vicinity of 75%.[16]

Table 6.4: **Bank non-performing loans and PIPs (properties in possession) versus total outstanding loan amounts by area**

Area	Outstanding loan amounts in 2001 (rand millions)	% total	Non-performing loans	Properties in possession
Low-income areas	R12 502	9%	10–15% depending on areas	4,4%
Suburban residential areas	R125 045	91%	5%	0,5%

Source: NHFC (2001).

The cost of lending also has a big impact. Figure 6.3 illustrates how, given plausible assumptions (made in 1998) about the cost of originating and servicing mortgage loans, a mortgage loan of less than R50 000 was just not profitable to the average large bank. This threshold would have grown substantially in the past six years, with CPI inflation alone moving the breakeven closer to R70 000; hence the relative lack of mortgage lending below this level.

So who can do affordable housing?
The breakeven analysis in Figure 6.3 reflects the cost structure and prevailing lending rates of large banks at the time. Smaller, more specialised lenders could perhaps reduce these costs—at least the fixed-cost element inherent in the infrastructure of a large bank. On the other hand, large banks have the advantage of economies of scale. It is not clear, therefore, that the breakeven loan size would be so different for other types of organisation.

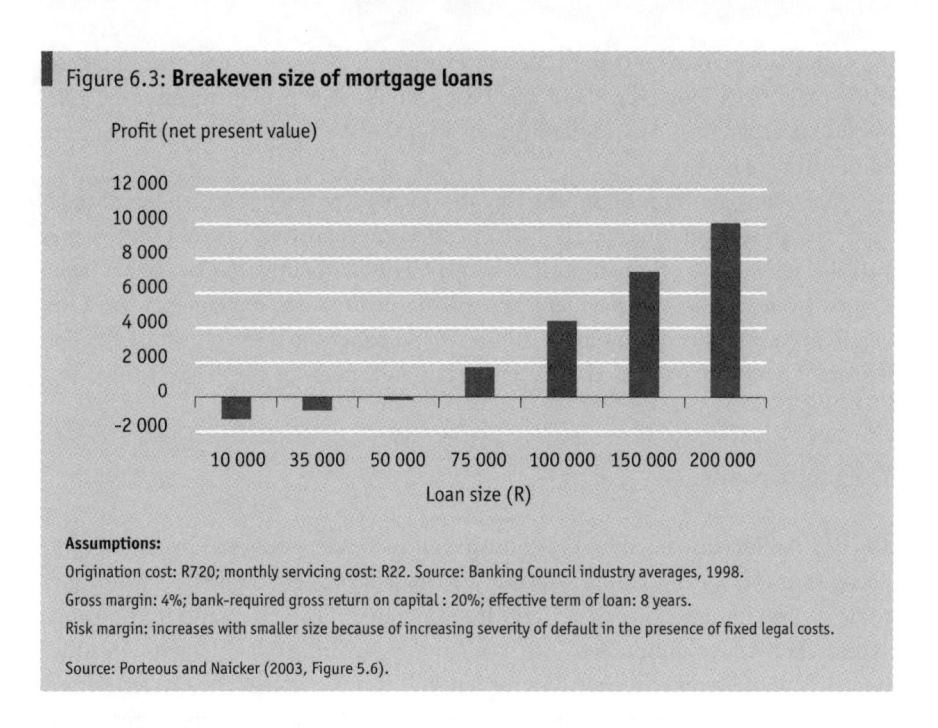

> Figure 6.3: **Breakeven size of mortgage loans**
>
> Profit (net present value) vs Loan size (R): 10 000, 35 000, 50 000, 75 000, 100 000, 150 000, 200 000
>
> **Assumptions:**
> Origination cost: R720; monthly servicing cost: R22. Source: Banking Council industry averages, 1998.
> Gross margin: 4%; bank-required gross return on capital : 20%; effective term of loan: 8 years.
> Risk margin: increases with smaller size because of increasing severity of default in the presence of fixed legal costs.
>
> Source: Porteous and Naicker (2003, Figure 5.6).

What is clear, however, is that lenders other than large banks have an essential part to play in the housing finance system. Alternative lending and origination networks can offer a distribution network that is closer to buyers and their communities. They can also manage some of the risks of home lending better, since they understand borrowers' situations.

This was part of the conclusion of a study, financed by FinMark Trust, into the servicing of affordable mortgages undertaken by US mortgage giant Fannie Mae in 2004.[17] Fannie Mae gave the example of successful, specialised, non-bank housing lenders such as Su Casita in Mexico, which faces similar swamp-like conditions around affordable housing. These lenders have capacity, such as kiosks in the housing projects, from which intensive management of borrowers, especially high-risk ones, can take place. Specialised entities like this have attracted international standard servicing ratings from rating agencies.

However, they must still be able to fund their home loan portfolios. Home purchase loans are relatively large and longer-term, certainly compared with micro loans, and this creates special financing challenges for small entities. Today, the only option for alternative home lenders is NHFC financing. But, as pointed out earlier, this is limited to R100m per institution, which is likely to be too little to make origination and servicing entities viable. A network of specialised home lenders requires financing solutions, such as securitisation, which would enable the lenders to on-sell standardised loans. Securitisation has been much debated over the past ten years, in the light of the SA Home Loans experience at the high end of the suburban market, and the Gateway experience at the low end (see the case study on p.147). However, there can be no doubt it will play an essential role because it separates financing and its associated risks from the operational and administrative issues.

Discussions continue about the way in which government and lenders should share risk in difficult markets, but the most serious constraint is that there is no available network of originators and servicers. The competitive landscape has been shaped by access to the payment system for debit order repayments. And, as researcher Kecia Rust has pointed out in several papers, it is tilted against smaller lenders.[18] Several have closed in recent years. And nothing else has yet filled the gap.

The way forward

Meeting the increased demand for housing and services, generated by an ongoing decrease in average household size, is a key challenge for government.[19] Ironically, some success in new-housing delivery has generated further demand for housing, as households have 'unbundled' into smaller units, creating more demand. In addition, SA's population is already 55% urban, and this percentage is expected to rise sharply in the next decade, increasing demand for housing in urban areas. The HIV/AIDS epidemic adds uncertainty to demographic projections, however. And housing finance, which is typically long-term, is especially vulnerable to the infection and death of a borrower during the term of the loan. This is why initiatives such as those by the Home Loan Guarantee Company (HLGC) to provide forms of cover to mortgage lenders against losses resulting from the borrower contracting HIV/AIDS are so welcome (see the case study on p.163).

In recent years, suburban home owners countrywide have enjoyed the fruits of house prices rising: since 1993, average home sale prices in real terms, tracked by Absa, have risen by over 25%, with most of the increase coming after 1999.[20] This development has created much new wealth. However, in the absence of a secondary market, most of the population has not tasted the fruits of this. Old township stock, in particular, has been left behind, although there are signs of progress in other market segments, most notably the newer privately developed houses. The wealth creation opportunity locked up in these defective markets offers one of the largest broad-based black economic empowerment opportunities of the next decade.

To unlock the 'dead capital' in these areas, the vicious cycle that continues to cause 'swamp-like' conditions will have to be reversed. This cannot be achieved by turning on the taps of housing finance alone. Reversing decline will also require a concerted effort by government at all levels, especially local authorities, where service levels and charges are set. Parastatals like the NHFC have an important role to play in risk absorption, and indeed in market creation, in order to encourage private lending to flow. The required level of public–private coordination cannot be achieved on a high-level national basis alone, such as through the Charter process. An area-by-area approach is necessary, where the most promising areas in terms of agreed criteria are prioritised for new private-home lending flows and public investment in infrastructure such as tarred roads, electricity and water. A credible central database, accessible to government and lenders, will be required to monitor trends in these areas. In prioritised areas as well, new points of presence are needed for the origination and servicing of home loans in the area. This township-by-township approach is no quick fix, but there are no alternatives to reversing spirals of decay. As house value is unlocked in an area and residents experience the benefits, so the demonstration effect should encourage other areas to participate in the process.

Housing in SA has witnessed various attempts at the quick fix over the past ten years. But housing is inherently a longer-term process, with longer investment and lending horizons. There is no easy walk to freedom in this area. Determined, co-ordinated, incremental steps will achieve more in democratising housing finance than any further attempt at the big quick fix in the next decade.

Endnotes

1 This chapter draws on a longer background paper by Rust (2004b).
2 Presidency (2003, p.25).
3 Renaud (2003).
4 Shisaka (2004).
5 This low level of trade is further substantiated by an analysis of Deeds Registry data. In the past five years (1999–2004), secondary registrations took place in respect of 7,5% of proclaimed properties in 12 of the 18 survey sites in which the Household Survey was undertaken. Of the 7,5%, 37% were as the result of becoming bank properties-in-possession, indicating the high level of dysfunction in this market.
6 Figures include banks and those of state-owned retail lender Khayalethu Home Loans (Porteous & Naicker 2003, p.192).
7 For a complete breakdown of reasons for mortgage default at this time according to the experience of mortgage insurer HLGC, see Porteous and Naicker (2003, p.193).
8 Numbers are drawn from NHFC annual reports (1997–2002), plus data supplied by the NHFC by e-mail for 2003. For 1997–2001, RHLF lending data has been deducted, given the independence of the two institutions currently. The various peaks in 2002 are overestimates, which were readjusted based on the 2002 Corporate Impact Report in 2003.
9 NHFC (2003c).
10 Rust (2004).
11 Rust (2002a).
12 Shisaka (2003).
13 Hawkins (2003b).

14 Rust (2004b, p.15).
15 Porteous & Naicker (2003).
16 De Ridder: personal communication based on Banking Council statistics, June 2004.
17 Available at www.finmarktrust.org.za/research.
18 Rust (2002, 2003 and 2004).
19 Presidency (2003).
20 See *Financial Mail* (17 January 2003).

CASE STUDY
The Community Bank: building society Mark 2

COMMUNITY BANK

Bob Tucker

Cas Coovadia

In 1991, with political negotiations on track and the new SA on the horizon, a community bank looked like an idea whose time had come. It was a concept that had worked in certain other developing countries, providing loans and banking services to low income households. And it seemed that many of the preconditions were in place, in SA, for a bank designed for the poor and financially underserved. A new dispensation was at hand, determined to empower the economically dispossessed, and the new democratic government was expected to be supportive of a cooperative initiative, as were private-sector banks, which were under pressure to serve a market they perceived to be high-cost, high-risk and unprofitable.

A community bank was seen as a way to fill the gap in community financing left by the demise of building societies—and more. In the 1980s, then Finance Minister Barend du Plessis introduced legislation that required building societies to hold the same ratio of capital (against the risk profile of their assets) as banks. Bob Tucker, then MD of the Perm Building Society and now CE of the Banking Council, says this was inappropriate and impractical. 'There was no way that building societies, without access to equity capital, could build up enough reserves out of retained income to meet that requirement.' The move spelt the end of the building society movement in SA, as the building societies started changing from mutuals to companies, most of them listing on the stock market. So, at precisely the point at which a building society movement was needed to serve the black community, it was washed away by events. 'I find it hard to believe the change in legislation was coincidental,' says Tucker. 'I believe it was deliberately designed to prevent blacks from using financial institutions to become property owners.'

In 1991, Tucker and civic activist Cas Coovadia, now transformation GM at the Banking Council, started working on the concept of a community bank. 'We decided to look at the international experience of banking low-income people,' says Coovadia. 'We identified Hank Jackelen of UNDP to advise us. Hank was renowned as one of the experts in community banking. He had advised the

Grameen bank, he had advised a number of institutions in South America, he had advised the Get Ahead Foundation and the Small Enterprise Foundation in SA.'

With Jackelen's input, a task team, headed by Tucker, developed a business plan, which distinguished between operations which should eventually be profitable, and those that would have to be considered developmental. The banking functions were placed in the Community Bank, which was regarded as a commercial venture, while the developmental work was placed in a Section 21 (not-for-profit) company—the Community Bank Foundation—and was donor-funded.

'We got support from the banks,' says Coovadia. 'The Big Four undertook to put in R5m each.' The state-owned Industrial Development Corporation contributed R15m, the Independent Development Trust R15m, and the Development Bank of Southern Africa R75m.

The Community Bank inherited the banking system previously used by Allied Bank, now a part of the Absa group, and key staff was seconded from various banks, especially Allied. It registered in July 1994 and opened its first branch for business in Benoni. The first products offered were:

- A low-end savings account
- A mortgage loan, similar in profile to conventional mortgages but smaller
- SME loans.

However, problems arose before the bank even got off the ground, when Tucker parted company with the donors and went on to head E Plan at Standard Bank. His experience in the deposit-taking and loan arena, combined with his insights into developmental imperatives, would have been invaluable in an organisation committed to both commercial viability and development.

The scene was set for the internal conflicts that were to tear Community Bank apart in less than two years. Coovadia believes the undertaking was fundamentally flawed by its dual structure and his inability to coordinate their activities. Tucker says the problem was twofold. On the one hand 'developmental gatekeepers, who believed that loans should only go to those who needed them most', were allowed to take control of the trust. With little regard for sound credit criteria, they steered the bank towards poor credit extension. On the other hand, a conventional building society executive was imposed on the banking operation. And he proved inflexible and unresponsive to the needs of a market that was very different from the traditional one to which he was accustomed.

'The conventional building society executive should never have been allowed in. The developmental gatekeepers had a role to play but they should have been obliged to comply with sound financial standards for granting credit,' says Tucker.

When its first financial reporting period ended, eight months after launch, Community Bank reported a R20,1m loss. Its MD said the bank had borne the cost of 'setting up a head office, with staff who had the required skills to lay the foundation for the branch and computer networks prior to receipt of the capital'.[1]

But the problems were more fundamental. 'We grew too fast,' says Coovadia. 'We immediately expanded to 17 branches, which was just too ambitious.' Coovadia also believes that the structure was too complex. His role was to co-ordinate the activities of the two arms. 'But both organisations were accountable to their own boards. This left me with virtually no power to play the role I was supposed to play.'

The rapid expansion was a symptom of the internal dissension, says Coovadia. 'The foundation would begin to interact with community groups, without strategising with the banking side,' he says. 'So expectations would be raised and the bank would be forced to open an outlet in the area without having conducted a sound market and economic analysis as to what investment would be necessary and how soon they could reach breakeven.'

With the benefit of hindsight, Coovadia says one unit should have been responsible for both banking and developmental functions. 'The bank must see the building of capacity as part of its business model.'

The expansion process drove up the cost-to-income ratio, as did the decision that the bank must look like a bank. 'There was a view that, to instil confidence, there must be a substantial investment in infrastructure. I don't believe that was a valid assumption,' says Coovadia.

Contributing to the problems was the absence of people with sufficient skills to guide the bank through its teething problems. 'The banks gave us key people in the planning stages but they pulled them out when we started.'

The final nail in the coffin turned out to be the absence of a 'sufficiently good funding strategy', says Coovadia. Though it was easy to extend small mortgage loans it was difficult to mobilise retail deposits. In addition, the margin on mortgages proved insufficient to fund the full costs of running a retail banking network.

Major funders began to lose confidence in the model on which the bank was based, refusing to provide further funding. In the absence of further wholesale funding, and with a rapidly growing long-term loan book, the bank started to experience liquidity problems.

Even Labour 'didn't come to the party', Coovadia recalls. 'The SA Clothing and Textile Union approached us for housing loans for their members. They indicated they would be willing to put money into the institution, in the form of members' savings. On the basis of their assurance, we opened a branch in Salt River primarily to service their members. But, when it came to signing on the bottom line, they backed out. They said they were not too sure about the future of the institution, and couldn't deposit members' money in it.'

In May 1996 the Community Bank, with 37 000 depositors, ran out of funding and was placed in curatorship by the Registrar of Banks. The mortgage book was eventually bought by Unibank, which itself collapsed six years later as the result of bad micro-lending decisions.

Coovadia says a fundamental problem for Community Bank was the environment. Unlike those developing countries where successful community banking models were implemented, SA has a strong and sophisticated formal banking sector.

'In other countries, the institutions had a significant untapped market, without having to compete against a formal banking sector. In Bolivia and Bangladesh they were able to sustain high interest rates. Here we couldn't sustain rates that would cater for the risk because the formal sector determined interest rates. In those countries, the institutions grew very quickly, becoming among the biggest in their countries and soon achieved economies of scale. We couldn't do that.'

However, valuable lessons were learned.

'We need to understand what we mean by community banking,' says Coovadia. 'There is space for niche banking in the low-income market, but not for a broad-based bank with a whole range of products.' As to the failed Community Bank: 'I think it was premature,' says Coovadia. 'The environment is more conducive today for a diverse range of institutions to service a diverse market. But they will need to be more flexible than we were under the Mutual Banks Act.'

Tucker believes the Community Bank concept would have worked if it had had access to the big banks' electronic distribution network, allowing its clients to use any ATMs. This suggests that an early version of the new basic bank account may have made the concept workable.■

Endnote

1   *Business Day* (21 July 1995).

CASE STUDY
CashBank: gobbled by Goliath

In many developing communities, the honour and standing of individuals takes the place of collateral in securing a loan. The system is known as peer sanction, and it has a long and reasonably successful track record in stokvel-type organisations in SA. In the 1980s, when financial and developmental institutions in SA started looking for ways to bring banking to poor people, peer sanction seemed a mechanism worth exploring. Christine Glover, formerly an urban and regional planner and later MD of CashBank, was among those to test its potential in the formal sector.

CashBank was set up originally as a niche provider of home loans to the low-income market. It was registered as a bank in 1995, following the first commercialisation of a micro-finance NGO in SA, the Group Credit Company (GCC). This route of NGO-to-bank conversion followed closely on developments in leading micro-finance markets such as Bolivia, where BancoSol had been formed from an NGO, Prodem, in 1991.

In 1989, Glover was seconded from the Urban Foundation (which was actively seeking ways to fund low-income housing in urban areas) to set up the GCC, with initial funding of R500 000 from the Urban Foundation and R1m from the Development Bank. 'We were based in Cape Town, with branches in the Eastern Cape and Gauteng,' says Glover. As the name suggests, the GCC offered a loan facility of 60 months, and up to R6 000 per borrower, to a group of up to 20 people who were jointly responsible for repayment. Once approved, the group triggered a loan by instructing GCC to pay an approved amount to a particular member. And within a year, by October 1990, GCC had advanced R1,78m to 57 groups made up of 919 people.

However, the operation was not large enough to serve as a demonstration pilot for conventional banks, which, it was hoped, would take up the challenge of lending to business opportunities in the low-income market. As that was part of the rationale for the project, Glover attempted to expand business to a scale that would make the outcome more influential. However, the attempt was halted in June 1992 when an arrears problem emerged.

The peer sanction system works well in small, cohesive communities, but does not necessarily migrate to a more complex type of organisation. The problem was one that GCC had not foreseen. 'Members were experienced in managing loans worth hundreds of rands for periods of less than a year,' says Glover. 'A group cycle is normally no longer than 12 months, usually 11. Human dynamics being what they are, groups change fundamentally over a longer period and it's not reasonable to expect the group to be stable. Maybe they are in rural areas, but not in the urban areas where we were operating.'

Member turnover and lack of experience with larger, longer-term loans made group sanction ineffective. 'As the sums of money moved beyond commonly used limits, the basis of assessing affordability became need, and not ability to pay.'

To address the problem, 'we started lending small sums of money for periods of less than a year,' says Glover. 'That worked very well operationally but, for the board, it didn't provide an acceptable risk return, considering the high management input required,' she says.

Glover decided that, if GCC was to become commercially viable, it would need to offer a diversity of products—low- and high-risk. An opportunity to explore low-risk opportunities arose in 1993 when unions operating in the metal industry approached GCC. 'They liked the institution but they didn't like the product we were offering,' says Glover. 'They suggested pension-backed home loans.'

GCC negotiated with the Metal Industry Pension Fund and the three Port Elizabeth companies whose employees were fund members to offer home loans to members against the security of their pension fund assets. But the lower-risk, secured product needed relatively high volumes to generate returns. And high volumes made it cash-hungry.

'The product took off and I started borrowing from the institutional market to fund it. It was at an opportune time because people were looking for brownie-point investment opportunities ahead of 1994,' says Glover. But she soon encountered legal obstacles to this source of funding: only registered banks are allowed to take deposits from the public. 'What we were doing was illegal in terms of the Banks Act. And, eventually, the Registrar of Banks insisted we register as a mutual bank,' says Glover.

GCC registered a banking arm as a mutual bank, named CashBank (Credit and Savings Help Bank) in 1995, with Norwich, Southern and Metropolitan Life as shareholders. In May 1995, it had total deposits of R10,6m and total assets of R75,8m. GCC remained as the non-profit research and development arm of CashBank.

Set up primarily as a niche provider of corporate and home loan financial products, CashBank was committed to providing 'appropriate banking services to the lower income communities, through the provision of savings as well as credit—mostly for housing, small business, education and personal loans'. However, the main growth, according to Glover, was in home loans; especially, at first, those secured by a retirement fund guarantee.

Increased participation of investors raised primary capital from R43m in 1996 to R82m in 1997. Investors included major private institutions (Southern Life, Metropolitan Life, Norwich Life, Fedlife, Nedcor, Sanlam) as well as the Eskom Pension Fund, the Independent Development Trust and the International Finance Corporation from the US.

The capital base potentially allowed the bank, which had assets of R250m in 1997, to grow to R1bn. Two years on, the bank had almost doubled its balance sheet to R474m, although it incurred a loss, in part due to the failure of retail lending activities.

CashBank's focus remained on the low-income market—in 1997, nearly 70% of its borrowers earned less than R2 000 a month. 'Mortgage loans initially averaged around R60 000, for the purchase of full standard housing. We never lent for the purchase of reduced standard housing in township areas, which was relatively high-risk because people valued the properties very much less,' says Glover.

'We continued offering micro and small individual loans and small business loans for a while. But, eventually, my board closed that down. We were in a high-risk arena anyway, so the board wanted us to concentrate on employer-based lending, with repayments collected via payroll deductions, because administration costs were lower.'

In 1998, the bank embarked on mortgage lending, finding a niche in the employer-backed small-mortgage market. It marketed the product through developers in the affordable-housing sector, to clients, usually first-time home buyers, who qualified for a state capital subsidy. The loan went towards the purchase of an R80 000 two-bedroom house, with A-grade finishes, and full electrical, water and sanitation services. By the end of the financial year, 30 September 1998, CashBank already had R82m in mortgage loans on its balance sheets.

However, this activity proved very draining on cash flow. By the late 1990s, the favourable fund-raising environment that dated from before 1994 had evaporated. 'Exchange control had softened, creating greater investment avenues for institutions, and there had been a lot of consolidation in the financial market, so there were fewer potential investors,' says Glover. As a mutual, CashBank struggled to build its reserves. It converted to a conventional commercial bank in 1999 because this institutional structure allowed it to issue equity to institutional shareholders. An additional advantage of its equity structure was that it could set up a share incentive scheme to enhance acquisition and retention of core staff.

By 2000, CashBank was struggling to fund its growing mortgage book. With total assets at over R550m in August 2000, the bank was outgrowing its resources. Efforts to structure off-balance-sheet funding did not succeed. In June 2001, CashBank was bought by the BoE Group and became a wholly owned subsidiary, carrying the group's low-end housing brand. BoE was itself subsequently bought by Nedcor in 2002, following the banking crisis triggered by Saambou. As a result, CashBank has disappeared as a brand and an entity. After more than ten years of innovation and perseverance in the affordable housing and banking markets, one of the earliest pioneers had finally been laid to rest. GCC, which had remained alongside the bank to initiate product innovation and testing, was wound up with the sale of the bank to BoE.

As to the future of small players like CashBank, Glover regrets that the major banks now treat pension fund lending as a loss leader. The product is priced down to get companies as clients. This makes it difficult for small players to compete. Another hazard small banks face, she says, is the uncertainty and declining formal employment profile of their potential markets. 'A 20-year loan is not practical in a volatile economic situation, especially where resale is poor and underdeveloped. While there has been rapid development of the middle- and high-income sector, there has not been much development in the low-income market.'

And as for the group-lending schemes with which GCC had been born, while they may work in rural areas, GCC's experience had shown that there were real problems with replicating a group-based approach to longer-term credit in urban areas.■

CASE STUDY
Gateway Home Loans: showing SA a new way home

'Pilot projects must have clearly defined objectives and timelines, with the guillotine if necessary, so that the landscape does not become dotted with institutions which have lost their way but which no one is prepared to put to death,' says David Porteous, MD and founder of Gateway Home Loans.

Gateway was a public–private partnership in the housing finance sector, which ran for a two-year pilot period between 1 April 1999 and 30 June 2001. It was designed and promoted by the National Housing Finance Corporation (NHFC) to fill the credit gap in housing finance, which in 1998/9 was loans for house purchases that were mainly worth less than R60 000. NHFC was majority shareholder and funder, with private institutional shareholders holding 15% of the equity.

'Gateway set out to do two things,' says Porteous. 'One was to test demand for a new type of non-mortgage home loan, called the Makhulong Home Loan, which relied largely on retirement funds and bought-in guarantees for security. The second was to test securitisation as an ongoing funding process for affordable home loans. These overall objectives were translated into the concrete target of accumulating a portfolio of 20 000 loans, at an estimated average size of R25 000, allowing a securitisation issue of R500 million to take place.'

But, by March 2001, Gateway had a total portfolio of only 2 000 home loans, amounting to around R200 million. These were of three types:

- The original Makhulong loan, although this proved to be a niche product which was successfully sold by only a few primary market lenders.
- The so-called Makhulong Institutional loan, which essentially derived its cash flow from an instalment sale agreement. It enabled refinancing of agreements, without the need to transfer the property—something that was increasingly in demand from private landlords, especially in inner-city and new-project environment.
- Smaller mortgages, which were of considerable interest to smaller mortgage lenders who were not able to fund mortgages easily on balance sheet, among them Cashbank, Unibank and Saambou.

Porteous says two years was 'long enough to establish critical facts with sufficient clarity'. However, it was not long enough to reach critical mass. No securitised funding was ever placed, owing to the small size of the portfolio, although Gateway did develop fundable deals around (i) a retirement-fund-guaranteed home loan book, owned by one of the banks, which was effectively turned down by the NHFC board; and (ii) a mortgage multi-lender conduit to fund smaller lenders such as CashBank, which was designed but never put into practice.

'Perhaps the original targets for loan purchase were too ambitious; and perhaps not enough attention was paid initially to the underlying incentives for banks to participate, something which might be different today,' says Porteous. Moreover, a dominant public partner (in this case NHFC) can restrict the flexibility which is so necessary at a pilot stage of any new venture. However, opportunities emerged in unexpected areas of housing finance, such as instalment sales and small mortgages. Unfortunately the NHFC was reluctant to support Gateway in pursuing them. When the NHFC rejected a business plan to build on new areas of momentum beyond the pilot, Porteous recommended the guillotine.

'Gateway started the pilot with a fairly prescriptive product (Makhulong) and approach, but also with high levels of expressed commitment by primary market banks (most of the retail banks, large and small, with the exception of Absa),' says Porteous. 'But the product proved complex and very difficult to introduce in large organisations with other priorities at the time. Gateway was forced into a high-innovation mode. It amended the features of the Makhulong product itself, and also developed the alternatives which went well beyond the original design, and helped players who needed liquidity.'

Towards the end of the two-year pilot, Gateway management commissioned an independent evaluation based on interviews with its clients. This review concluded: 'Despite the fact that Gateway has not managed to build a sufficiently large loan book to launch initial capital market funding, substantial progress has been made, particularly in the last six to eight months, since Gateway became more responsive to the market. A basis has been established for momentum to build.'

Proposals to revamp Gateway in the light of the lessons from the pilot period were made by the Gateway board to major shareholder, NHFC. But the NHFC would only agree to continue the pilot for a further three months. Porteous resigned at the end of the original pilot: 'I had no confidence that this response addressed the market need we had seen, or the lessons which came from the pilot period, and I believed it did not create a viable model going forward,' he says. Gateway was absorbed into NHFC in 2001, where, to this day, similar basic products have continued to be offered, in what has become a less hostile environment.

Interestingly, at about the same time as Gateway launched, South African Home Loans (SAHL) was started at the high end of the mortgage market. Using an approach that had been successful in Australia, SAHL offered mortgagees the opportunity to refinance at interest rates that were generally below prime. The first major issue of AAA-rated mortgage-backed securities in SA, backed by over R1bn of SAHL's mortgage loans, was successfully placed in 2001. Since then,

SAHL has successfully placed two further issues. The concept of securitisation of low-risk mortgages has become thoroughly accepted in SA; and even mortgage banks are now following suit.[1]

Gateway differed from SAHL in a number of ways, not least its focus at the lower end of the market, which was perceived to be, and is in fact, more risky than SAHL's suburban market. Nevertheless, Porteous believes valuable lessons were learnt from the Gateway pilot. 'The original objectives were too ambitious, since they involved both the creation of a new primary market product in two years, working through other institutions, as well as the new secondary market funding aspect. During the pilot, we came to see the need for both issues to be addressed, but each had, and has, a very different focus and resourcing requirement. The end of the Gateway pilot did not mean that securitisation does not work for low-income housing, since it was never actually tried. However, as the result of Gateway, the complexities and issues affecting securitisation at the low end were understood much better; and securitisation per se, as opposed to structured funding and risk sharing, was seen as less of a panacea than it was in the heady days of the late 1990s.'

Another lesson was that banks need incentives. 'We relied too much on the moral commitments made at the Job Summit in 1998 and at the launch of Gateway,' says Porteous. 'In practice, such moral commitments proved worthless in the face of other organisational priorities. Only where there was a serious business case for all parties was there effective engagement. I would therefore never rely on moral commitment alone. Having said this, it is not the case that Gateway did not work only or even mainly because "the banks did not come to the party". The truth was that there were large differences in the willingness, the ability and the desired outcome among the five banks which we had as primary market lenders.'

He believes these lessons could be applied successfully in future to the packaging of home finance at the low end of the market. They are informing some of the discussions around housing initiatives arising from the Financial Sector Charter.■

Endnote

1   See Cole et al. (2004).

Insurance

Introduction

The concept of insurance rests on an insurer's ability to pool defined risks and to spread those risks across a broad base of insured people.[1] Because the risks are pooled and diversified, the price of cover—the premium—can be much lower than the potential financial impact of the risk. In this sense, insurance improves the welfare of those insured and reduces their vulnerability to risk. Unfortunately, only around one-fifth to a quarter of adults in SA today have any form of formal insurance policy. This situation will have to be addressed by the insurance industry, if it is to meet its Charter commitments; and more importantly, if it is to be relevant to the evolving market in SA as a whole.

To be sustainable, insurers must be able to measure and price for risk; and they must also have the ability to collect premiums and pay claims cost-effectively. They will have to find ways to do this as they enter new markets about which they know comparatively little. The problem is twofold:

- In a new market, the risks are inherently uncertain and therefore hard to calculate. In the face of uncertainty, the natural tendency is to set a higher price, and this will affect affordability.
- Efficient collection of premiums is a transactional issue more than an insurance issue. Given the high cost to companies of receiving cash, and to clients of paying in cash, the reach of insurance is largely limited to those who can transact electronically—for example, through debit orders to make regular payments on their accounts.

Insurers have responded to the high cost of collection with schemes that cover defined groups of people, usually employees in a workplace. A single, aggregated amount is paid monthly to the insurer, significantly reducing collection costs. Group schemes have grown substantially in the past decade and have come to cover most formally employed people, many of whom have group life cover built into their retirement savings.

But, in SA, broadly defined formal employment applies to a minority of all adults—perhaps one in three. Hence, informal associations, known as burial societies, have evolved as a means of insuring against one major risk faced by households: the cost of a funeral. After the bank account, the burial society is today the most widely used financial product in SA, with almost one in four adults involved. This financial mechanism is an important means of risk pooling, especially for poorer people.

There is a further problem about broadening access to insurance: risk pooling does not work well when the risks rise above a certain threshold level. For example, the crime wave of the 1990s led to substantially increased premiums on short-term insurance, often pricing the product out of the market and prompting clients to effectively self-insure. In this situation, the remaining insured risk pool becomes less diversified but is still subject to certain fixed costs of administration, which further increases premiums. And a vicious cycle sets in, undermining the core value proposition which insurance offers.

In this context, the major issue for life insurers is HIV/AIDS, which is infecting an estimated one in eight people in SA and affecting most, if not all, South Africans. While many individual life policies address this problem by specifically excluding AIDS-related deaths from coverage, group policies do not. The result is rising group premiums and reduced levels of cover. Even insurance policies that do cover AIDS-related death do not cover the real risk which many households face: living with HIV/AIDS. In the absence of treatment, the infected person is likely to lose his or her job due to AIDS-related illnesses, some time prior to death, which means that the policy would likely lapse anyway. In the absence of income, the infected person and the family may be unable to cover regular payments such as mortgage loan repayments, quite apart from the significant additional medical costs. New product innovations, especially in housing, are looking at addressing this (see the case study on **Home Loan Guarantee Company** on p.163). But HIV/AIDS remains the frontier issue for insurers to address today.

In the Charter, the insurance sector signed on to the general access objectives. However, only short-term insurers set an explicit access target for 2008. Life assurers left their target to be determined later. The reason for the delay was that defining effective access for insurance, and setting appropriate targets, is no easy issue, as this chapter will show. The chapter will not, however, address the issues of medical schemes, since these schemes are formally excluded from insurance and are a complex and rapidly evolving subject in their own right.

It is worth noting that the insurance sector, somewhat like credit, is large and diverse. The main distinction is between life and short-term insurance. But even within each of these categories, there is considerable variety: funeral policies, for instance, fall into a sub-category of life assurance known as assistance business. Different regulations and market practices apply across each of these. Here, as elsewhere in the book, our focus is on those forms that are most relevant at the lower end of the market. In addition, this chapter focuses on insurance as a functional product category, and not as the business of insurers. The business of insurance includes offering substantial savings products such as retirement funds and annuities, which were considered earlier, in Chapter 3.

Perceived risks and coping strategies

The heart of insurance lies in people's perceptions of the risks they face and how they believe they can manage them. But insurance is only one among several coping strategies.

In FinScope (2003), respondents were asked to select, from a coded set of risk circumstances, which of the set they thought was most likely to happen to them. The top five risks across the whole population in order of precedence were:
1. Theft, fire or destruction of property
2. Loss of job of main wage-earner
3. Death of main wage-earner
4. Serious illness of family member
5. Flood destroying house or property.[2]

There are few surprises on this list. Even the differences in ranking across different sub-groups are easy to explain: for example, wealthier people are more likely to be concerned about the loss of movable property, such as a car or a cellphone, than about flooding, which concerns around one in ten of the poor.

More interesting are the coping strategies proposed for each eventuality. In the case of flood, drought and livestock theft (the last two in the 'top ten' list of risks), a majority of respondents looked to government assistance. This probably reflects personal experience or knowledge of government drought and emergency relief for poorer communities when natural disasters occur. However, a sizeable portion of those who fear theft, fire or destruction of their house or property also look to government for relief.

In general, the commonest coping strategies across risks, other than natural disasters, include:
- Taking a loan from family and friends
- Withdrawing savings
- Selling assets
- Claiming/cashing insurance policies
- Taking a loan from a bank.[3]

This list illustrates that insurance, whether short-term or long-term, is one of a broader set of household strategies to cope with defined risks, which includes borrowing and saving. Any plan to promote formal insurance has to consider the risk proposition, not only of available insurance products, but also of these alternative mechanisms, given their utility and accessibility.

Who insures and how?

Measuring insurance usage accurately is beset by various problems. First, there is a distinction between the number of policy holders (who are quite likely to have multiple policies) and the number of lives covered. Measuring policy holders alone clearly understates the effect of insurance coverage on lives, and hence also the value of insurance to the lives covered. Furthermore, certain types of insurance are embedded in other products and those insured are less aware of them. As a result, household surveys may not pick them up clearly. For example, credit life assurance is commonly bundled with micro loans, retail credit accounts and mortgage loans.

Various initiatives are under way to refine the available data. However, this chapter uses the best available data, based on the profile of policy holders, who after all are still the direct clients of insurance companies.

1994–2003: ten-year view
AMPS figures show that the overall number of people with any type of formal insurance has been stagnant at around six million (see Figure 7.1). And they show that the proportion of adults with insurance policies has been declining for the past decade: from almost a quarter to just over a fifth today. To some extent, this decline in number of clients underlies the statistic reported earlier (on p.11) that the ratio of insurance company assets to GDP has not grown over the past decade, unlike bank assets where the ratio has almost doubled. In part, this is because some of the earlier tax and regulatory advantages of insurance companies, as investment entities, have been eroded over the decade by the rise of new investment vehicles such as unit trusts. And relatively poor investment performance has not helped asset growth either. This is why there is pressure on insurance companies to address their core business of developing and offering risk-based products.

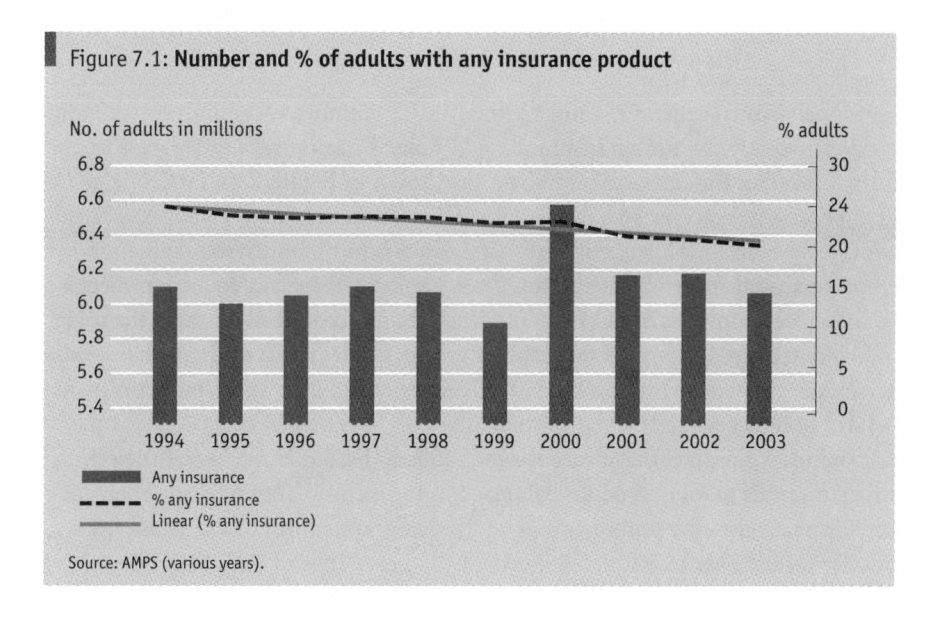

Figure 7.1: **Number and % of adults with any insurance product**

Source: AMPS (various years).

A breakdown (see Figure 7.2) shows that 'whole life' policies have stagnated as a product category, while the drop in the number of clients with short-term insurance has been quite marked: there are 20% fewer clients now than there were ten years ago. The only product category showing growth in numbers is funeral insurance, which has added 600 000 policy holders, to become the largest single formal insurance product category.

Figure 7.2: **Policy-holder breakdown by product**

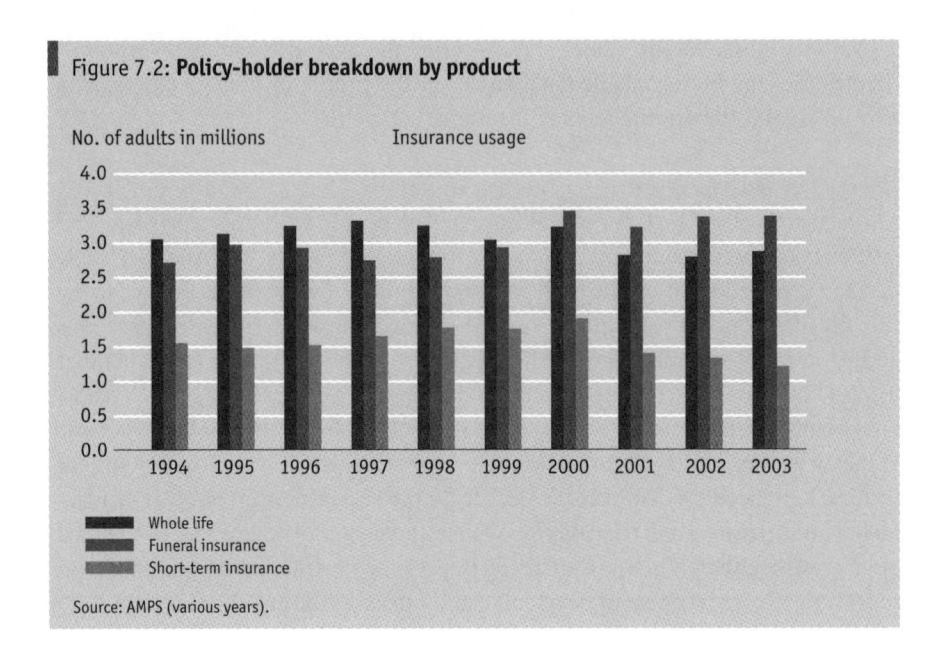

No. of adults in millions — Insurance usage

- Whole life
- Funeral insurance
- Short-term insurance

Source: AMPS (various years).

So who insures and why?

FinScope results generally confirm the AMPS numbers—around six million people currently use formal insurance; and funeral insurance is the biggest single formal product line by client numbers (as shown in Figure 7.2). FinScope gives further insight, however. In Table 7.1, formal insurance is almost totally correlated with being banked. This is not surprising, since other than payroll deduction by employers (and most of the employed are banked), the main collection mechanism for premiums has been a debit order on a bank account. In any case, the reach of insurance is really limited to wealthier groups—one in two of the higher LSMs versus one in ten of the lower LSMs. The penetration of short-term products below LSM6 is negligible.

The most far-reaching insurance mechanism, by far, is the burial society, to which over one in four SA adults belongs. It is the inclusion of burial society membership that raises the proportion of adults using some form of insurance from a quarter to just over two-fifths. Because of the prevalence of burial societies, they are given separate detailed attention later in this chapter.

There is a sizeable group of previously insured, just as there is a sizeable group of previously banked. The ratio of previous users to current users varies by product category (see Table 7.2) from almost one in three to one in seven. For one thing, the table tends to confirm the AMPS figures, which show a decline in short-term insurance policy holders. However, the extent of lapsed life assurance policies is, perhaps, surprising. It implies that there must be considerable churn of policy holders to maintain the product numbers at around the four million mark. The insurance regulator, the Financial Services Board (FSB), reports that as many as 23% of life assurance policies lapse in the first year, with a further 11% in the second year.[4]

Table 7.1: **Usage of insurance products**

% are the % of each column who use the product category in the respective rows

	Total	Banked	Unbanked	LSM1–5	LSM6–10
Formal—long-term					
Life assurance	4,0m	3,96m (29%)	0,06m (0.5%)	4,6%	34,1%
Funeral policy	4,2m	3,9m (28%)	0,3m (2%)	8,4%	29%
Formal—short-term					
Home owner	1,8m	1,8m (13%)	NA	0,2%	19%
Household	1,9m	1,9m (14%)	NA	0,3%	20%
Car	2,3m	2,3m (17%)	NA	0,2%	20%
Informal					
Burial society	7,7m	4,7m (35%)	2,97m (23%)	30%	27%
Any formal insurance	6.7m	6,3m (46%)	0,4m (3%)	11%	51%
Any insurance	11,9m	8,8m (64%)	3,1m (23%)	35%	61%

Source: FinScope (2003, Q19).

Table 7.2: **Previously insured**

	No. of previous users	% previous/current
Disability insurance	274 789	32%
Life assurance	964 638	24%
Car insurance	512 234	22%
Home owner insurance	366 830	20%
Household insurance	274 789	14%

Source: FinScope (2003)

Life Offices Association (LOA) and FSB research independently suggest that the inability to afford the premium is the biggest cause of lapses, as is the case for bank account abandonment. However, the profile of the previously insured is more likely to be wealthy and white than the profile of the previously banked. This suggests greater elements of discretional abandonment in the case of lapsed policies than is the case in transaction banking.

Informal insurers: the role of burial societies

Burial societies are member-based informal associations that provide funeral benefits to their members. They have traditionally provided not only financial support for the costs of the funeral, such as the coffin and food for mourners, but have also fulfilled important social needs, including solace to members at times of bereavement. They also provide a link between the rural roots of migrants and their urban lives. Burial societies are therefore much more than financial mechanisms, depending on the extent and type of assistance provided and on the structure and governance of the society. University of Witwatersrand academics Rob Thomson and Debbie Posel have identified no fewer than seven traditional, hybrid and commercial forms of burial societies.[5] Nevertheless, the dominant reason for belonging is to receive financial assistance, in cash or kind, at times of bereavement. And the majority of societies do pool contributions and accumulate funds to pay out at such times.

There has been uncertainty about the size of this sector during the past decade. But a relatively consistent number of current members has emerged from at least two independent recent surveys, FinScope (2003) and Futurefact (2002): around eight million. Based on an estimate of an average of 88 members per society, this implies almost 100 000 societies countrywide. The profile of burial society members is shown in Table 7.3.

Table 7.3: **Profile of burial society and stokvel members**

% are the percentage of people in each row category who belong to a burial society/stokvel

	Member of burial society	Member of stokvel
Young (18–24)	7%	5%
25–65-year-old	33%	10%
Elderly (65+)	45%	9%
Black	31%	12%
Male	26%	7%
Female	32%	11%
LSM1–5	30%	10%
LSM6–10	27%	7%
Banked	35%	14%
Unbanked	22%	4%
Metro area	28%	9%
Rural area	32%	10%

Source: FinScope (2003, Q8a, 9a).

The majority of burial society members are black, and almost one black person in three belongs to one, although one coloured person in eight also reports belonging to such a society. Almost two-thirds of members are personally banked, which is lower than the banked proportion of stokvel members. One rural person in three belongs, which is much higher than reported for stokvel membership. A joining fee of anywhere from R20 to R600 is typically charged, and monthly contributions vary widely. On average, members contribute R61 a month, implying that around R6bn a year flows into these associations. Over half the members report that their society has a group savings account, while 18% report that the group uses an individual member's account. Like stokvels, burial societies are therefore mainly integrated into the formal financial system.

As with stokvels, burial societies are not without their problems. One in three members reports some form of difficulty associated with the group, although this proportion is lower than in the case of stokvel members (where it is 43%). Again, as with stokvels, the problem of members not paying their dues ranks highest; while 10% report running out of money owing to 'the death of too many beneficiaries'. Fraud or theft by a committee member has affected around 5%, with similar proportions reporting misuse of money or false claims. The case study on p.167 provides further perspective on burial societies in practice.

Strictly speaking, the first example in the case study is not a burial society, because members have no control over the operations. However, it illustrates how the burial society concept has evolved into a profit-making operation in some cases. Many burial societies have agreements with funeral parlours (often contractual), where the burial society will operate as a stand-alone entity but will have an agreement to use the services of the parlour, usually at a discounted price for members. In some cases, the funeral parlour will help with the administration of the burial societies. The second example in the case study is described as a 'friendly society', which is how burial societies could be legally categorised, though they could also be described as co-operatives.

The challenge of HIV/AIDS to insurance

The parties are particularly concerned about the need to end unfair discrimination against people with HIV and develop appropriate services for them. Following the Summit, they will work together to achieve this end, and especially to ensure that people with HIV have improved access to housing finance and other services.
NEDLAC Financial Sector Summit Declaration 3.10

The HIV/AIDS pandemic is a formidable challenge to society as a whole. And, because it directly affects the risks and livelihoods of a sizeable section of the population, it is a particular challenge to the life assurance industry. The estimated prevalence of HIV infection across LSM groups is shown in Figure 7.3 on p.158, together with current usage of life assurance, funeral policies and membership of burial societies.

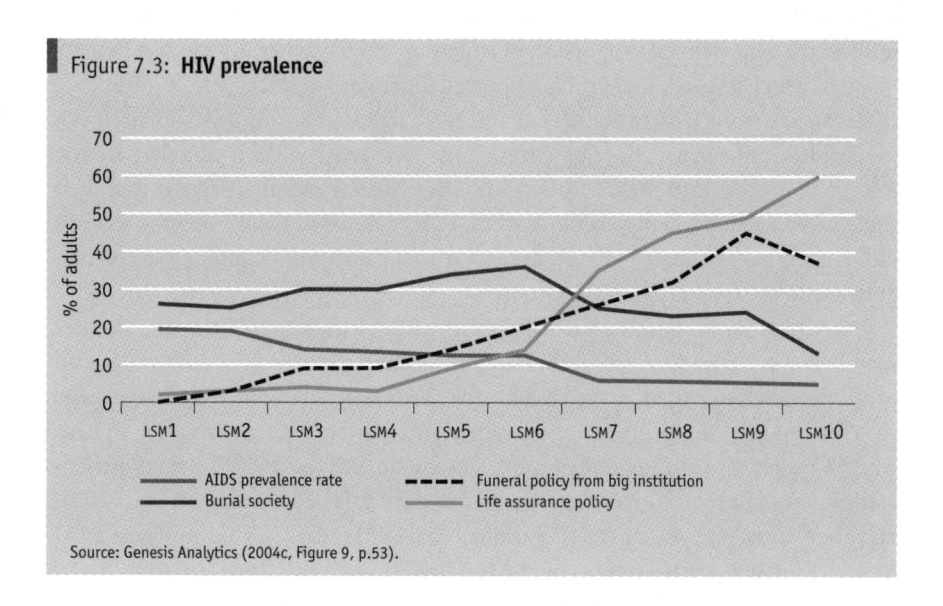

Figure 7.3: **HIV prevalence**

% of adults (y-axis: 0–70) vs LSM1–LSM10

— AIDS prevalence rate
— Burial society
---- Funeral policy from big institution
— Life assurance policy

Source: Genesis Analytics (2004c, Figure 9, p.53).

In a recent report for the MFRC, ECI Africa has mapped the financial pressure experienced by a household in which a member is infected with HIV/AIDS.[6]

> Though an individual might have HIV/AIDS for 10 years, the greatest financial pressure occurs in the six months prior to death and shortly thereafter ... The three scenarios (of varying financial pressure) following death depend on the availability and level of safety net at household level. Financial and social safety nets facilitate the financial recovery of a household, relieving the financial pressure.

Insurance can, in principle, cover three risks facing affected households. They are: loss of income coupled with medical expenses following the loss of a job or inability to work; the cost of a funeral; and continued loss of income to the household following the death of a breadwinner. However, the current usage of formal insurance is too low to make much impact. The current HIV/AIDS prevalence rate is highest among LSM1–5, which are the target groups for Charter access initiatives. If insurance does not cover some of these risks, then they affect other sectors. For example, banks will not grant a mortgage loan if the borrower cannot get credit life assurance on the loan.

The Genesis insurance report cautions that we must be realistic about the ability of the insurance sector, both formal and informal, to relieve the risks and costs of an epidemic as widespread and serious as *untreated* HIV/AIDS.[7]

Were AIDS to remain largely untreated, it would have a devastating effect on the informal provision of insurance to low income households, as burial societies would find it very difficult to stay afloat. It would also have a strongly negative effect on attempts by the formal sector to service the low-income market, as all barriers to that market (high risks, high costs and low-unit revenues) would rise.

But there is far more scope for insurance of all kinds to service communities where HIV/AIDS is normally treated and the industry should be encouraged to design products for such an environment. Perhaps more important, the industry should be strongly encouraged to develop products that enable carriers and sufferers to obtain effective treatment. These products are commonly referred to as wellness interventions.

Developments in both the state and the private sector offer opportunities. Recently, the government announced the provision of anti-retroviral therapy (ART) to all infected individuals, in a programme that will develop to full capacity over the next five years. ART does not provide a cure for HIV/AIDS but reduces it to a manageable disease and can significantly extend the productive life of the affected individual. In addition to the social and personal benefit, it means that skilled labour can be retained for longer in the economy. From the perspective of financial services, it sharply reduces the risk profile of the infected person, while increasing the period over which the person can save, contribute to insurance products and repay loans. This has a dramatic impact on the effective access of that person to a wide range of financial products.

The Home Loan Guarantee Company (HLGC) has developed an innovative form of mortgage cover, which allows the infected borrower to stay in his house provided he enrols on a wellness programme including ART. It will support the mortgage instalment if he is unable to work, and pay out on death (see the case study on p.167). However, due to restrictive provisions in the medical schemes environment, the provision of ART in this way by an insurer which is not a medical aid scheme can take place only through a charitable foundation using donor funds. The demarcation debate between the role of insurance and medical schemes deserves further attention.

Access and Charter targets

The Charter defines first-order retail services, which are the subject of the access commitments, to include life assurance, funeral insurance, household insurance and risk insurance.

The concept of effective access, which was comprehensively applied to transaction banking earlier, is harder to apply to insurance. For one thing, the category of products included under the rubric of insurance is much more diverse. For another, the needs and requirements for geographic access differ across the three main types of insurance transaction:

- Signing up the policy—which could happen anywhere, through mobile sales people.
- Paying regular premiums—which is usually remote as it is dependent on the employer or debit order to the bank account.
- Paying claims—which requires the submission of some proof; the payment usually being made into a bank account.

Even if these criteria were defined precisely in each case, the harder issue would still be affordability. What is a reasonable proportion of salary for people to spend on life assurance? Since we know that large numbers of people are willing and able to spend around R60 a month on burial society contributions, one may surmise that this represents a threshold of affordability. However, almost 60% of adults today do not belong to burial societies, let alone have formal insurance. And industry figures reported by Genesis put the annual operating costs of individual life business in 2003 at R198 per policy.[8] So over R16 a month is needed simply to administer a life policy, before pricing for risk or profit.

Insurance seems to be one of the financial service areas in which it is better not to create elaborate and hard-to-measure definitions of access. The alternative is to identify product categories that are applicable to poorer people, and set basic norms and standards within these categories for products to qualify as being 'poor-friendly' or 'basic'. For example, affordability could be based on whether the premium, per R1 000 of cover, is reasonable for that class of insurance. This approach—benchmarking basic terms of charges, access and terms (the so-called CAT standards) on a simplified class of product designed for broader usage—is essentially the one taken in the UK for savings and investment products.[9] It would address one of the core difficulties of insurance products: the terms are often complex to understand; and the range of choices of product and provider is overwhelming and confusing.

Nonetheless, the current Charter approach is based on numerical targets around access. Box 7.1 shows the targets and the current levels of usage. In part

---

Box 7.1: Charter target as agreed October 2003

% of LSM1–5: Effective access to:	2008 target	2003 actual usage
life assurance	TBC	5%
short-term insurance	6%	Negligible

Source: Financial Sector Charter 8.3; usage: FinScope (2003).

because of the definitional and data difficulties, the life assurance target has continued to be debated long after the signing of the Charter. The target for short-term insurance (6% at the time of writing), while seemingly modest, would represent a big increase from the almost negligible proportions today.

Interestingly, certain developing countries, such as India, mandate annual targets by law.[10] This 'directed insurance' approach has hitherto been commoner for bank lending. However, it shows a possible state response if broader access to insurance is not achieved through consensual means.

The way forward

Formal insurance in SA is at a crossroads. Insurance products have reached most formally employed people who want them; and the overall client base today is largely stagnant or declining. As Capital Alliance CE Ian Kirk says, 'there must be enough capacity in SA to run businesses five times the size of the market.'[11] The result, as *Business Day* has headlined, is 'Shake-up in insurance sector looms as business growth stalls.'[12]

Business growth for insurers is constrained by the almost complete reliance on the client having a bank account or a formal employer as a conduit for premium collection. In addition, new regulations, such as the Financial Advisory and Intermediary Services Act (FAIS), designed to protect consumers from abusive selling practices, are adding new cost and complexity to the insurance sales process. And the life assurance sector faces the tidal wave of HIV/AIDS-related risk, which has to date largely been addressed by exclusions on individual life policies, or by reducing the cover provided on group schemes.

Despite the obvious advantages of being low-cost and flexible, informal mechanisms cannot adequately address the extent of risks faced by many households and communities. Although burial societies are the most used single insurance type in the country today, only one in four adults takes part; and the nature of the cover—funeral costs pooled among relatively small groups—is too limited to address the main household livelihood risks significantly, following prolonged illness or death of a breadwinner. Formal mechanisms will be necessary to spread these risks more widely if the cover provided is to be anything like adequate.

Some question whether insurance, as we know it, is appropriate at all to address such risks. Perhaps the scale of risks brought by HIV/AIDS requires a state mechanism to redistribute the burden through the tax system. Certainly, there are forms of risk that require state intervention to address adverse selection and ensure a large enough risk pool to work, as pointed out by David Moss in his recent book, *When All Else Fails*.[13]

On a broader level, Yale economist Robert Shiller has questioned the relevance of most insurance available today to the real risks in the lives of ordinary people. In his new book,[14] he says: 'Risk sharing has been used primarily for certain narrow kinds of insurable risks ... We need to extend the domain of finance ... to cover the risks that really matter in our lives.' He proposes the use of derivative instruments, currently being used by large corporations at an unprecedented rate, at a retail level. They could provide ordinary households with better effective cover for risks, such as the decline in the value of their house; or a decline in lifetime earnings. Shiller outlines a broad agenda for a new era of innovation in risk mitigation, which is an essential element of democratising finance.

Even locally, it seems that the challenges faced by the insurance industry are calling forth innovations: greater workplace education to increase awareness and reduce the risk of contracting HIV; wellness programmes to manage risk; and forms of cover such as that developed by HLGC to provide living insurance.

In the absence of successful innovations which increase the reach and relevance of insurance, the political pressures caused by widespread HIV prevalence are likely to cast a shadow over the life assurance industry, at least over the next decade, as AIDS mortality peaks. After all, government can change the rules of the game with respect to the ability of insurers to exclude clients from cover.

In the decade ahead, SA's insurance sector faces a struggle for relevance. Unless formal insurance finds ways to break out of its current market bands, it is likely to remain a limited and probably declining product category. In this sense, the challenge of the Charter is useful in forcing the industry to address one of the central issues ahead: how to grow its market sustainably.

Endnotes

1   Much of the background material for this chapter was drawn from Genesis Analytics (2004b), a comprehensive scoping study on insurance.
2   FinScope (2003, Q54a, b).
3   FinScope (2003, Q54c).
4   Genesis Analytics (2004b).
5   Thomson & Posel (2002).
6   ECI Africa (2003c, p.i).
7   Genesis Analytics (2004b).
8   Genesis Analytics (2004c, p.97, Table 20). By comparison, the operating cost for in-force group business is R38 per year.
9   See Sandler (2002), which recommended this approach for savings and insurance products.
10 IRDA Regulations (2000) place obligations on Indian insurers to meet targets on rural clients as a percentage of total; and an absolute number of so-called social sector clients.
11 *Business Day* (29 June 2004, p.1).
12 *Business Day* (29 June 2004, p.1).
13 Moss (2002).
14 Shiller (2003, pp.1, 2).

CASE STUDY

Home Loan Guarantee Company: the Starship Enterprise

Homeloan guarantee company

Nkululeko Sowazi, chairman of Home Loan Guarantee Company (HLGC), describes it as the 'Starship Company'. Its mission, he says, is to 'boldly go where no man has gone before'. The task is to assume 'affordable housing' finance risks. The person responsible for the bold voyages of exploration is, in fact, a woman: CE Charlene Lea. She was brought into HLGC in 1993 to straighten out processes, which she did in short order. She also started sorting out the affordable housing market. Lea has a reputation for being robust in her approach to the lending community. 'Give them any excuse and they won't lend,' she says. Her job is to deprive them of excuses. HLGC provides guarantees of last resort to providers of home loans, where conventional collateral is not available.

Charlene Lea

A Section 21 company formed in 1989, HLGC originally provided only deposit replacement for mortgage loans—lending institutions generally require a borrower to put down a 20% deposit. To assist people who did not have the funds available, HLGC replaced the deposit by providing guarantees of up to 20% of the purchase price of the mortgaged property. The scheme proved viable because 'one of the things HLGC has been good at is managing risk,' says Lea. 'The banks distance themselves substantially from the end-user. When they do interact, it's by letter or phone. When there is a default, we sit in front of each defaulting borrower to determine the reason for the default. And, if you know the reason for the default, you can often fix it.'

In the mid-1990s, banks and others (see the case studies of **CashBank** on p.143 and **Rural Finance Facility** on p.118) started lending against cession of pension and provident fund benefits. A top-up need emerged because, in many cases, potential borrowers did not have enough accumulated in their retirement funds to secure a loan. HLGC provided guarantees to the lenders for the unsecured part of the loan.

'The product was not well used at the time, because the lenders found loans simpler to administer when there was only one source of collateral; and they focused on the fully guaranteed market. But there is renewed interest in the concept and we are negotiating with one of the large lenders for a significant top-up kind of programme,' says Lea. The HLGC guarantees are anything but vanilla. While the basic 'look' might be the same, the guarantees have had to be tweaked to match the specific needs and idiosyncrasies of the lenders and their systems.

Another area of innovation in the late 1990s was providing instalment-based credit guarantees, under rent-to-buy schemes. 'We provided guarantees to housing associations which had access to subsidies for housing development. The idea was that individuals were able to rent their homes to start off with, and take ownership at a later stage, with most of the rent offsetting the eventual purchase price of the home.'

This guarantee product was reasonably successful, until the ruling of the High Court on the Prevention of Illegal Eviction Act and the Unlawful Occupation of Land Act. 'Effectively, the ruling made the eviction of non-paying tenants and mortgage defaulters extremely difficult,' says Lea. 'It extended the operation of the Act to borrowers defaulting on home loans, and to defaulting tenants. One of HLGC's precepts is "no pay, no stay". There has to be discipline in the market or you will never normalise it. We will still provide indemnity where there are alternatives to eviction to create discipline, but the take-up is small.'

HLGC's latest foray into innovative territory is HIV/AIDS-related. AIDS sufferers generally lose their jobs long before they die and, unable to meet their home loan repayments, they go on to lose their houses. HLGC's objective is to keep people with HIV/AIDS in their homes as long as possible.

A few years ago, Lea realised that banks would perceive the pandemic as creating an unacceptable risk in certain market segments. 'I saw it as another reason for not lending and I said, "No, you are not going to use AIDS as a reason not to lend." We have put together a programme that will allow us to guarantee lender loss, where the reason for default is anything—including HIV- and AIDS-related illness.' The target market is people earning less than R7 500 a month.

'It's simply about how you manage your risk,' says Lea. 'We figured that, if we could manage the AIDS risk, we could manage the default risk in an affordable way.' Lea designed a programme that achieves this and neatly avoids the legal obstacles of medical aid legislation. Two programmes work in tandem.

'The guarantee programme, that includes HIV- and AIDS-related cover, is pure insurance, covered by the HLGC—a registered insurance company. Housing for HIV is a US-based not-for-profit foundation that facilitates access to appropriate HIV- and AIDS-related treatment, essential to managing the risk of housing loans,' says Lea.

'The Housing for HIV Foundation is a grant-making institution, and where treatment is not available through existing employer programmes, medical aid or government roll-out, the foundation will fund as necessary. We are not creating new capacities in SA. The treatment programmes the foundation is buying into are already up and running, and will be managed by specialised organisations.'

The innovation is also in managing the risk proactively, starting from the education of the borrowers, through voluntary counselling and testing, to whatever treatment is appropriate to manage the disease. 'It could be multi-vitamins, it could be treating secondary infections or it could be anti-retroviral therapy (ART),' says Lea.

She is putting together international funding to create a constant sustainable income stream, through the Housing for HIV Foundation. 'The concept is ground-breaking, because nowhere in the world has anyone used treatment of AIDS to manage the default risk. We are putting together a significant amount of money through a structured finance mechanism, which in itself is new because structured finance mechanisms have never been used for philanthropic programmes before.'

Lea says that actuarial calculations put the peak of HIV/AIDS-related defaults in 2010. 'There's going to be a serious financial risk to lending unless lenders take cover. It is primarily the existing book that is under threat; their new books can be more easily managed.' HLGC is currently negotiating with banks, which all have commitments to lend for affordable housing. Cover is available for existing as well as new loans.

> It's been difficult to put together and it's been a long process, because we have had to get reinsurance capacity specifically for AIDS-related illness. And getting the money into the foundation for treatment is not the easiest thing I have ever done. But the most difficult part is trying to get the lenders to wrap their minds around the problem. While they might want government to bail them out, the reality is it's a manageable, commercial risk that can be covered in the market place.

Another programme in the HLGC incubator is shelter replacement cover. 'We would work with Sasria (SA Special Risks Insurance Association) and government so that, in the face of disaster, we would replace the shacks or informal homes lost through the disaster,' says Lea. 'But it's very early days and there is a lot of work to be done.'

Top-up of conventional mortgage loans remains HLGC's main business and it is prepared to take on whatever loans banks regard as poor risks. 'In the early days, our approach was "cover one, cover all". Then we allowed the banks to choose which 10% they wanted to keep. But about five or six years ago, we said, "You just give us the loans you think are lousy because we understand the risk." And it's not difficult to manage. Our loss is less than 1% of our book. That's why I question the lenders' claims about their bad experiences—especially if they are palming only their perceived high-risk loans onto us.'

Lea says that HLGC is a tight-run ship; testimony is its AA+ rating from rating agency Fitch. And the company has maintained this, despite facilitating more than R3bn in home loans over its lifetime.

Lea has a simple philosophy: 'Square pegs, square holes; round pegs, round holes.'

And, with this philosophy, she went on to introduce a series of innovative business models to ease access for low-income people to housing finance, models which are designed to make the risk profile of affordable housing more suitable for housing lenders. ■

CASE STUDY
Burial societies: social capital

Jim Roth has over ten years' experience as a researcher, policy analyst, manager and consultant in the development field. His interest in micro insurance began after research work on informal indigenous insurance mechanisms such as burial societies. In 1999, he surveyed burial societies in Grahamstown, Eastern Cape. His report gives some fascinating examples of these mechanisms, which play an important role in the lives of so many South Africans, as the chapter has shown.[1] Two cases from this report are cited below.

Jim Roth

Informal for-profit funeral parlour insurer: Shoba & Shoba

The brothers Shoba started their insurance scheme when they purchased a township funeral parlour in 1995. One of the brothers had worked for the municipality and the other had worked for the previous owner of their funeral parlour.

The brother leaving the municipality received a large payment when he left. The brothers used this as a deposit to secure a bank loan that they used to buy the parlour. They will finish paying off the loan this year (1999). Their insurance scheme operates as follows. Members pay a joining fee of R10 and a monthly premium of R15. They can nominate up to 10 people for cover, who need not be related to the main policyholder, nor do they even need to reside at the same address as the main policyholder. The main nominee qualifies for immediate cover. Shoba 'underwrites' the main nominee by observing him or her when he/she applies for membership. To avoid moral hazard problems, policyholders must wait three months before they can claim benefits for other nominees. The benefits are paid only if Shoba & Shoba arrange the funeral. This crucial clause ensures that Shoba & Shoba are able to keep the cost of their payout to a minimum.

The benefits members receive on the death of a nominee are: a coffin with a retail price of R350, along with an immediate payment of R200 in cash. Shoba & Shoba cover the cost of refrigeration of the corpse (which they collect immediately), all cemetery fees, the radio announcement, and they take care of all official bureaucracy. It is difficult to put a price on the cost of the service they provide but it is unlikely to cost them more than R200 (an employee of another informal insurer reported the wholesale cost of the coffin as R90).

Their policy has no exclusions. The brothers rely on word-of-mouth marketing and thus have no marketing costs. The clients bring premiums to them when they have them in cash. The client is issued with a booklet. When a premium is received, the booklet is stamped and dated. If clients fail to pay a premium, they are given three months to pay. If they fail to do this, then they need to re-join by paying a new membership fee and the waiting period will then re-apply.

In the event of death, the funeral parlour is the first port of call for the remaining relatives. In the majority of cases, they recognise the deceased or at least have a person they trust who can confirm the identity of the deceased. Payment of the R200 is immediate. In cases where there is uncertainty about the identity of the deceased they wait for the death certificate.

Their record keeping would be regarded as very poor by the standards of formal institutions. They have no up-to-date record of all the members who have paid premiums (records only reflect joining fees). The onus is on the client to prove that he/she is up-to-date with his/her premiums—by means of a booklet that they have stamped whenever they make a payment. Joining the scheme is a very simple matter. Terms and conditions in Xhosa and English are printed on a single sheet of paper and are explained in Xhosa to the client.

Township informal friendly society: Grocery Umgalelo

Extension 2 Grocerey Umgalelo was started in 1998. All members live in Extension 2 (Makana's Kop), part of the greater Grahamstown township of Rini. The friendly society has 34 members, all of whom are women. To join the society, an initial fee of R40 is paid once off. The monthly premium is R10. Members nominate officials to collect premiums. The nominated officials collect the premium door-to-door and bank the cash at the local post office. Each member nominates 12 beneficiaries of the scheme. The beneficiaries do not need to come from the members' own household. To overcome moral hazard problems of someone who is about to die joining at the last minute, three months must pass after a member has joined before a claim can be made. On the death of a member, the nominated beneficiary receives R500 in cash, plus all the groceries for the funeral feast (excluding the cow, sheep or other meat purchased for the feast).

It normally takes three days to receive a payout from the umgalelo. Claiming is a relatively simple process. The beneficiary or member of the household writes or has someone help her write a letter to the president of the friendly society. The president ensures the premium has been paid and, if all is in order, pays the member R500 and convenes a meeting of the society. At this meeting different members of the society are given funds and assigned the task of buying groceries. The buying of groceries is very convenient in that it saves both time and transport costs.■

Endnote

1 Roth (2000).

Chapter 8

SA Financial Institutions and the Region

Introduction

One of the key changes in the SA financial system since 1994 has been its increasing internationalisation as foreign banks entered the SA market—some for the first time and others returning after a sanctions-driven departure.[1] However, almost all entered wholesale or investment banking; only recently have two returnees, Standard Chartered and Barclays, tentatively entered retail niches. While the immigration of financial institutions to SA has been important, the story of the increasing presence of SA financial institutions in the region is often overlooked.

By and large, during the apartheid era, SA banks were not welcomed, or allowed to establish a presence, elsewhere in Africa, beyond the immediate common monetary area (CMA) markets. But the advent of democracy opened the doors to international expansion. By comparison, insurers such as Old Mutual have long had a wide African footprint. However, in different ways and at different speeds over the decade, most large banks and insurance companies increased their presence significantly in the Southern African Development Community (SADC) and beyond. The result is that, in 2004, SA banks (and to a lesser extent insurers) have a significant presence in most SADC countries. And their influence appears to be growing.

This regionalisation of financial sectors has happened against a broader political and economic backdrop which has encouraged greater convergence in standards and even integration within the region. A variety of regional groupings has been formed, or re-formed, over the past decade as part of explicit SA government foreign policy to look to Africa as a sphere of economic and political influence (see the Appendix on **Regional integration mechanisms** on p.216). The Southern African Customs Union (SACU)—made up of SA, Botswana, Namibia, Lesotho and Swaziland—is one of the oldest customs unions in the world. But even this venerable body has changed substantially during the decade. Other bodies were created: the New Partnership for Africa's Development (Nepad), for example, with a continental vision for growth and stability. Around the increasing diplomatic and economic ties, regional groupings of financial regulators have emerged to share knowledge and build capacity, especially among the southern and East African countries that make up the SADC. These various regional groupings and their significance for financial access are summarised in the Appendix on p.216.

The importance of the SADC region to SA financial institutions has become clear: the SADC is a potential market of some 210m people, four times the combined population of the SACU countries, many of which could be considered functionally integrated into the SA economy, and especially the financial system. While many SADC countries are poor, banking in them can still be highly profitable. In fact, banks in Africa report, on average, one of the highest returns on equity of all the continents. This reflects a risk premium, to be sure. But it also reflects underlying structural conditions that have made wholesale banking, in particular, very profitable. As some of these factors change, so increasing weight is being placed on retail banking strategies to generate growth and profitability. The linkage between foreign-bank entry to a market and expanded access is still tenuous, however.

In general, reliable information on the state of access to financial services across the SADC is very patchy. However, FinMark Trust has focused on mapping both the supply and the demand side of the state of access in the four BLNS countries around SA (Botswana, Lesotho, Namibia and Swaziland). As a counterpoint to the detailed analysis of the landscape of access in SA which runs through this book, this chapter will review the landscape in each of these countries.

SA financial institutions in the SADC, 1994-2004

Box 8.1: Chronology of key events

1993	Comesa launched
1994	SA joins SADC; African Economic Community established
2001	Nepad adopted by OAU (Lusaka Summit)
2002	African Union launched (Durban Summit)
2004	New SACU agreement finalised

SA Banks in the SADC

Over the past decade, SA banks in particular have moved aggressively into other SADC countries. This was especially true for countries on the immediate border: Botswana, Namibia, Lesotho and Swaziland, which make up SACU with SA; three of them comprise the CMA based on the rand. The process was at first opportunistic, as banks took advantage of opportunities that presented themselves. Later it became strategic, as they started to take the longer view of the market outside SA's borders.

The process in fact pre-dated the arrival of democracy in SA. Both Standard Bank and First National Bank (FNB)—formerly Barclays—had been constrained in their African operations by agreements with their international parent companies. After 1987, when the UK parent companies of both banks exited SA under apartheid-era disinvestment pressure, this constraint was removed. However, until the political situation in SA changed with the release of Nelson Mandela in 1990, there was little scope for SA banks to move beyond the immediate SACU region.

Standard Bank entered BLNS countries in 1988, with a 70% purchase of Swaziland Bank. Its next opportunity came in 1992 when international bank ANZ

Grindlays sold its wholesale operations in six African countries. Absa acquired its first operation outside SA in the 1991 merger with Volkskas, which left it with a substantial and continuing stake in Bank Windhoek. After the split from Barclays, FNB was left with an operation in Namibia. But FNB also took advantage of an early opportunity: the chance to acquire the Bank of Credit and Commerce in Botswana in 1992, after the spectacular collapse of its parent company.

However, the advent of democracy legitimised and made possible broader and more systematic expansion. SA banks have an increased presence in most SADC countries (see Table 8.1) except Zimbabwe, where their presence has decreased slightly; Angola, where the lone SA bank has pulled out; the DRC, where the presence is marginal; and the Seychelles, which no SA bank has yet entered.

Table 8.1: **Summary table of per country snapshot analysis, 1994–2004**

	Namibia		Botswana		Swaziland		Lesotho		Mozambique		Zimbabwe		Angola	
	1994	2003	1994	2003	1994	2003	1994	2003	1994	2003	1994	2003	1994	2003
Total no. of banks	6	8	9	7	5	4	4	2	3	12	12	11	3	4
State	2	2	2	2	1	1	2	0	2	0	2	1	2	1
Local	1	3	2	1	0	0	0	0	0	2	5	2	0	1
Foreign	1	0	3	2	3	0	2	0	1	8	4	7	0	2
SA	2	2	2	2	1	3	0	2	0	2	1	1	1	0
SA assets/ total assets	82%	72%	9%	22%	18%	72%	0%	87%	0%	30%	9%	3%	sus-pended	0%
SA deposits/ total deposits	81%	72%	7%	30%	14%	54%	0%	88%	0%	29%	9%	4%	sus-pended	0%

	Malawi		Mauritius		Zambia		DRC		Tanzania		Seychelles	
	1994	2003	1994	2003	1994	2003	1994	2003	1994	2003	1994	2003
Total no. of banks	5	9	9	12	19	17	10	8	7	25	3	4
State	1	1	1	3	4	2	3	2	4	6	3	3
Local	4	3	5	4	9	4	2	3	0	11	0	0
Foreign	0	3	3	3	5	10	4	2	3	6	0	1
SA	0	2	0	2	1	1	1	1	0	2	0	0
SA assets/ total assets	0%	17%	0%	40%	7%	12%	9%	7%	0%	21%	0%	0%
SA deposits/ total deposits	0%	16%	0%	26%	5%	12%	8%	7%	0%	23%	0%	0%

Source: Genesis Analytics (2004a, p.72), drawing on Sifida Banking Directory and BankScope.

Over the decade, the *modus operandi* of banks within the region has changed. Traditionally, foreign banks in Africa have followed the 'suitcase' and 'armchair' business models.

Armchair banking refers to a focus on the wholesale market, gathering the deposits of major companies and reinvesting them at a higher margin. What made armchair banking so attractive in Africa, for so long, was the prevalence of high interest rates in the government bond market. Partly as a result of high inflation and partly as a result of their need to fund budget deficits, African governments were willing to pay high rates to attract private bank funds. Thus, substantial profits could be made on the turn. This meant that there was little need to enter the retail market and certainly little attraction in the lower-income segment of the market.

Suitcase banking describes arm's-length banking, where banks offer services that require limited or negligible physical presence in a country—such as servicing sophisticated trade and project finance deals, mainly from a home base.

But times are changing and, with them, the business models of banks. Over the past decade, most African governments (with a few flagrant exceptions) have embraced the core principles of the 'Washington Consensus', which call for conservative monetary policy (inflation reduction and price stabilisation), a balanced budget (or reduced deficit) and trade liberalisation. Though the last pillar will encourage further SA engagement, the first two present various challenges.

Suitcase banking may continue to provide low-risk, high-return opportunities, especially in growth areas like telecommunications. But the era of armchair banking is drawing to a close: reduced supply of government bonds has cut the yield. The deposit spreads—the difference between what banks pay for deposits and what they earn on risk-free Treasury bills—have fallen quite substantially in a number of African countries. This development places pressures on banks to gather deposits more cheaply and lend at higher margins, which can only be achieved by greater penetration of the retail market. Important technological innovations in retail banking, such as those highlighted in Chapter 2, will cause retail products to diffuse faster through the region and to be more viable.

Today Standard Bank, which is represented in 16 African countries, leads in regional presence through its subsidiary Stanbic Africa, so called to avoid confusion with former parent Standard Chartered. Typically, Stanbic Africa has concentrated on wholesale banking in these countries, although its subsidiaries closer to home are more likely to have a retail presence. But the only subsidiaries that have more than 20 branches are Namibia (22), Lesotho (23), Mozambique (24) and the notable exception, Uganda (65).

Stanbic Bank Uganda is considered the 'poster child' of Stanbic Africa, and demonstrates the increasing retail focus of its African operations. Standard Bank has had an excellent wholesale operation in Uganda since 1997, with average return on equity of more than 50% and a cost-to-income ratio below 30%—the result of armchair and suitcase banking. However, acutely aware of the need to move into the larger retail space, Standard Bank took the opportunity to buy an 80% stake in the largest bank, Uganda Commercial Bank, when it was privatised in 2002.

FNB has so far expanded into Swaziland, following the failure of Meridien Bank in 1995, and in 2004, into Lesotho. FNB has, however, given much more emphasis recently to the development of its banking strategy in Africa north of the Limpopo.

Other than their stakes in Namibian banks, which pre-dated democracy in that country, Absa and Nedcor had no substantial presence in the region outside SA in 1994. Since then, Nedcor has bought 93% of the Commercial Bank of Namibia and has majority stakes in banks in Malawi, Lesotho, Swaziland, Madagascar and Mauritius. It maintains substantial minority shareholdings in Zimbabwe. Since 1994, Absa has retained its minority shareholding in Namibia, acquired another in Zimbabwe and has majority ownership of banks in Mozambique and Tanzania. It is focused on acquiring retail banks in Africa at the rate of one a year. And it is considering innovative ways to reach untapped markets in Tanzania and Mozambique, including cellphone banking.

A *Business Day* article headed 'Local banks look to expand by chasing African footprints' showed that operations from elsewhere in Africa yielded headline profit to all the Big Four banks ranging from R75m (Absa) to R489m (Standard).[2]

SA insurers in the SADC

Compared with the bankers, there has been less new engagement by SA insurers in SADC countries in the past decade. For example, while Old Mutual has long had a strong presence in four other African countries (Namibia, Malawi, Zimbabwe and Kenya), it has not made a single acquisition in the region in two decades. However, SA firms completely dominate the Namibian and Botswanan insurance markets and have strong influence in Zimbabwe and Malawi. There is currently only a small SA insurer presence in Mauritius and Tanzania. And SA insurers are completely absent from the Seychelles and the DRC.

This is because insurance sectors in these latter countries (and Swaziland) are still controlled by state monopolies that block entry. Besides, SA insurance companies generally require an established banking system before entering another country, because they rely on processing premiums through bank accounts and payrolls, rather than through the local cash-based system.

The case study of **African Life** on p.182 highlights the regional expansion path of this entrepreneurial mid-sized life assurer. From no regional base, African Life has grown rapidly outside SA to develop a diversified portfolio of businesses across four other SADC countries, and as far afield as Ghana and Kenya. African Life's target customer is in the lower end of the market and its revenue model is based on selling and administering large volumes of small-premium policies. It aims to continue expanding and will take minority stakes in pre-existing companies. But it requires management control, at least.

Metropolitan Life, which had had a presence in Lesotho and Namibia since the 1970s, expanded to Botswana in 1996, where it now has 30% of the life market. Metropolitan has also bought a health insurance company in Kenya, and, via concessions from the Swaziland regulator, operates under limited circumstances in that country. Like African Life, it specialises in offering life products to the lower- and middle-income groups. But it has a broader product range, including funeral cover, family care and education policies.

SA short-term insurer SA Eagle has two subsidiaries in Botswana and Zimbabwe and two associates (minority stakes) in Mauritius and Swaziland. SA's biggest short-term insurer, Santam, has a subsidiary in Namibia and has minority shareholdings in Malawi and Zimbabwe.

The landscape of access in SACU countries

Greater entry by foreign institutions into previously closed financial systems may be expected, a priori, to lead to an expansion of access—primarily through increased competition. However, as the Genesis report outlines, there are many reasons why this may not materialise.[3] This has to be watched carefully over time—which requires developing the means to monitor access and usage patterns.

The BLNS countries show a high degree of economic integration with SA, including the financial system. However, because of their different histories and levels of development, the landscape of access differs among them. The shape of their landscape was largely unknown until quite recently. Since its formation in 2002, FinMark Trust has commissioned several pieces of work to shed light on this issue.

In 2002, Genesis Analytics conducted scoping studies covering all categories of financial services, to document levels of usage of various financial products.[4] It was based largely on numbers from service providers—a supply-side view. In addition, the studies considered the barriers to the expansion of access as well as private- and public-sector initiatives attempting to overcome them. The studies found an absence of clear market information on the potential size or profitability of the lower-income market. This data gap restricts the activities of financial institutions to the familiar markets—the urban, higher-income and commercial markets.

To address the information gap, FinMark Trust initiated FinScope surveys in these countries on a pilot basis in 2003. The samples were limited to between 500 households (Botswana, Lesotho) and 800 (Namibia). Although the samples were drawn on a nationally stratified basis, the relatively small sample sizes limit the power of results at this stage. In each case, the head of the household was interviewed. This implies that, even if weighted, findings can only be generalised to all households' heads.

In addition, due to insufficient or outdated census data, it was not possible to calculate weights that would allow the data to be extrapolated to national level. Hence, FinScope BLNS (2003) yields a volume of highly indicative data that will require further checking to confirm its accuracy.

Nonetheless, the demand-side findings from FinScope BLNS compare quite well with the supply-side estimates, on individual products, from the original scoping studies—which gives greater credence to the FinScope findings. A comparison of the countries, based on FinScope (2003) in Figure 8.1, shows that Botswana is generally ahead in usage, as might be expected from its higher level of development; but that the gap between Namibia and the remaining two countries is smaller than originally estimated. This is mainly due to the addition of informal market figures.

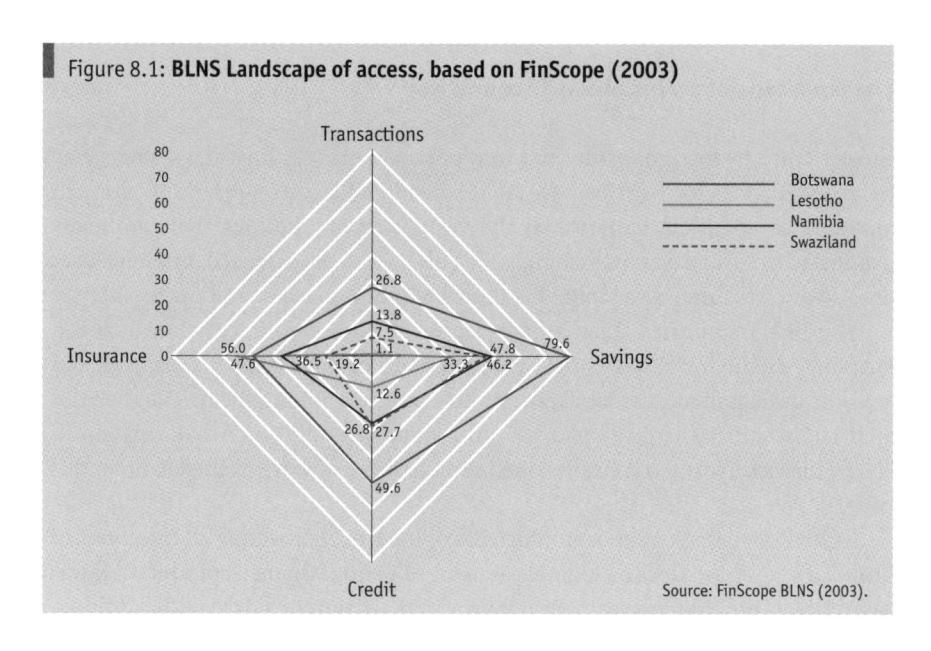

Figure 8.1: **BLNS Landscape of access, based on FinScope (2003)**

Source: FinScope BLNS (2003).

The four BLNS countries are dominated by foreign (particularly SA) financial institutions, and all have a growing, largely unregulated micro-lending sector. The national payment system is underdeveloped and inefficient in all four countries, which has made payroll deduction (particularly from government payroll) important for contractual savings and insurance products. Until recently, government was a major player in the retail financial markets in Botswana, Lesotho and Swaziland. It still is in Swaziland and to some extent Botswana. Government provision was mainly focused on credit to stimulate economic development. The failure of government-run institutions, and the continued cost of subsidising their inefficiencies, have prompted governments to start withdrawing from the market. However, with the exception of Namibia, there is still a fairly low level of private-credit provision.

Figure 8.2 unpacks the landscape of access for each BLNS country, to highlight the comparison of formal and informal product types. While the formal could be estimated by comparing the supply-side and demand-side figures, the informal can only be picked up from the demand side, as a result of the FinScope (2003) household surveys. Informal organisations, such as burial societies, co-operatives and rotating savings associations, are quite substantial in these countries and, as in the SA data, should rightly be counted in the relevant product category. The result is the larger usage in the insurance and credit axes in particular. The difference is especially marked for the two lowest-income countries in the SACU, Lesotho and Swaziland.

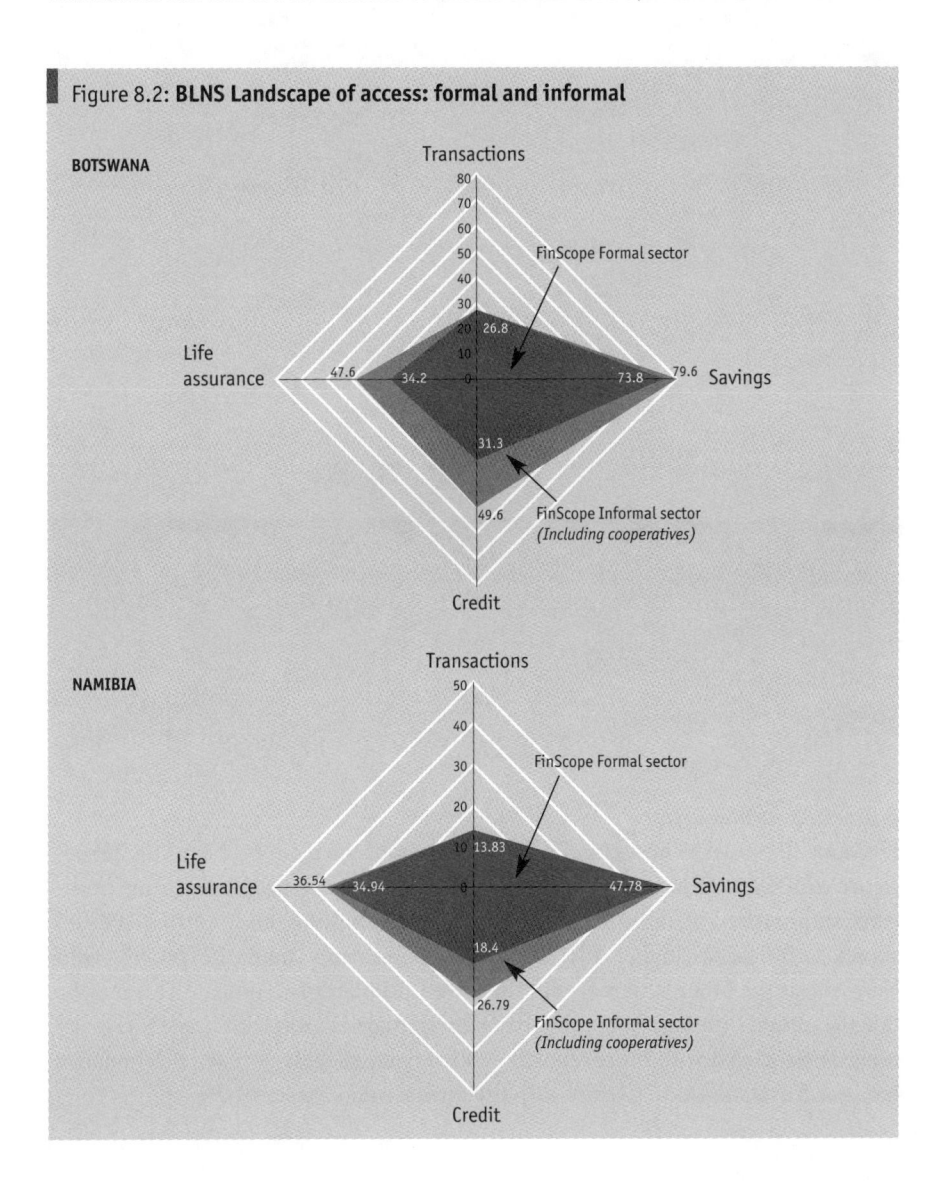

Figure 8.2: **BLNS Landscape of access: formal and informal**

BOTSWANA

- Transactions: 26.8 (Formal), 31.3 (Informal)
- Savings: 73.8 (Formal), 79.6 (Informal)
- Credit: 49.6 (Informal)
- Life assurance: 47.6 (Formal), 34.2 (Informal)

NAMIBIA

- Transactions: 13.83 (Formal), 18.4 (Informal)
- Savings: 47.78
- Credit: 26.79
- Life assurance: 36.54 (Formal), 34.94 (Informal)

LESOTHO

[Radar chart with axes Transactions, Savings, Credit, Life assurance showing values: Transactions 19.7/1.1, Savings 33.3/1.3, Credit 12.6, Life assurance 56/10.5, comparing FinScope Formal sector and FinScope Informal sector (Including cooperatives)]

SWAZILAND

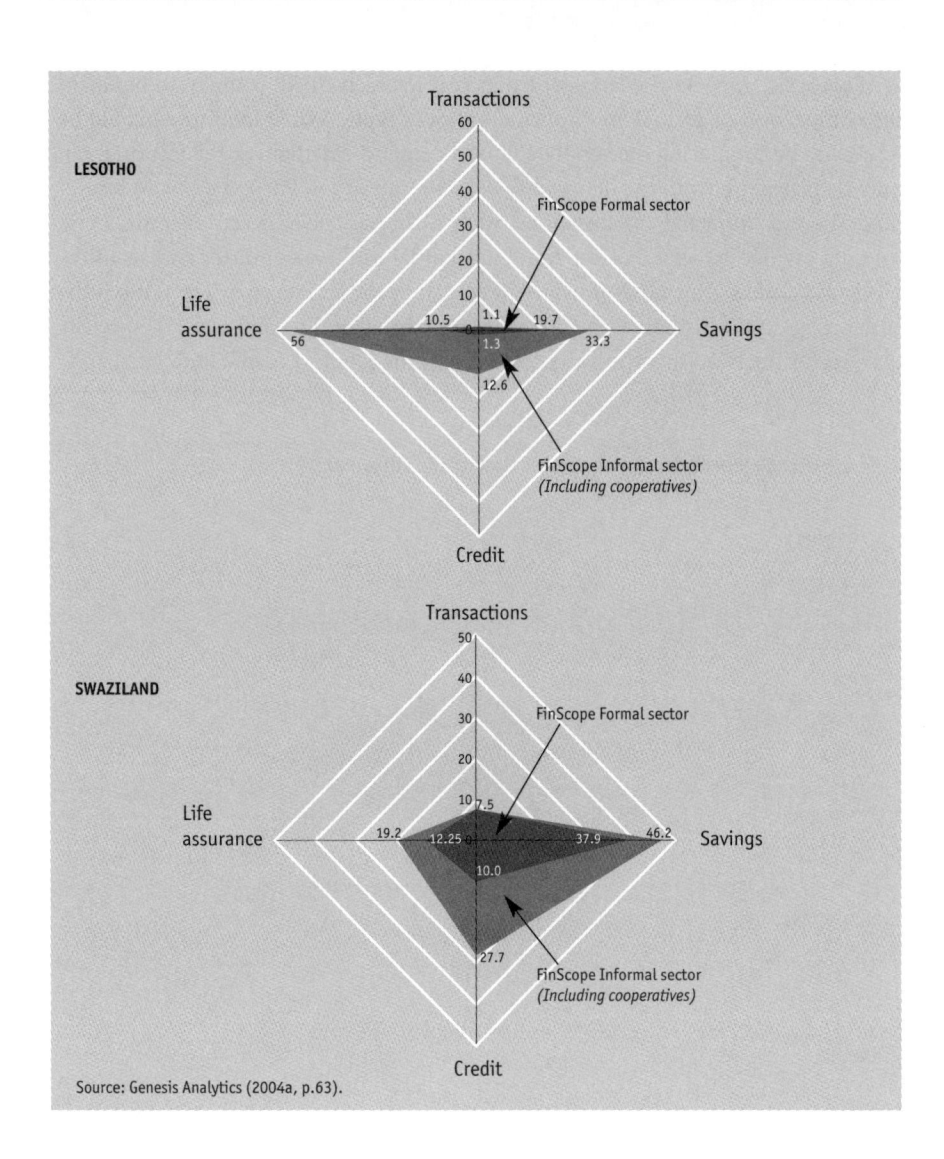

[Radar chart with axes Transactions, Savings, Credit, Life assurance showing values: Transactions 7.5, Savings 46.2/37.9, Credit 27.7/10.0, Life assurance 19.2/12.25, comparing FinScope Formal sector and FinScope Informal sector (Including cooperatives)]

Source: Genesis Analytics (2004a, p.63).

Barriers to formal access

FinScope BLNS asked household respondents about the main problems they experience with formal financial institutions. The percentage of people reporting problems, summarised in Table 8.2, differs substantially among the countries. Lesotho shows significantly higher identification of problems than the others, with Namibia, at the other extreme, with the lowest number of responses. This may be due to cultural differences, but the strong inverse correlation with usage (i.e. lower usage is associated with more reporting of barriers) suggests it may reflect relative levels of frustration experienced with the formal financial sectors.

Table 8.2: **Main problems reported with formal financial institutions**

% of adults in each country agreeing with the problem stated in each category

Statement:	Botswana	Lesotho	Namibia	Swaziland
Qualification	%	%	%	%
They force me to keep a high minimum balance.	52,3	76,6	37,5	63,6
I don't qualify for their services.	57,2	57,7	40,4	51,8
I have to have credit references.	25,8	47,2	24,3	32,5
I have to have a pay-slip.	21,0	56,9	11,6	32,4
I have to fill in forms.	14,9	39,5	10,3	2,7
I need a permanent address.	6,2	12,7	13,6	8,1
I have to have an identity document.	4,0	18,2	8,1	10,1
Access to the service				
I cannot get the money immediately if I need it.	57,6	88,8	52,7	63,9
They are too far away for me and expensive to get to.	45,6	77,6	48,4	57,2
I have to stand in queues for service.	52,7	74,4	37,4	55,9
Their technology can be difficult to work with.	46,6	68,6	23,8	38,4
Perceived value/benefit				
My money does not grow quickly.	55,8	87,4	47,9	63,1
My money is taxed.	42,7	81,4	40	63,3
They only offer a good return over a period of years.	53,2	77,1	20,6	59,1
Their ATM machines are not always safe.	39,2	84,6	40,1	38,5
The big institutions are not always safe.	44,5	84,6	37,3	30,0
I have to pay to deal with them.	34,2	66,7	23,3	41,6

Source: FinScope BLNS (2004).

Although magnitudes differ, the relative order of issues is similar in all four countries. The exception is that qualifying for services was a bigger problem than having to maintain minimum balances in Botswana and Namibia; while the opposite applied in Lesotho and Swaziland. This, however, corresponds to the differences in the general level of financial development reported in the supply-side study and confirmed by the usage figures.

The common problems that respondents ranked high across all four countries were that:

- Financial institutions force them to keep high minimum balances.
- They do not qualify for services.
- They cannot get immediate access to their money, if needed.
- The institutions are far away and expensive to get to.
- Money saved or invested does not grow quickly.

The way forward

The past decade has seen important changes within the SADC region. The creation of new political bodies, on a regional and continental level, has signalled the explicit aim of achieving greater economic integration within and across Africa. However, the aspirations of many of these regional bodies await effective implementation in the next decade.

Meanwhile, SA financial institutions have taken decisive steps outside their home market. From relatively low bases, except in Namibia, they have come to dominate most SACU financial markets, and have an increasing influence in SADC markets beyond SACU. Much of the expansion has been of a wholesale banking nature, but this is starting to change as wholesale margins narrow, and large, under-banked retail markets beckon. The wider SADC market, four times the population of SACU alone, offers considerable expansion opportunities to SA banks and insurers in the decade ahead.

Products developed in SA to serve the low end of the market may also be appropriate elsewhere. As the potential market becomes larger, so does the potential return on the fixed costs of new-product development, making it more likely that a product will be tried than otherwise. In this sense, regionalisation may encourage greater innovation and therefore be positive for financial access.

As retail banking markets integrate, Johannesburg, already the financial market centre for the continent and the head-office location for all the big SA banks, has started to assume a new role: as the base for the financial product factories and support hubs that will sustain retail penetration into other markets. Two other international banking groups with major African retail banking interests (Barclays and Standard Chartered) have recently moved their African headquarters to Johannesburg, further reinforcing this trend. The expanded labour market, skilled in this area, is again likely to be positive for access.

In addition, SA financial institutions are increasingly drawing on human capital from elsewhere in Africa to supplement and grow their management teams. This flow of skills from other countries will enrich the search for access-enhancing solutions in SA.

Increased regional integration across the SADC countries, at least, is clearly likely to continue apace over the next decade. But it is as likely to be driven by banks, insurers and other private businesses seeking market expansion opportunities, as it is to be led by unfolding intergovernmental agreements.

Endnotes

1 This chapter is drawn in large part from Genesis Analytics (2004a).
2 *Business Day* (24 June 2004, p.15).
3 Genesis Analytics (2004a, pp.46–47).
4 Genesis Analytics (2003a, b, c, d).

CASE STUDY
African Life Assurance: exploring the region

John Burbidge

African Life's (ALA's) core business is providing cover for financial needs arising from 'life events'. Its basic product is a funeral policy. Its target market is typically LSM5–7, a demographic sector in which blue-collar workers, nurses and teachers are heavily represented. And its revenue model is based on low costs, high volumes of small value, and high margins.

'In the early 1990s, we had experienced considerable growth,' says John Burbidge, executive director and formerly MD of Botswana Insurance Holdings (BIH). 'To replicate that growth, we either had to move into new markets in SA or into similar markets outside SA.' It was a time when political changes in SA had made regional expansion a possibility for the first time in decades. And ALA realised there was a vast, underserved market in Africa.

Opportunity knocked internationally in 1995. 'We were looking at setting up an operation in Botswana when Southern Life, at that time a majority shareholder in African Life, decided it wanted to exit from its investment in Botswana,' says Burbidge. ALA acquired 25,2% (a stake later increased to over 50%) of the BIH Group, a composite insurer, quoted on the Botswana Stock Exchange. It stripped out the short-term operations and secured a management contract for the life and fund management operations.

BIH, which includes a fund management and employee benefits company, is now ALA's flagship operation outside SA. 'BIH has seen huge growth since we acquired it,' says Burbidge. 'Assets in 1996 were R594m and net premium income was worth R162m. By 2003, total assets were R7bn and premium income was R531m.' BIH is unique in the group because it is the only company that serves a wide range of the population.

In 1996, ALA took a 10% stake in the Lesotho National Insurance Company, also a composite insurer, and a 40% stake in its life arm. However, ALA did not secure a management contract, and 'this experience confirmed our view that we should only invest when we can take management control,' says Burbidge. 'We want to ensure our model—from distribution, to product design and customer relationship management is replicated as closely as possible, given local conditions.'

Domestic acquisition ambitions were thwarted when takeover target Norwich Life fell to Fedsure in 1998. And once again, ALA focused beyond SA's borders. The next move was into Namibia in 1998. An opportunity came its way, through the International Finance Corporation (IFC), which had taken a 7%

stake in ALA in 1994. By virtue of its charter, as the commercial arm of the World Bank, the IFC is a significant provider of capital to the private sector in the developing world. It is a 'strategic partner in the ALA group,' says Burbidge.

The IFC suggested that Namibia was a suitable site for a greenfields operation, and ALA's original intention was a joint venture with a consortium of prominent local business people. 'However, that didn't happen and we are still trying to transfer ownership into Namibian hands. We believe local participation is important,' says Burbidge. ALA has 70% of the Life Office of Namibia, and the IFC has 28%, while the rest is locally owned.

Once again the IFC pointed the way, this time to Kenya in 2000. ' It has a population of over 30m and its life industry was less than 50% the size of ALA's life business in SA. So, irrespective of political and economic circumstances, there was a strong case for investment,' says Burbidge. ALA took 46% of Pan Africa Insurance Company, a Nairobi-listed composite insurer. 'Growth has been good: in 2000 we sold 4 000 life policies and last year we sold 300 000. The market is stable because it is predominantly civil servants. Diversifying into the broader market is the next step.' However, some of the downside of venturing into unfamiliar territory emerged when ALA had to contend with lapses in corporate governance. 'It absorbed a lot of management time,' says Burbidge

In 2001 ALA took a 39% stake in a new company, Enterprise Life Insurance, in Ghana. With the IFC as a partner, ALA negotiated management control. 'We have built up a 16 000-customer base and there is huge potential, especially through associations and church groups,' says Burbidge.

In 2002 ALA was able to take advantage of a link to Zambia through its Botswana Insurance Fund Management (BIFM), which had a 50% share in Zambia's African Life Financial Services. A joint venture between BIFM and Anglo American Central Africa, it gave BIFM control of Anglo's Zambian pensions administration and asset management operation. 'We were able to harvest the benefits of this association and were ready to produce life products in Zambia. We invested 100% in African Life Zambia, to complement the BIFM investment,' says Burbidge.

ALA is now preparing a greenfields venture in Tanzania, which it plans to open in 2005.

Currently about one-third of the group's revenue comes from its diversified portfolio of countries across the border.

'ALA is more like a local player than a foreign participant in the regional market,' says Genesis Analytics associate Doubell Chamberlain. 'Our interaction with various insurers in the SACU region has shown us that ALA's approach is quite different from that of other SA financial institutions. It actively seeks local partners rather than relegate operations to branch status. And it realises insurance markets are sensitive to different national and cultural contexts.' ■

Conclusion

For us, this day is a very significant one that signals a new beginning ... we commit ourselves to working in service of the broad interests of the economy of which we are merely a reflection. The time for excuses—political, practical or otherwise—has passed and has been replaced by an urgent need for sound decisions and delivery in all sectors.
Derek Cooper, chair of the Standard Bank Group, speech at Nedlac Financial Sector Summit, August 2002

1994–2004: a decade in review

Financial services play an important role in achieving society's overarching objectives: growth, economic citizenship and the elimination of poverty. However, the message of this book is decidedly not that greater access to financial services is enough to address these objectives.

Finance alone cannot solve underlying structural flaws. In fact, turning on the taps of supply-led finance to address a complex problem—SMME finance, for example—can do much more harm than good. In many ways, the focus on financial services in the first decade of freedom reflects the bifurcated nature of SA's financial system. One part is well developed by most international standards; the other is underdeveloped. If the financial system in SA had not been as developed, would as much attention have been given to re-channelling or transforming it? But the reality that SA has a stable and profitable financial sector has encouraged the dangerous illusion, in some quarters, that finance alone can solve many problems. The message of this book is that the binding constraints on growth must be addressed if there is to be progress. And in some cases, such as SMMEs or housing, finance is often not the real constraint.

If finance per se is not the main constraint, then what is? It is coordination failure: the lack of coordination between public and private sectors in order to produce mutually desired outcomes to complex problems. Private finance and financial services flow when there is a stable environment and when the expected rate of return is reasonable for the perceived risk. Just as water does not flow uphill without the help of a pump, private finance ceases to flow where the return is too uncertain or too low. Where vicious cycles have set in, for example in redlined areas such as township housing markets, substantial public–private coordination is required to reverse the cycle. While the public sector can remove some of the obstacles, it cannot address all; in some cases, private finance must commit to flow in advance of the realisation of full solutions, since normalisation is itself dependent on that flow. Because it is simpler not to coordinate, the state is often tempted to provide the finance directly; but its resources are inevitably limited.

Coordination failure is even more likely in the presence of the strong network effects in the financial sector. For instance, the value to an individual of having a bank account is related to the number of other individuals and entities who have a bank account, since the account facilitates payment between accounts.

In the presence of strong network effects, the quicker the initial take-up, the more likely the product will succeed. But getting big fast requires considerable investment—and therefore risk—which is unlikely to be undertaken without stability and coordination among market players and regulators.

Other examples of coordination failure come from state development finance intermediaries (DFIs). Some are intended to assist financing flows to move over uncertain (and sometimes uneven) risk-return terrain, but their credit policies are more risk-averse than those of market investors. The lack of coordination in approach to risk-bearing results in waste and inefficiency.

Other DFIs compete unsuccessfully with private-sector players. As a result, they become obsolete and cease to play the role of financial 'pumps'. The roles and policies of ineffective DFIs should be revised so that they can play major market-leading roles in the next decade—following discussions on the finalisation of Charter-linked programmes in housing, SMME and other areas.

Financial literacy or consumer financial education is another area in which there has been little coordination. It does not fit neatly into any one of the sectors covered in the book, since it underlies and encompasses all of them. As the Appendix **Financial literacy** on p.222 relates, there have been various initiatives, public and private, at many levels—from high school to adult education. Yet despite these efforts, results from FinScope (2003) on an indicator question showed that overall levels of financial literacy are very low. Financial literacy has strong features of a public good. For instance, though financial-service providers will benefit from a more literate client base—in terms of lower origination costs and lower lapses—no one provider will benefit *fully* from offering consumer education to clients. After all, clients might choose to go to a competitor who has not incurred the cost of educating the client, and can therefore offer the product more cheaply. So the market alone will never provide enough (or indeed appropriate) financial literacy training.

One way to resolve this market failure is through collective action by the industry so that all share the cost; and the Charter levy of 0,2% of profits to fund consumer education is a step in this direction. However, coordination must go well beyond voluntary taxation, if duplication and waste are to be avoided. Leadership is needed to align the diverse initiatives, including those by the state in the areas of school curriculums and adult basic education. There must be ongoing monitoring of initiatives to assess impact and information on what is happening. Consumer financial literacy is therefore a litmus test of the forms of coordination required under the Charter.

The Charter Council is the governance mechanism, established in terms of the

Charter, to oversee and monitor adherence to the Charter. The Council is composed of representatives of government and other Charter signatories. As such, it offers a vehicle for enhancing coordination in the sector; and it is vital that it plays this role alongside the roles of Charter umpire and scorekeeper.

Movement on the landscape
This book has been a guided tour across the landscape of access to financial services. It has highlighted areas of change and innovation, as well as the areas where, despite much activity, there has been little real change. Two sectors stand out as having experienced material expansion in levels of access, driven by legislative or technological change (or both) over the past decade. They are transaction banking and micro lending. In both areas, millions more people are using financial services in 2004 than in 1994.

Why did these sectors, and not others, see progress? For one thing, they have several interesting features in common:

- Neither area received much state support or subsidy. This is clear in transaction banking where state agencies such as PostBank and Ithala have been minor or regional players in the expansion. However, the statement must be qualified somewhat in the case of micro lending. Some segments (payroll lending) benefited from state financing support for incremental housing, in the early days. But private firms, using their own capital, are responsible for much of micro lending today, and have been for most of the decade. In both transaction banking and micro lending, feasible models were developed early on by innovators—E Plan and the payroll and cash (PIN card) lending models date back to the early 1990s. These models could not be patented or protected; and their success had a strong demonstration effect.
- Strong competitive forces ensured rapid and large-scale diffusion. Entry to micro lending was initially unregulated and there was rapid entry after the legalisation of high-interest loans. In the banking sector, competition between the major retail banks ensured that the basic debit card platform was soon rolled out widely to new, employed clients.
- Growth in clients of these two sectors was overwhelmingly among the formally employed. It was salaried workers who received micro loans for the first time in the past decade; and salaried workers who were pressured by their employers to open a debit card bank account, to access their salaries via ATM. This trend is not surprising. On the demand side, the arrival of democracy raised the lifestyle aspirations of these new salaried clients. From the supply-side perspective, they were much easier to reach profitably, with bank accounts and loans—and often at the place of work with employer support.

Innovation played a critical part in the process since it reduced the cost of delivering the services. For this reason, this book has intentionally showcased successful and failed innovation. Across all the categories of financial services, not only in transaction banking and micro lending, successful innovations had the following characteristics in common:

- They were based on demand-side need: successful innovation is ultimately about delivering products or services that people want, at a price they are willing to pay. In the nature of SA's historically divided society, many innovations have been driven by a vague sense of what people 'ought to have', rather than what they actually want. In this sense, the market is a great discipliner: innovations that do not meet real needs will not survive; nor should they. Successful innovations have usually started by being very close to the needs of target clients.
- They were driven by individuals or teams of people, rather than by institutions. The case studies in this book have sought to reflect some of the views of the innovators themselves. Their motivations have differed—some have been profit-driven, others have been driven by social awareness. But, in each case, it was the vision and determination of key people that made something happen.
- Successful concepts were flexible and evolutionary: successful innovations evolve over time, adapting to feedback from the market. The case studies highlight several examples of organisations that went through progressive phases of product innovation (such as HLGC) or institutional innovation (such as Group Credit Company/CashBank). Organisations that did not have this flexibility failed (such as Gateway). This characteristic is far more important as a determinant of success than private or public ownership per se: public organisations have succeeded (such as MFRC) and private ones have failed (such as RFF). However, it is likely that publicly owned entities will struggle to evolve as quickly as privately owned ones. Though certain NGOs have been quick to evolve, this has been dependent on the quality of their leadership and governance.

Harvard Business School professor Clayton Christensen has introduced the term 'disruptive innovation' (as opposed to incremental innovation) to describe innovations which radically change markets, and often take incumbent firms by surprise.[1] We have seen few disruptive innovations in the financial sector over the past decade. However, we have seen disruptive innovation in other sectors, particularly in telecommunications. The introduction of cellphones to SA, at around the time of the first democratic elections in 1994, has led to explosive growth in the number of people who have wireless service—at the cost of the older fixed-line service. Many of these are people who were regarded as too poor to afford the service. But people pay for what they value. The disruptive innovation at work in cellular telephony was a mechanism that reduced the credit risk—namely, prepaid airtime—and that bundled the product in different-sized packages—airtime vouchers of various denominations, which a range of consumers could afford. The successful take-up of cellphones (which is also subject to network effects) offers a clear challenge to the financial sector to emulate, by allowing disruptive innovation in the next decade. And as the second chapter explained, cellphones are likely to become important channels for payments and financial transactions over the next decade.

... and beyond

Are we likely to see disruptive innovation in the next decade? Disruptive innovation is especially difficult in the tightly regulated financial sector where regulators do not welcome disruption. But disruption may well have a dramatic impact on the access outcome, especially in areas where there is no obvious incremental solution available.

To answer this question (and others), FinMark Trust conducted a scenario-building project known as Vision 2010 in 2002/3. Scenarios were seen as a way to encourage Charter negotiators and others to think about the impact of current trends and choices on the medium- to long-term future of access.

Three main scenarios were built. But they are merely stories about developments in the state of access to financial services from 2004 to 2010.[2] They are less important than the 'laws of motion' or scenario logic which created them. This logic is built on understanding the 'rules' of the game, the largely unchangeable trends; and also the key hinges, or uncertainties that could alter outcomes decisively.

The two main uncertainties identified were the following:
- Who pays for expanded access? This question refers to the way in which the risks and costs of extending access are shared between government (and therefore taxpayers) on the one hand, and shareholders and depositors in financial institutions on the other.
- Will the architecture for the sector be open or closed? In other words will the policies and norms adopted facilitate entry and innovation in the sector or not? Will disruptive innovation be allowed?

It is still too early to predict which scenario is more likely to emerge. Even though the Charter was finalised in October 2003, various important issues which could determine the answers to these questions are still not clear or public. In particular, the risk-sharing mechanisms at the heart of the renewed thrusts in housing and SMME finance have not yet been finalised. The architecture of the sector has not changed decisively yet, in part because the general election of 2004 curtailed legislative programmes; and in part because government and regulators had to await the outcome of final post-Charter negotiations. However, there are signs in pieces of proposed legislation that a more open architecture is possible, even likely, in the next two years.

One is the proposed Dedicated Banks Bill, which creates a new second tier to the commercial banking system. It comes in the form of core and narrow banks, which are required to carry less capital, in return for operating only in prescribed areas of business—mainly retail deposit-taking and lending. This bill could open the architecture of the payment system to other providers such as retailers and cell-phone companies. They already have trusted brands and extensive online distribution channels where cash can be withdrawn or deposited. The entry of such players would decisively change the geographic landscape of access. And it would make basic bank accounts more affordable by using largely existing infrastructure to carry instructions or provide cash points.

The second is the Consumer Credit Bill, which integrates previously disparate pieces of legislation that have fragmented the consumer credit markets into uneven niches, including the Usury Act exemption, which allowed micro lending to flourish. The bill must carefully balance the need for consumer protection with the need to develop new and innovative credit products, at least in areas such as housing and SMME. And therefore it should maintain the balancing-act approach started by the MFRC. By integrating sub-markets under one main, stable regulatory regime, the Consumer Credit Bill may make new forms of competition possible across credit niches.

These two pieces of legislation should help open the financial architecture in the next decade and, in that sense, make the positive access scenarios more likely. However, openness in and of itself is not an unqualified good, as the mixed effects of the original usury exemption have shown. While the state can open the financial architecture, it has to monitor and balance the resulting outcomes against broader societal goals. In this era, when the spotlight again falls on the activist role of the state in social delivery, it is appropriate to consider this issue in the light of the past decade.

Role of the developmental state
It is unusual among middle-income developing countries for as much of the retail financial sector to be privately owned as it is in SA. State retail financial initiatives, such as Postbank or Ithala, are presently weak or area-specific. Clearly, one option for the state in the next decade is to expand these initiatives so as to broaden access. In this, initiatives that mobilise savings must be distinguished from those that provide credit. There are good international examples of the former, such as the Caixa of Brazil, discussed in Chapter 2; but precious few examples of the latter. The reality is that any state is usually ill-equipped to lend directly to its citizens: it lacks the incentives to ensure consistent collection and enforcement of credit contracts. Ultimately, it is more expensive to 'pretend' to lend, without the intent of recovery, than to give grants. All too often in certain BLNS countries, state credit schemes have contributed to bad attitudes towards repayment, which limit the extension of private credit long after the particular schemes have collapsed.

The private sector must therefore be harnessed, if access to credit is to be sustainably extended. Even in other areas such as savings, it is unlikely that direct retail initiatives would be successful alone—indeed, they may have the perverse effect of ghettoising low-end clients, as the banking system happily offloads unprofitable clients onto a state bank, rather than finding new ways to serve them sustainably.

The challenge of the developmental state, which desires to promote access, therefore remains how to make (largely private) financial markets work for the poor. This means neither crowding out the private sector, nor leaving it alone, but catalysing its better functioning, in line with social priorities. The record of the last ten years helps define the potential boundaries of this role.

The traditional role of the state, which it cannot abrogate, is to provide a stable, clear legislative and regulatory framework. This, of course, assumes a stable political economy. Only with such a framework will large-scale capital be deployed by reputable providers in a way which ensures the sustainable expansion of access in the medium-to-long term.

However, the developmental state would and should go further in pursuit of access goals. It should actively create legislative and regulatory space for change, that is, an open architecture. This requires that the state act as the guardian of the delicate trade-offs involved: between stability of the financial system on the one hand, and broader societal stability, through the realisation of legitimate economic aspirations, on the other. The trade-offs require careful investigation and monitoring within a coherent policy framework. But too much caution will mean that the status quo prevails.

The developmental state also faces tough choices, balancing the need for adequate consumer protection with the need for extended access. Currently, financial regulation tends to protect better-off consumers who do not need it as much as poorer consumers, who have no protection at all. Large parts of the financial system, which touch millions of lives, such as burial societies, are effectively not regulated at all. Not that they necessarily should be: the developmental state should be cautious about extending its limited regulatory reach if the effect is to add unnecessary costs with little benefit to the target consumer group.

In the next decade, the developmental state also faces strong pressure to introduce new laws in alignment with international norms, for example to counter money laundering and terrorism. The objectives may be unobjectionable, but as we have seen, well-intended laws in areas such as these can have perverse effects. The developmental state must balance the benefits against the costs in terms of extending access.

The developmental state must also not confine itself to the role of legislator or regulator. As the past decade shows, it is where the state or state institutions have actively led in finding fair and sustainable solutions to market development that there has often been progress. State development finance institutions (DFIs) have a potentially valuable role to play in assuming appropriate risk, so that new markets can be catalysed. Over the past decade, state-sponsored entities, such as the IDTFC, NHFC and even Khula, have played a very important role in financing the early development of micro credit. But a number have lost their way. There is therefore a need to realign and rationalise the DFIs responsible for addressing access-related issues.

In the light of the Charter, various reviews of DFI effectiveness and their roles are already under way. The recently announced merger of two state small-business support organisations (Ntsika and the National Manufacturing Advisory Centre) may herald other welcome changes. The state, as shareholder in well-endowed DFIs, should refocus DFIs to achieve maximum impact and gearing on its funding. This may mean closing defective institutions in favour of new-generation approaches to public–private partnership.

Starting the journey

Much of the high-profile energy and activity around the Charter is focused on transforming the ownership of financial institutions. But the Charter's success will ultimately be judged at the bar of history in terms of its impact on access. In his 2004 budget speech, Finance Minister Trevor Manuel referred to the Charter as 'an important milestone in the evolving framework for empowerment and broadening participation in the economy'. The only specific Charter target that he mentioned in his speech related to access: 'It aims to extend financial services to 80% of lower income people by 2008.' This is of course a simplification of the elaborate Charter framework and targets for different categories of financial service, as the book has discussed; but it proves the point. In the private sector, statements such as that made by Standard Bank Group chair Derek Cooper at the Nedlac Summit, quoted at the beginning of the chapter, increase the expectation that the financial sector will deliver on these targets.

It is the access targets of the Charter that catch the political and public imagination in ways that the other targets do not. However, it is also in this area where progress is hardest, since coordination is needed. In other targeted areas, like the transformation of ownership and of management, the Charter is most likely to reach its targets for one of two reasons: because the process is dependent only on individual organisations doing deals (ownership); or because it has been under way for a while in somewhat less focused form (management). Not surprisingly, perhaps, there was criticism, even from within the sector, that the original targets in these areas are not demanding enough. And targets in these and other areas had to be raised.

But, unless there is demonstrable progress, especially in flashpoint sectors such as housing finance and SMME finance, the access debate is likely to erupt into the political arena again before the next election in 2009. The industry's self-imposed access targets, if unmet, would become easy weapons in the hands of those who would compel private organisations to provide social solutions. And there would be little defence.

In this sense, SA ends the first decade of freedom—of democratising finance—on a high. It is not a mountain-top high, because we have certainly not arrived at the end goal. In a sense, we have only reached broad consensus on starting the journey. The opportunities created by a stable economic and political framework are much greater than they were ten years ago; but the stakes are also much higher.

The road to increased access from here will not be easy or quick. It will require striking a delicate balance—between over- and under-regulation; between no state involvement and too much state involvement, for example. It will incur costly investment—both public and private. Above all, it will require a new generation of innovators with vision, passion and determination, who will find ways around every obstacle. As long as there is space for and encouragement of innovation in the financial sector, the ascent to increased access, while not quick, will be sure.

Endnotes

1 See for example, Christensen (1997; 2003).
2 *Vision 2010* can be ordered on request from www.finmarktrust.org.za.

APPENDIX 1
Stokvels: making social cents

'Stokvels: Making Social Cents?' evolved from an earlier project by the UCT Unilever Institute, entitled 'Stockings and Stokvels'.[1] The initial research aimed to discover what really happens at Christmas time among black South Africans, and uncovered the important role of stokvels in funding Christmas purchases for many people.

The Institute followed this up with a major research project, which fills in some of the shades and colours of the stokvel phenomenon in SA. Twenty-four focus group meetings were held in rural and urban areas of the country in May and June of 2003. Of those people taking part, 60% were aged 30 years or more. Groups were gender-specific and three consisted of non-stokvel members. Audio-visual research was conducted in 18 in-depth interviews with various stokvels in Gauteng, KwaZulu-Natal and Cape Town.

The roots of stokvels lie deep in SA history. In early colonial days, banks were opened by settlers, for settlers—they were simply not an option for the indigenous population. It was this lack of access to formal financial services that saw the spontaneous development of community-based group savings schemes or stokvels—called rotating savings and credit associations (Roscas) internationally.

The term 'stokvel' is in fact a corruption of 'stock fairs', the rotating cattle auctions held by British settlers in the Eastern Cape during the early 19th century. Black farmers and labourers visiting these fairs took the concept back to their communities, and the stokvel germinated there as an indigenous alternative to the formal banking introduced by the settlers. When gold was discovered in what was then the Transvaal towards the end of the century, many joined the gold rush and brought the concept with them to the Witwatersrand. Destined for further hardship, both the migrants and those remaining fell back on the *ubuntu*-enriched stock fair concept as a form of insurance against calamity, and the true stokvel was born.

Eight different kinds of stokvels were identified by the research:
1. The **contributions stokvel** is a forced savings (rotational) scheme. Money is contributed weekly, fortnightly or monthly, in fixed amounts of cash, to the member next in line. This means members wait their turn for payouts. They are free to choose what they spend their payout on. This creates big-ticket opportunities for consumers who generally have little money to spend but, once a year, have access to a lump sum.
2. The **basic stokvel** is similar to the contributions stokvel, although it is sometimes split as a savings scheme for the end of year, and also for death. The money is either rotated or paid out at the end of the year (sometimes half in

December and half in January for back-to-school purchases). Food and drink is provided at some stokvel meetings. These groups of like-minded consumers share brand loyalty and relay both good and bad experiences to one another. Because of their year-end bulk buying, they create opportunities for sellers of groceries and household goods, for instance.

3. The **grocery stokvel** collects cash or grocery coupons bought from Shoprite or Pick 'n Pay. A profit may be made from free additional coupons. Money is paid on an ongoing basis, through the year, for necessary grocery purchases. At the end of the year, members buy groceries in bulk and there is a big get-together for which they buy food and drink.
4. In a **purchasing stokvel**, members pool money and decide upfront what they are saving their money for. They get paid out on a rotating basis and use the money for big-ticket items (as in a contributions stokvel) but often one person, the chairperson or treasurer, buys the big-ticket item on behalf of the member, to ensure that the money is used for its intended purpose.
5. A **family stokvel** invests money in interest-bearing accounts or money schemes. Payouts are flexible, to meet needs of the family as they arise. Money is used for a range of purposes, from cars, to land, to supporting new business ideas and bank loan deposits.
6. An **investment group** invests money in various ways and profits from the interest. Not all the capital is necessarily repaid, as some may be reinvested for future growth. Investment group schemes are often entrepreneurial.
7. A **party stokvel** arranges street parties, jazz evenings (in Gauteng) and stadium parties. It invites members and friends of members to fund-raising parties where an entrance fee is charged and food and drinks are sold. Members share the profits. In a sense, a form of catering micro enterprise, some of these stokvels have evolved into sophisticated business entities.
8. **Borrowing stokvels** generate additional income by lending money to members and sub-members who are recruited by the stokvel members. This money is loaned out at a rate of 20–50% a month. FinScope results suggest that borrowing stokvels are rare in SA.

The UCT report concludes that both stokvels and burial societies are alive and well, and will continue to play an important role in the lives of members. They will adapt as and when members require them to. They are often successful micro businesses because they are financially efficient, provide social support and fit in with the community-focused culture of *ubuntu*. They are often far more efficient for a member as a savings-and-credit mechanism than any bank or financial institution. This has been highlighted by the fundraising arms of a number of stokvels, in the form of sophisticated micro-lending schemes or fundraising entertainment parties. The profits from micro lending and party schemes are channelled back into the profits of the stokvel and, in some instances, stokvel members see their money increase threefold on their actual contribution.

The UCT report concludes with a challenge to marketers: formal offerings at the low end of the market are often product-driven, Eurocentric, focused on the individual, inflexible, and remote from their customers. Marketers believe they can 'educate' the stokvel customer to understand their existing products. This is arrogant and extremely bad marketing, says UCT. Rather, marketers should recognise that stokvels are here to stay, change their mindset away from selling 'white' products and appreciate a market where they can serve 12 to 20 customers instead of one.

Endnotes

1   UCT Unilever Institute of Strategic Marketing (2003).

APPENDIX 2
Village banks: democratic banking?

Democracy is a form of governance that allows diverse and even contradictory social interests to be collectively expressed in the realm of civil society.[1]

Village banks are a relatively recent development in SA.[2] The concept was introduced by the International Fund for Agricultural Development (IFAD) about ten years ago, and substantial energy and donor funding has been expended on it. Associations, which are democratically governed and mutually owned, are formed in remote villages to set up village banks. Each village bank is linked to a formal bank in the nearest town, where the savings are kept on deposit. Local infrastructure reduces transaction costs to members, who would otherwise have to travel to the nearest bank; and loans to members keep the funds in the areas in which they are mobilised.

Three village banks, all in the North West province, were registered in 1996 as financial service co-operatives. The Financial Services Association (FSA) was formed as an umbrella body. Its brief was to develop and implement new products and services, provide training, and direct financial contributions to new village banks.

A milestone in the development of village banks came in 1998 when they were granted an exemption under the Banks Act and allowed to accept deposits. Because of their potential to provide rural financial infrastructure to the poor, the National Department of Welfare (now the Department of Social Development) approved a project grant of R7m in 1999, to establish 70 village banks in seven provinces. The grant allowed the FSA, which took the role of regulator, to formalise its activities and improve its capacity.

Twenty-nine communities set up financial service co-operatives over 30 months. But at the end of the period a departmental project review revealed a lack of proper management, poor training and inexperience. Funding fell away and the FSA closed operationally in 2001/02. Some village banks, which had belonged to the FSA, had developed enough capacity to continue operating.

A second stream within the village banking movement was started in KwaZulu-Natal. FinaSol was originally conceptualised as an umbrella body to transform the clients of South African Sugar Association's Financial Aid Fund (FAF) into village banks. Funded by donors and registered in 1999, FinaSol was recognised by the Registrar of Banks as a regulatory body with more or less the same functions as the FSA.

Because development initiatives often founder in the early stages, FinaSol, as franchisor, provided start-up assistance and ongoing support to the village banks. A village bank did not have to buy the franchise. It registered as a financial service co-operative and, once it had an acceptable business plan, FinaSol advanced R40 000 to cover the initial operating expenses, and a grant of R8 000 to buy a safe and set up an office. The village bank was responsible for all operating costs, including the salary of the teller or administrator, who was trained by FinaSol.

Theoretically, the franchising concept allows communities to jump-start financial services, without the trial-and-error period associated with a start-up. However, the process was not free of trial and error.

In 2001, following a large grant from the UK Department for International Development, FinaSol's head office was relocated to Johannesburg, a new management was appointed for the project and First National Bank (FNB), which undertook to implement the project as the link bank, set up a village banking department. The operation barely got off the ground. FNB's objective for the project was not achieved and the funding was not tapped. FinaSol's operations were discontinued in July 2002. Nevertheless, most of the village banks it established continued to operate.

In 2002, the National Department of Agriculture (NDA) attempted to refocus the programme. It set up a national task team to look at how to build capacity, and a Cooperative Development Fund to mobilise rural deposits and channel them into productive rural enterprises.

Today, about 62 village banks are registered with the Registrar of Cooperatives. Of these, 32 were members of the FSA and 30 were members of FinaSol. A number of communities have established local structures, five of which have applied for registration. The movement has an estimated 60 000–80 000 members and an estimated total portfolio worth R30m–R40m.

With no support services, some village banks are reportedly experiencing difficulties, including mismanagement of funds, administrative problems, a shortage of stationery and lack of training. And almost all are in dire need of auditing services. Despite these problems, some of the very first village banks, such as Motswedi, with its 1 552 members and a savings portfolio of R1,8m, are continuing to expand their portfolios.

A number of lessons were learned from the FSA and FinaSol experience.

The impact of member-based banking goes beyond financial services, as it has a decided influence on empowerment at grassroots level. It develops human resources and improves the ability of people involved to interact with the government and other stakeholders. Moreover, the contribution of members entrenches the community's sense of ownership and lowers the local-level institutions' transaction costs.

To test the proposition that village banks offered genuinely democratic banking, social researcher Anthea Dallimore, of Development Research Africa, undertook a study of the governance of four village banks in 2002.[3] The banks were chosen to represent different types in terms of geographic location, population group served, length of operation and services offered. The rural communities in which they were based were: Bhambanana in KwaZulu-Natal; Mathabatha in Limpopo, Motswedi in the North West Province; and Sakaletfu in Mpumalanga. Focus groups were held with different groups of members of each bank.

Research probed understanding of the governance procedures at each bank, such as how the board of directors was elected.

A litmus test of democracy is how conflicts are resolved. To establish that systems and procedures were in place, participants were asked how problems were solved. There were similar response patterns across the groups but, within each group, participants were divided. Some had never heard of any problems and did not know if there were mechanisms for solving them. Others said there had been problems and explained how they were resolved. Comments from participants who had never heard of problems suggested inadequate communication between members and bank management.

Another key indicator of a healthy democratic institution is a wide range of community participation and a healthy tolerance of other people's views. Questions in this section were designed to identify the types of people receiving the bank's services and establish whether people would be excluded because they were poor or illiterate or came from a different tribe. Rather than ask directly, the researchers asked why certain people would not use the bank's services. Responses varied across banks. In Bhambanana, pensioners said members were the 'people who could save', while board members recognised that it was primarily poor people who were members. In Mathabatha, most respondents described members according to vocational status, such as 'pensioners' and 'small business people'. However, the men recognised that the bank primarily served poor people. In Sakaletfu, people were described in terms of their actions: 'any person who saves'. Women from Motswedi recognised that the bank was open to anyone over 16, regardless of employment status and that there was 'no discrimination'. The pensioners said it was 'good people' and 'people who behave' who were members.

Dallimore also probed the benefits offered by the village bank to the community. Her conclusion from the focus group discussions was that, regardless of the extent to which any of the banks are managed democratically, they have all rendered a great deal of social and economic benefit to the communities in which they are located. In all four groups, and in each different focus group, mention was made of the long distances to the closest (non-village) bank, the cost of getting there, the danger of keeping money and the inhospitable nature of commercial banks. Alternatives to the village bank included travelling long distances to a commercial bank and traditional methods like digging a hole in the ground to hide the money. Some of the banks had also played an important role in the distribution of social grants to beneficiaries.

The governance assessment was taken further in Dallimore's study of poor households in one of the four rural communities,[4] where some members also used the nearest commercial bank branch some distance away. This study provides a useful snapshot of households and their finances in a rural area. A stratified cross-section of over 200 households in the community was interviewed. The households fell into three segments: commercially banked households, village-banked households and unbanked households. Various demographic and poverty indicators were collected on each household, together with a wide range of data about financial-instrument usage.

The research found that commercially banked households were the wealthiest (and most likely to have formally employed members), followed by village-banked households, with unbanked households the poorest in the community. Furthermore, the report found some evidence of the beneficial impact of village banking on savings habits, in that the inverse relationship between savings and poverty was strongest among village-banking clients. Although Dallimore is careful not to claim that this is conclusive evidence of causation—i.e. that village banks cause higher savings—she says the correlation is significant and is a starting point in 'unpacking the complex relationships between savings, poverty and access to financial services'.

If village banks are to be viable, some structure is needed to represent them at the national or policy level, because individual banks lack the capacity. But people in the community must accept full ownership. Similarly, operations at secondary level require a degree of technical expertise beyond the general capacity of local members. But the introduction of expertise must be managed properly, or the process may create tension and endanger effective participation.

Establishing village banks is a developmental process. There is little chance that they can be established without at least some external support and funding. But experience has shown that, with the right initial support and emphasis in the early stages, a village bank can go on to operate independently.

Whether the experiments in 'democratic banking' over the past decade will lead on to larger roll-out in rural areas in the next decade will depend on the level of support received—from the state, the financial sector and donors.

Endnotes

1 Community Agency for Social Enquiry (CASE) (1998). The State of Civil Society in South Africa: Past Legacies, Present Realities, and Future Prospects.
2 This case study is drawn from ECI Africa (2003a, b) and two research papers: Dallimore & Mgimeti (2002) and Dallimore (2003), available via www.finmarktrust.org.za.
3 Dallimore (2003).
4 Dallimore (2003).

APPENDIX 3

The macro picture: why saving matters but has declined

Johan Prinsloo, senior economist at the SA Reserve Bank, has a useful definition of savings.[1] They are 'the amount of income that is not consumed immediately but is put to use in a way that will provide returns to the economy in years to come'. There are other ways to describe savings. They can be explained as the equivalent of a country's trade surplus. Or they can be defined as a pool of domestic funds that can be drawn on, to finance investment in the real economy.

But savings is more than a technical issue. For households, they represent a buffer in times of adversity. For economies, they are a driver of economic growth and possibly of jobs. 'Most of the recent studies on strategic guidelines for achieving an adequate rate of economic growth and development indicate that the aggregate saving rate will have to be raised above 20% of GDP to support a sustained growth rate in real incomes of more than 3% a year,' says Prinsloo.

So the level of saving in a country has important implications for ordinary people. This is why it is of great concern that South Africa's saving rate is low, both by historical and international standards. Aggregate saving declined from a fairly stable average of about 24% during the 1960s and 1970s to an average of 16,3% in the 1990s,[2] and continued to decline to 15,6% in 2000–2003.

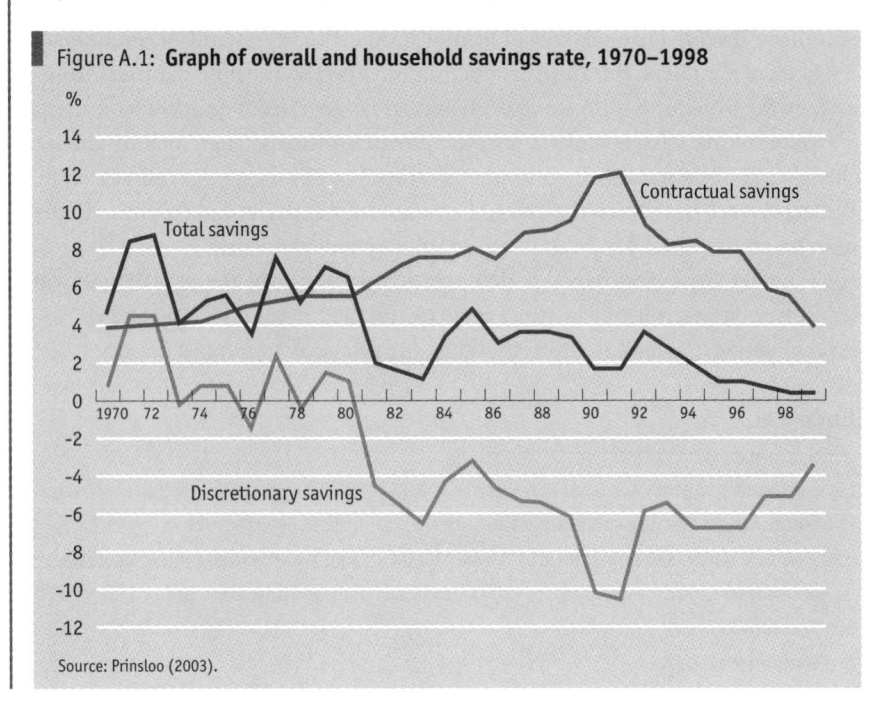

Figure A.1: **Graph of overall and household savings rate, 1970–1998**

Source: Prinsloo (2003).

This decline was coupled with a change in its composition: a rise in corporate saving has been offset by a decline in saving by households, while government's performance has been mixed. It started dissaving towards the beginning of the 1990s but has reversed the trend recently.

Figure A.1 shows that, within the household sector, which is the focus of this chapter, the relative composition of savings has changed too: discretional savings have been negative since 1980, although they have improved during the 1990s; and while contractual savings have compensated to some extent, they have declined since their peak in 1991.

The ratio of total household savings to GDP has been on 'a decisive downward trend' since 1984, says Prinsloo.[3] And he cites a number of factors that would have influenced savings behaviour over the period:

- Rising marginal personal tax rates which reduce disposable income.
- Easier access to credit facilities, which increases household borrowing.
- The after-tax interest rate on depository-type investments, which has been low or even negative in real terms for long periods in the past 20 years.
- The slowdown in households' real income growth during long periods of high inflation.
- The impact of high inflation on income tax: fiscal drag eroding real income.
- The increase in prices of households' assets.
- The redistribution of income. Poorer households need to spend a greater proportion of their income: in economic terms their propensity to consume is greater than that of middle- and high-income families.
- Demographic trends, including a higher dependency ratio, a relative rise in the number of younger people in the total economically active population and, recently, the impact of HIV/AIDS.

IMF research confirms this analysis, to some extent, by finding that the decline in personal savings experienced in SA is in line with: a decline in real per capita income; declining income inequality and greater social transfers; and fewer liquidity constraints and greater household borrowing. It is also in line with portfolio shifts because of the relative attractions of contractual saving vehicles.

However, there is no clear policy prescription to address the decline. Some factors responsible for the deterioration in saving no longer apply: marginal personal tax rates have been declining for several years, as has the burden on individual taxpayers, in real terms. Exceptionally high inflation is no longer an issue, which means personal disposable income is no longer deteriorating in real terms.

Other forces undermining saving lie outside the ambit of policy: for instance increases in prices of households' assets, which are the result of rising stock market and property prices over a period. In other cases, the remedy may do harm. Domestic consumption spending, for instance, is an engine of growth, and keeps the economy growing when rand appreciation erodes export income. So a decision to stifle consumption may incur a considerable cost.

Another complication is that, in at least one case, the deterioration in savings is a by-product of a positive development for the economy: the redistribution of income from wealthier to less wealthy households, which have a higher propensity to consume. Households with low incomes will spend proportionately more, simply on survival, while wealthier households have more resources and are more likely to save. This redistribution of income will continue as the legacy of apartheid recedes. And, positive as the process will be for the economy as a whole, it will have a negative impact on savings for many years.

However, some good news for the future comes from the ipac/IDC Savings Barometer, which tracks quarterly changes in the environment affecting the propensity to save. At a household-only level, the barometer has shown continuous improvement since 1998 as a result of positive household income growth.[4] While actual savings performance has shown an opposite trend to date, the barometer may be pointing to improvements to come.

Endnotes

1   Prinsloo (2000).
2   Genesis Analytics (2004d).
3   Prinsloo (2003).
4   Savings Institute. Available via www.savingsinstitute.org.za/ipac.html; quoted from 4th Quarter 2003.

APPENDIX 4
Was there a credit bubble in the late 1990s?

Many observers of micro lending and retail credit in the 1990s casually refer to the 'consumer credit bubble'. The claim that this bubble existed is an important one, since the scale and impact of a burst bubble are different from the fall-out of credit distress in particular market segments.

The concept of a credit bubble requires analytical definition at the outset. A credit bubble occurs when the rate of credit extension to a particular market exceeds the long-run debt-bearing capacity of that market, *measured at the time of grant*. The italicised text is important. It requires irrationality in borrowers and lenders (i.e. borrowers borrowing more than they can afford and suppliers of credit lending more than borrowers can afford) at the time of the loan. This distinction regarding timing matters since, without it, there would be no observable difference between the effects of a burst bubble (which usually come only when a bubble is identified and named) and the effects of credit distress as the result of outside factors, such as a large unforeseen interest hike or adverse shock to employment, which had little to do with over-lending at the time.

There are at least two necessary conditions for the formation of a credit bubble:

- *Borrowers must be willing and able to borrow at a rate which exceeds their long-run repayment capacity*: if consumers are even partly rational, this would imply a structural change in consumer expectations about future income.
- *Lenders must be willing to lend without taking a view of consolidated borrower indebtedness*: this could happen as result of the information not being available, though the more typical lender response is to withhold loans in the face of unknown risk. Or it could result from a desire to increase market share through consciously lax credit policies—though for a bubble to form, it would require conditions which prompted more than one lender to chase market share.

Together, these preconditions are sufficient for a credit bubble.

One further definitional question remains—the extent of over-indebtedness needed to qualify as a bubble. Clearly, bubbles can assume various sizes, with policy implications, if any, varying accordingly. Figure A.2 shows the quarter-on-quarter, annualised nominal rate of increase in household credit in SA over the past ten years, decomposed into bank credit and retail credit. The graph shows rates of increase in retail credit of more than 30% per quarter between 1994 and 1997, and a subsequent decline to much lower rates. Bank credit also increased relatively fast during the period in question, then declined, and has shown some increase since 2000.

A high rate of increase is not evidence per se of a bubble forming, since one would have to control for:
- Inflation, typically running at 10% during the period in question.
- Real increases in wages, which would give consumers the ability to afford more.
- Access to credit by those who have not had access before, i.e. expansion of the credit universe, which would lead to more rapid expansion.

Undoubtedly, all these factors have come into play, and if they were sufficient to explain the increases, it would mean that there was no bubble. But there is a further factor: black consumers' expectations of an improvement in their conditions, as tracked by the University of Stellenbosch's Bureau for Economic Research index, mirror very closely the rate of retail credit extension. This is not the case among white consumers, whose expectations remained largely flat over the period. The pattern suggests that at least part of the increase in credit was driven by a change in the expectations of a large consumer group that became credit-active during the period. Unduly positive expectations could cause consumers to over-borrow, and hence constitute a necessary condition for a bubble.

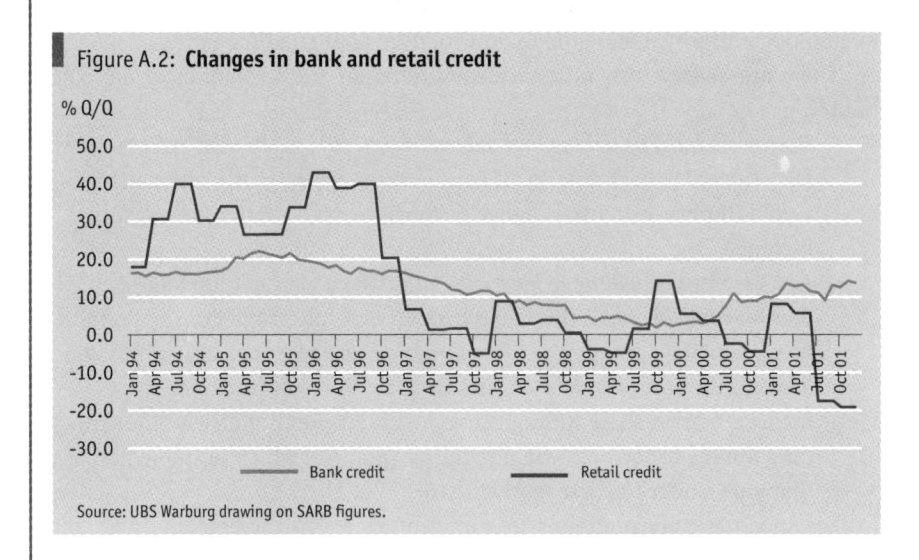

Figure A.2: **Changes in bank and retail credit**

Source: UBS Warburg drawing on SARB figures.

Since, as Figure A.2 shows, rates of increase in household credit have been relatively muted since 1998, any evidence of a large credit bubble must lie further in the past than 2000/01.

In terms of the second necessary condition for a bubble, that lenders lend irrationally: the two significant new collection technologies, payroll deduction and PIN card holding, were deployed widely in the 1990s. This significantly fuelled the profitability and hence growth of the micro-lending industry. One consequence of these innovations was that many new lenders regarded traditional credit-checking methodology, such as a credit bureau check, as unnecessary. Furthermore, the validity of bureau data was seriously questioned, especially for black consumers, since a bad credit record was sometimes evidence of participation in politically motivated credit or service charge boycotts.

The super-profitability of early pioneers in the field caused others to follow, including banks such as Unibank and Saambou, and indeed to pursue market share. During 2000/01, the market continued to reward evidence of book growth and certain lenders were happy to deliver this, even after the collapse of one of the major collection methodologies through the state payroll system, Persal, in June 2000.

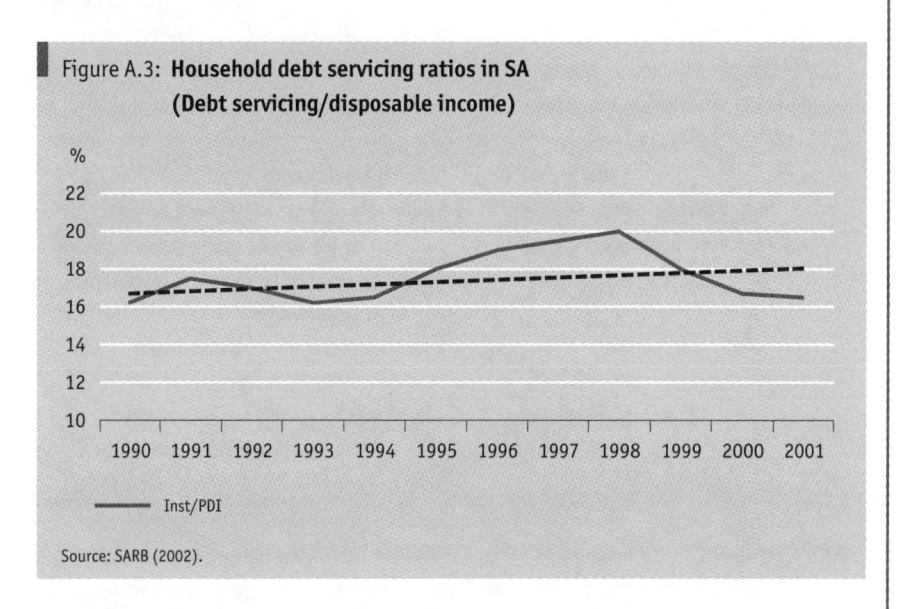

Figure A.3: **Household debt servicing ratios in SA**
(Debt servicing/disposable income)

Inst/PDI

Source: SARB (2002).

So there are some indications, in terms of both the borrower and lender, that the necessary conditions for a consumer credit bubble may have been in place. But the evidence of a generalised bubble lies further back than most people would date it—in the mid-1990s, rather than in the late 1990s.

Finally, since bubbles are only usually recognised in hindsight, i.e. by the symptoms of their bursting, rather than upfront, it is relevant to ask whether the symptoms of a burst bubble are shown in current credit conditions.

In general, the evidence does not support the view that a large consumer credit bubble built up in the late 1990s and burst in 2001/02. Instead, the evidence appears to support the following:
- There were very rapid increases in consumer credit earlier on, correlated especially to changing black consumer expectations in post-apartheid SA.
- There were poor lending practices, by at least some lenders in the micro-loan sector, who failed to consider the repayment ability of

Table A.1: **Expected features of a burst bubble, and the evidence**

Expected burst bubble symptom	Evidence
1. Losses and exit by lenders in the affected market.	1. MFRC data shows that the overall number of lenders and outlets in the registered micro-loan sector has been roughly stable.
2. New credit disbursements would either increase (due to distress borrowing) or decrease (due to lender reactions to reduce their risk) sharply.	2. Again, MFRC disbursement and balance-outstanding figures for 2001–2 are fairly stable: quarterly disbursements fell from an average of R3,6bn to R3,2bn, but outstanding balances rose between 2001 and 2002.
3. The instalment-to-income ratio for consumers would be expected to rise rapidly and stay high as the bubble burst.	3. Figure A.3 shows no recent rapid increase in the ratio; in fact, it has decreased since the credit distress of high interest rates associated with the Asian crisis in 1998.
4. Increasing evidence of distressed debtors with multiple indebtedness.	4. Even in one of the most heavily indebted sub-markets (Persal), the percentage of consumers who had borrowed via payroll and who were distressed per the agreed definitions in June 2001 was only 6%, and has fallen due to rehabilitation measures since then.
5. Arrear and credit delinquency measures would rise, as consumers are unable to make their repayments.	5. Summonses and civil judgments for debt show no evidence of a large increase between 2000 and 2001; similarly, Consumer Credit Association data for retail credit providers shows little evidence of large increases during 2001 in arrears of more than three months.

borrowers, and some of these lenders are now being shaken out of the industry.
- There is some evidence of more localised credit distress, such as in the payroll deduction market, especially among larger employers. But, even in this segment, the extent of distress has been relatively low and is as likely to result from changing economic circumstances, such as retrenchments, as from irrational or irresponsible borrowing or lending.

In the face of the evidence, it is important not to reach simplistic conclusions about the negative effects of micro lending, and adopt swingeing policies in response. The evidence suggests a definite need to respond to and to curb certain abuses; but not as severe a crisis as the popular media portrayed at the time. This more considered view underlies the DTI panel recommendations for the future regulation of consumer credit in SA. It was also the basis of the MFRC submission (2003) to the Portfolio Committee on Finance, which said, 'There are indications of over-indebtedness in at least certain segments of the population ... However, the greater number of borrowers appears to manage their debts responsibly and there are indications of significant numbers of people who have reduced their level of consumption debt since 1995 ... a general clampdown on credit extension would be counterproductive as there is as great a need for an increase in access to finance.'

APPENDIX 5
SMME definitions

There are many ways of defining the categories of business activity that fall within the broad description of an SMME. Official SA definitions differ from international definitions, which generally distinguish only between micro enterprises on the one hand, and small and medium enterprises on the other. The main official categorisation in SA is contained in the 1996 White Paper on Small Business, in which SMMEs are broken down into survivalist, micro, very small, small and medium categories.[1]

- *Survivalist enterprises* are those with minimal asset value, no paid employees and little or no collateral, where the individual concerned depends on the marginal income generated in order to survive from day to day. These operations do require working capital to buy supplies and inputs (often for periods of less than a week) but in the absence of collateral, they are unable to access formal credit, and rely on alternative approaches, such as group-based micro lending and family and friends.
- *Micro enterprises* are those with turnover below R150 000 a year, with fewer than five paid employees. They may have access to collateral but are generally unwilling to risk it; and few have the type of collateral required by formal financial institutions anyway. They need small loans to acquire equipment such as sewing machines or deepfreezes, and working capital ranging from R2 000 to R30 000 for supplies and material inputs, for period of three months to three years.
- *Very small enterprises* are those that employ fewer than ten people. Their equity requirements are generally too small for equity financiers, so the only equity in the business is generally the owner's. They may have established relations with their suppliers but generally don't buy in large enough volumes to get credit. They are often considered formal micro enterprises by institutions, sometimes have access to formal financial institutions but are often constrained by collateral requirements. They may have some life insurance policies or pension funds and are often home owners but they are usually over-leveraged. And they are more prone than other SMMEs to failure. Debt-financing needs are usually for fixed assets, such as office equipment. For working capital, they need bridging finance or revolving credit facilities but they also need leasing finance. And their credit requirements typically range from R100 000 to R200 000.
- *Small enterprises* are those that employ fewer than 50 people, are more established than very small enterprises, have greater capital needs, especially for equipment and working capital, and often have some form

of acceptable collateral, though not enough to meet their needs. They rely on leasing finance for long-term outlays for machinery and equipment, and on factoring, overdraft facilities and suppliers' credits for working capital.
- Finally, *medium-sized* enterprises generally have established relationships with their bankers and may even aim for a listing on the stock exchange in time. Those with growth potential are targeted by equity financiers and have a range of institutions serving their financing needs.

The National Small Business Act of 1996 created a complex definitional matrix (using the basic categories above), but differentiates, by sector, in terms of number of employees, turnover and gross assets of the business.

The level of detail in official definitions has not led to effective targeting of services to SMMEs, as the *Ten Year Review* has recognised. It proposed a modified categorisation: 'It remains important to clarify the focus of strategies with regard to distinctively different sectors of the SMME community, i.e. micro businesses (often informal), small businesses, small technology start-ups and medium business.'[2] This is in line with calls by other expert observers such as the Global Entrepreneurship Monitor (GEM).

Two functional categorisations are especially useful in discussions about financial services for the wide range of entities that fall under the broad SMME label.

First, there is the distinction between formal business and informal business, which is based on whether there is a separate legal persona and whether the business is registered for VAT or other taxes or levies. If so, it is considered formal. For financiers, such businesses are in a different category from informal businesses, where financing the business is essentially indistinguishable, in risk terms, from financing the owner personally. Because the business is unregistered, it is also much harder to verify information about it; and, in addition to normal business risks, it may be exposed to regulatory risk in that it may be fined or shut down if it contravenes any laws. This distinction is usually signalled by dropping the second 'M' (for micro) from 'SMME' to get 'SME', referring to formal small and medium businesses only.

Table A.2 on p.210 shows GEM (2002) findings on the different characteristics, following a survey of 400 businesses, formal and informal, based in townships in four metropolitan areas.

Second, GEM distinguishes between opportunity and necessity entrepreneurship as the driver of new businesses. Opportunity entrepreneurs are those who desire to take advantage of a business opportunity, while necessity entrepreneurs are those who lack better choices. Necessity entrepreneurs are more likely to start and run informal businesses, are resource-constrained, and are likely to abandon the enterprise if offered a job in the formal sector. Necessity entrepreneurship corresponds to the 'survivalist' category of micro enterprise. State enterprise promotion agency Ntsika describes these activities as 'pre-

Table A.2: **Characteristics of informal versus formal businesses in townships**

Informal businesses (88% of respondents)	Formal businesses (12% of survey)
• 58% earn less than R2 000 p.m.	• 25% earn less than R2 000 p.m.
• 35% have matric or higher	• 73% have matric or higher
• 18% have own vehicle	• 67% have own vehicle
• 8% have fixed premises	• 45% have fixed premises
• 42% have a cellphone	• 67% have a cellphone
• average size loan needed: R1 000	• average size loan needed: R10 000

Source: GEM, Foxcroft at al. (2002)

entrepreneurial' because social barriers, a shortage of financial resources and a lack of access to markets prevent them from being entrepreneurial.[3] And their activities are generally limited to hawking, vending and household industry. Though some survivalists have grown into micro enterprises and formal SMEs, the majority are likely to remain poor, since they are constrained by various forces. GEM estimates that a third of all start-ups (0–3 months) and new enterprises (4–42 months) in SA are necessity-based.

These two functional segmentations of SMMEs highlight the need for different policy approaches. For example, in its 2002 report, GEM argues that policy interventions must distinguish between social upliftment and poverty alleviation programmes on the one hand, and targeted support of small business to increase employment on the other.[4] Different strategies are needed to address different constraints. And SMMEs within each category require specifically tailored financial products and services. Instead, all categories are often lumped together for policy purposes—which accounts in part for the limited impact of policy on SMME development in SA.

Even when the debate is narrowed to formal businesses, confusion over the main objective remains. Is it to create jobs? In which case, supporting the growth of established small and medium businesses, regardless of ownership, may make sense. Or is it economic transformation through the creation of a wider, black, business-owning class? In which case, the emphasis must fall on starting up and promoting specifically black-owned SMEs, rather than on micro enterprise.

It seems that the focus of SMME policy has swung towards the transformation objective. For example, the Financial Sector Charter explicitly targets investment in black-owned SMEs. This is defined in the Charter to mean those businesses that are black-owned (51% or more) or black-empowered (25%+), with a turnover ranging from R500 000 to R20m per annum. While the poverty alleviation objective remains for micro enterprise, state efforts to promote micro enterprise are still mired in confusion and uncertainty in 2004.

Endnotes

1. Source: Adapted from Department of Trade and Industry (1998), cited in Bathuthukazi Consultancy cc (2000).
2. Presidency (2003, p.40).
3. Ntsika Enterprise Promotion Agency (1999).
4. Foxcroft et al. (2002).

APPENDIX 6

Government support entities

The National Small Business Act established the National Small Business Council, which was intended to represent and promote the interests of small business and advise all spheres of government on social and economic policy relating to small business. However, it was closed after allegations of mismanagement in 1997/98.

The Act also set up Ntsika Enterprise Promotion Agency to facilitate non-financial support and business development for SMMEs. Ntsika ran into problems and repositioned itself in 2003 in an attempt to address its negative public image. It shifted its focus to market development and business linkages.[1] Ntsika has supported the providers of technical assistance to small and medium-size enterprise. (The assistance came in the form of programme design and research and information collection and dissemination.) The merger with its sister DTI support agency, the National Manufacturing Advisory Centre (Namac), announced in the opening of Parliament speech of 2004, is intended to rationalise state capacity and give it sharper focus.

In terms of the white paper strategy, the DTI set up Khula Enterprise Finance Limited in August 1996 as the main wholesale provider of finance, or apex body, in the sector. Khula operates as a company, with government as sole shareholder. It has had three main programmes over the past decade:

- Apex financing for retail financial intermediaries (RFIs) that lend to micro enterprise. The instruments include debt financing as well as seed loans or quasi-equity for capacity building. Loans range from R100 000 to R2m. At a lower level still, Khula Start is targeted mainly at the micro or survivalist sectors, making loans of R300–R3 500, mainly to groups of rural women in micro or survivalist enterprises through a broad range of intermediary micro-credit organisations.
- A credit guarantee scheme that guarantees bank loans to SMEs, where there is insufficient security.
- Provincial private equity funds for equity investments in SMEs, valued at R250 000–R5m. In 2003, the AngloKhula Mining Fund was launched to support junior mining companies.

The statistics for each programme from inception to March 2003 are set out in Table A.3 on p.213.

In 2001, Khula commissioned a major impact assessment from Unisa's Bureau of Market Research (BMR). The results put the gross number of jobs created by Khula loans at 787 697, of which 66% were in new businesses. Table 5.2 on p.108 shows that the RFI programme yielded the most jobs. If true, this would have been a relatively material number, in the face of declining total

Table A.3: **Khula performance statistics to 2003 (cumulative)**

	RFI programme	KhulaStart	Private equity funds	Credit guarantee
No. of entities financed	32	22	11	1707 (committed)
Total facilities approved	R549m	R28m	R18m	R344m
Total disbursed	R420m	R28m		
Bad-debt write-off	R40m	NA	R0	R47m
Job creation estimates	719 606	88 882	535	67 404

Source: Angela Motsa & Associates (2004b, pp.28–30) from Khula Annual Reports.

formal employment over the period. However, doubt has been cast on the reliability of the BMR figures. It is likely that there was substantial double counting due to the methodology used. Moreover, it is always difficult to attribute new jobs to Khula finance unambiguously when Khula provides wholesale funds only and does not support small business directly. In addition, it is hard to distinguish jobs which existed before Khula's support was given from genuine new creations. At most, it may perhaps be concluded that Khula has disbursed R448m for micro-enterprise finance, of which R40m has been written off to date.

Meanwhile, as a wholesale funder, Khula has suffered from a severe constraint because of the lack of retail capacity in the RFI sector: of 32 entities financed, only half are operating today—some with low capacity. Rural Finance Facility is one of the Khula clients that closed down during the period, causing losses (see the case study on p.118). In part because of frustration with these constraints, Khula commissioned a formal investigation by consultants Gemini into whether it should become a retail micro-enterprise financier.[2] This would have meant competing with its own clients. The mere act of commissioning the study compounded uncertainty and confusion in the sector. In 2002, disgruntled Khula clients proposed that the role of wholesale funder of RFIs be taken from Khula and placed in yet another financing apex.

The Khula Credit Guarantee Scheme has been an ongoing source of contention between Khula and the banking sector. The 2002 GEM report found that the concept of the guarantee scheme was sound but that it had been poorly implemented and ineffectively marketed. University of Stellenbosch professor A Schoombee cautions that generally poor international experience of credit guarantee schemes for small business should temper expectations that the Khula scheme would be genuinely additional; that is, would cause the lenders to do more than they were already doing.[3]

Although Khula has been the major state SMME funder over most of the decade, there are several other entities at national level, some of which are new creations.

The *National Empowerment Fund* (NEF), set up by the National Empowerment Fund Act of 1998, was established in 2001 as part of the DTI's group of development finance agencies. It has a strong BEE focus, offering finance for empowerment transactions, targeting medium-to-large and mature companies with a profit history; and providing smaller sums in the shape of debt, equity and quasi-equity, to be used as seed, early stage, start-up, expansion and acquisition finance.

However, despite high expectations, the NEF was slow to get started, and in 2003 lost its first chief executive, following a dispute over mandate and focus.[4] It was relaunched in May 2004 with additional funding pledged by government.

The *Industrial Development Corporation* (IDC) offers a wide variety of products aimed at the upper end of the market: i.e. medium-sized businesses requiring a minimum of R1m. Entrepreneurs must generally make a meaningful financing contribution of at least 33% or, if they are historically disadvantaged people, between 10% and 20%.

The *DTI* itself offers an overwhelming range of incentives and financing packages to targeted sectors, which are catalogued in Anicap.[5]

Apart from these DTI entities, there are several other parastatal initiatives in other ministries providing or supporting enterprise finance.

The *Land Bank* has a range of products for agricultural entrepreneurs. They include loan, equity and venture finance, targeting a wide variety of clients from start-ups to established commercial farmers, agri-businesses and micro enterprises. The bank focuses on BEE within the primary agriculture and agri-business sectors. And it also provides retail micro loans in smaller towns through its 'Step Up' lending programme.

The *Umsobomvu Youth Fund* (UYF) was established in January 2001 to help create jobs and develop skills among the youth.[6] UYF was financed by the demutualisation levy on Sanlam and Old Mutual. It provides business advisory services through its voucher scheme, and finance through partnerships with various service providers such as Nations Trust, FNB/Momentum, Nicro Enterprise Finance, and Business Partners. The types of funds vary from micro finance to loan or equity finance of up to R5m. UYF's 2003 annual report showed that the fund had spent only half its allocated R1bn in five years, as a *Business Day* article headlined.[7]

The *Small Business Development Corporation* was established as a public–private partnership between government and large business, as long ago as 1981—the first financing intervention in this sector.[8] It was relaunched as Business Partners in 1998, after a change in strategic direction and shareholding. As a result, it is no longer a state-controlled entity but a specialist investment group providing debt and equity investment, mentorship and property management services to formal SMEs. Government remains a minority shareholder with others, including corporates, banks, insurance companies and individuals. During the 2002/03 financial year, Business Partners invested R400m in 496 entrepreneurial businesses and planned to increase this to R500m in the 2003/04 financial year.

Endnotes

1   Wadula (2003a).
2   Wadula (2003a).
3   Schoombee (1999).
4   Wadula (2003c).
5   Anicap Venture Partners (2003).
6   See www.uyf.org.za.
7   *Business Day* (11 May 2004, p.3).
8   See www.businesspartners.co.za.

APPENDIX 7
Regional integration mechanisms

Following democratisation in SA in 1994, there has been a plethora of old regional bodies revamped and new regional bodies formed. The most important from the viewpoint of financial services are highlighted here.

SACU

Established in 1910 between SA and the regions that have subsequently become the BLNS countries (Botswana, Lesotho, Namibia and Swaziland), the Southern African Customs Union (SACU) is a customs-free zone. All import duties on goods (but not services) traded between members have been abolished, and a common external tariff is imposed against all non-members. The SACU arrangement provides for a common excise tariff. All customs and excise duties collected in the common customs area are paid into a fund and divided according to a revenue-sharing formula. Botswana, Lesotho and Swaziland receive a significant portion of their public revenue through this arrangement.

A new SACU agreement has been negotiated over the past few years and was concluded in mid-2004. SACU is also negotiating a free-trade agreement with the US, which may apply to trade in both goods and services.

Monetary and exchange rate policies are largely influenced by SA. Lesotho, Namibia and Swaziland also have a CMA Agreement, with currencies pegged against the SA rand. Botswana, a non-member, has pegged its currency to a basket of currencies, including the rand.

The SADC

Nine Southern African countries established the Southern African Development Coordination Conference in 1980, to reduce their dependence on the apartheid regime in SA. It was the precursor to the SADC, formed in August 1992, and it was joined by SA in August 1994. The SADC's goal is to form a common market by 2015. And the private sector is the strategic vehicle through which it will achieve its objectives. To attain this goal, the SADC will have to harmonise policies and legal and regulatory frameworks, and achieve macroeconomic stability.

Currently, the SADC has 14 members in southern, Central and East Africa. They are Angola, Botswana, the Democratic Republic of Congo, Lesotho, Malawi, Mauritius, Mozambique, Namibia, the Seychelles, SA, Swaziland, Tanzania, Zambia and Zimbabwe.[1] The SADC Secretariat, consisting of four functionally defined directorates, is located in Gaborone, Botswana. Financial markets fall under the Directorate of Trade, Industry, Finance and Investment.

The SADC strategic roadmap is called the Regional Indicative Strategic Development Plan (RISDP).[2] It was launched on 12 March 2004 in Arusha. The RISDP affirms that the private sector is a strategic vehicle through which the SADC region will achieve its objectives. And it focuses, in part, on facilitating trade and financial liberalisation and increased investment, by creating an SADC common market over a period. The document acknowledges that, to attain this goal, the SADC will need to harmonise policies and legal and regulatory frameworks, and achieve macroeconomic stability.[3]

From an access viewpoint, the RISDP expressly argues that:

- Financial institutions should be encouraged to provide a fuller spectrum of financial services to households, in both the formal and informal sectors, as well as in both urban and rural settings. For this purpose, they could develop and implement programmes to encourage household savings, for instance through (i) revisiting minimum deposit levels and discretionary administrative fee structures, in order to encourage small savers to use the formal financial sector institutions; and (ii) advertising campaigns;
- Government should encourage, directly and indirectly, the development of the microfinance sector to provide sustainable finance for the informal sector and financial services to the poor. On a regional level, member states should be encouraged to exchange information on best practices on policy and regulatory frameworks for microfinance; and
- Harmonisation of policies and regulatory frameworks at the regional level should be encouraged to create a larger market for microfinance industry.[4]

The RISDP is indicative rather than prescriptive, setting defined targets for goals to be achieved. These include: an increase in the share of credit accessed by women and by small and medium enterprises (although it remains silent about transaction services); the creation of an SADC monetary union by 2016; and a regional currency by 2018.[5]

The objectives of the SADC treaty and the RISDP are implemented through a series of protocols, including a Trade Protocol and draft Finance and Investment Protocol (FIP).[6] The FIP is being developed and its approval is expected in the second part of 2004.

The FIP's strategic objective is regional integration in the field of finance and investment, macroeconomic convergence, mobilisation of intra-regional savings, the coordination of central banking and the harmonisation of regulatory frameworks, such as payment and clearing systems. The FIP will create implementation commitments, which are likely to have an effect on the financial markets of SADC countries. Of particular interest, with regard to access, is the emphasis on improved infrastructure and payment systems, and more interaction between supervisory bodies. Also noteworthy is that the RISDP openly urges governments to encourage the development of a micro-finance sector, and urges financial institutions to provide a fuller spectrum of services to households, even going so far as to recommend a revisiting of minimum deposit levels and fee structures.

Comesa

The Common Market for Eastern and Southern Africa (Comesa) was founded in 1993, as a successor to the Preferential Trade Area for Eastern and Southern Africa (PTA), which was established in 1981, to achieve a full trade area with free movement of capital and finance. There are 20 members of Comesa: Angola, Burundi, Comoros, the DRC, Djibouti, Egypt, Eritrea, Ethiopia, Kenya, Madagascar, Malawi, Mauritius, Namibia, Rwanda, the Seychelles, Sudan, Swaziland, Uganda, Zambia and Zimbabwe. A number of members of Comesa have overlapping membership with the SADC.[7] SA was invited to join Comesa in 1995 but declined, as did Botswana. The Secretariat is situated in Lusaka, Zambia.

On 31 October 2000, the Comesa free trade area was launched, when Djibouti, Egypt, Kenya, Madagascar, Malawi, Mauritius, Sudan, Zambia and Zimbabwe agreed to eliminate tariffs on goods traded between them. Burundi and Rwanda joined the free trade area on 22 January 2004.[8]

In monetary and financial matters, the Comesa Treaty sets out a raft of aspirational commitments, including commitments to strengthen the payment system, to harmonise fiscal and monetary policy, to adopt macroeconomic convergence policies (deregulating interest rates and exchange rates, and harmonising tax policy), and to develop capital markets (including establishing stock exchanges, a region-wide network of national capital markets and a more attractive investment regime to draw private-sector investment).

A Monetary and Fiscal Policies Harmonisation Programme has been adopted to prepare for monetary union in the year 2025, which imposes further aspirational commitments on the members, including the phased introduction of currency convertibility, a regional exchange rate mechanism, macroeconomic convergence criteria and harmonisation of banking supervision and regulation.

The creation of a regional payment and settlement system has been investigated and awaits political endorsement. In 2000, the African Commerce Exchange was launched to provide a SWIFT Service Bureau to small and medium-sized banks, on a shared cost basis. Since 1985, the Eastern and Southern Trade and Development Bank has provided finance for trade and development projects. The Comesa Bankers' Association was formed in 1989, and acts as a forum for the exchange of information on banking practices in the sub-region. A clearing house has been set up to allow businesses to invoice their exports in national currencies. And the African Trade Insurance Agency, a multilateral export credit and investment insurance agency, was launched in August 2001. A reinsurance company, which services the needs of the insurance and reinsurance industry within the region, has also been established. While there is a comprehensive overlap of long-term financial goals between Comesa and the SADC, Comesa is further down the line in the implementation of its financial sector agenda.

The African Union

On a continental level, the African Union Treaty, signed at Abuja in June 1991, sets out a vision of a more stable, more politically and economically integrated continent. The Treaty provides for an African central bank and monetary fund. This implies not only greater macroeconomic convergence but also more closely integrated financial markets. However, clear steps towards these goals have not yet been mapped out.

The economic arm of the African Union, the African Economic Community (AEC), formed in 1994, aims to improve coordination among regional economic communities such as the SADC and Comesa. Its founding treaty sets out a structured, long-term agenda, with a number of obligations in the finance arena. These include the obligation to create a multilateral payment system and foster regional money markets; eliminate payment restrictions; establish an African clearing house; and ensure free movement of capital and the eventual creation of an African monetary union.

The New Partnership for Africa's Development (Nepad)

At the Lusaka Summit in July 2001, African leaders adopted Nepad, which provides a comprehensive, integrated development plan to address key economic and political principles for the continent. The objective is to eradicate poverty. The five initiating states were SA, Nigeria, Algeria, Senegal and Egypt, and a small secretariat is based at Midrand, SA.

The Nepad programme of action includes a number of initiatives, with several focusing on the facilitation of private-sector development and governance, a first in Africa. Arising from the acknowledgement that Africa needs to fill an annual resource shortage of 12% of GDP or $64bn, another initiative seeks to mobilise private capital flows into Africa. In respect of financial services, the Nepad strategy aims to mitigate the perception of investment risk in Africa. It includes 'credit guarantee schemes and strong regulatory and legislative frameworks'. Another priority is 'deepening financial markets within countries, as well as cross-border harmonisation and integration'.

Regional regulatory bodies

The Eastern and Southern African Banking Supervisors Group (ESAF) is a regional supervisory body set up in 1993, in close cooperation with the Basle Committee on Banking Supervision. ESAF aims to develop a harmonised system of bank supervision in member countries. All members of SACU are represented in the ESAF group, though a number of ESAF members fall outside the SADC region. Progress is reported in harmonising bank licensing requirements, in examining means of managing risk and regulatory governance and in sharing knowledge and training.[9]

The Eastern and Southern African Anti-Money Laundering Group (ESAAMLG) was launched in Arusha, Tanzania, in 1999. It is the regional arm of the Financial Action Task Force (FATF) and was set up to coordinate the implementation of anti-money laundering initiatives and standards, and also measures to combat the funding of terrorism. Member countries are Botswana, Kenya, Lesotho, Malawi, Mauritius, Mozambique, Namibia, the Seychelles, SA, Swaziland, Tanzania, Uganda, Zambia and Zimbabwe. Membership was formalised by a memorandum of understanding, signed in August 2003. The secretariat is based in Dar es Salaam, Tanzania.

Cisna, the Committee of Insurance, Securities and Non-banking Financial Authorities, was established in early 1999 as a forum within the SADC framework, to address non-banking regulatory and supervisory issues. Cisna consists of the regulators responsible for the regulation of insurance, securities and non-bank financial institutions in SADC member states. Members include regulators and supervisors from all 14 SADC states. Cisna has recently approved a Memorandum of Understanding on Regulating and Supervising the Non-banking Financial Services Industries in the SADC as part of the Finance and Investment Protocol process.

Commentary

The expansion in the number and scope of regional bodies has not yet led to full implementation of their ambitious agendas and targets, outlined for regional integration and growth. Partly, this is because the more ambitious framework agreements are relatively new. And it is partly because tensions among member states and even between regional bodies militate against rapid change. There is implicit conflict in objectives between the SADC and Comesa, for example. These two share members, although it is not logically possible for a state to belong to two overlapping customs unions. To date, little action has been taken to eliminate the conflict.

Meanwhile, the SACU remains one of the most effective regional bodies—perhaps because of its smaller size, the presence of a dominant anchor state (which is often the key to successful regional economic integration) and a long history of implementation. Moreover, the possible conclusion of a Free Trade Agreement with the US may further enhance the SACU's standing. However, it is likely that continued expansion of SA businesses, including financial services, into markets to the north will encourage convergence of regulatory regimes beyond the SACU.

Endnotes

1. The Seychelles has given notice that it will leave the SADC in July 2004, while Madagascar and Rwanda have applied for membership.
2. SADC Secretariat (2001).
3. SADC Secretariat (2001, p.xiii).
4. SADC Secretariat (2001, pp.126–127).
5. SADC Secretariat (2001, pp.103–107 and pp.126–127).
6. Protocols are formal agreements between member states that create binding legal obligations. Twelve protocols have already been developed and signed in a number of areas, including Energy, Mining, Combating Illicit Drug Trafficking, Transport, Conservation and Trade.
7. Namely, Angola, the DRC, Malawi, Mauritius, Namibia, the Seychelles, Swaziland, Zambia and Zimbabwe.
8. The DRC, Eritrea, Ethiopia, the Seychelles, Uganda, Angola and Comoros are yet to join the FTA. Namibia and Swaziland were seeking the approval of the Southern African Customs Union (SACU), of which they are also members, and are at present exempt from full application of the trade-related provisions of the Comesa Treaty.
9. Interview with Christo Wiese, ex-registrar of South African banks and former member of ESAF, 1 April 2004.

APPENDIX 8

Financial literacy

Financial literacy is an issue that cuts across all the dimensions of the landscape of access. However, owing to the nature of the SA financial system, it has usually been considered in product silos only, such as home buyer education or debt-related education. Because of its importance to expansion of access and because it does not fit under any of the categories of services considered previously (nor should it), it will be considered briefly here.

Private-sector providers would benefit from improved standards of financial literacy. For individual financial institutions, it costs more to reach financially illiterate consumers than informed consumers. The high rate of lapsed life policies and the high levels of dormant transaction accounts, often the result of low levels of financial literacy, are costly to providers. It is clear that financial services require financially literate consumers if they are to be sustainable.

However, financial literacy has strong 'public good' characteristics. Enhanced consumer literacy is widely recognised as the best way to protect consumers and prevent abuse without over-regulation. Moreover, it is hard for any one firm to capture the benefits of educating consumers—who might well use their new-found knowledge to choose a more competitive product, after all. So financial literacy will always be under-provided by private providers. Or, at best, it will end up entangled in product marketing.

Benchmarking the level of financial literacy is not easy, as there is no agreed definition. FinScope (2003) used one indicator of financial literacy: the ability to name inflation as the concept of 'annual goods price increases'. Respondents were then asked what the rate of inflation had been in the preceding year. Results are shown in Table A.4.

One in three South Africans was able to define inflation correctly but fewer than one in ten knew roughly the correct range in 2002. The range of results is predictable in many ways: people with more education (matric or higher) and wealthier people (LSM6–10) were much more likely to get it right than poorer or less well-educated people. What is most striking about the table, however, is that the overall levels of literacy are so low. Even when offered a pre-coded answer list to choose from on both questions, so that guessing was possible, most people simply professed ignorance: 49% did not even guess the word 'inflation' and 82% had no ability to guess the rate at all.

A scoping study of financial literacy in SA for FinMark Trust, by ECI Africa, found a wide range of programmes in place at different levels—by financial providers (Standard Bank and Old Mutual in particular), by the regulators (Micro Finance Regulatory Council and the Financial Services Board), by NGOs, and by government (MongiMali campaign for civil servants) itself.[1]

Table A.4: **Financial literacy levels**

% are the percentage of people in each column who answered in the row category

	All	LSM1–5	LSM6–10	Elderly (65+)	Young (18–24)	Below school-leaving	School-leaving or higher
Correct naming of inflation	34%	19%	62%	31%	36%	19%	58%
Inflation name: don't know	49%	64%	21%	57%	50%	63%	26%
Correct guess of inflation range in 2002	9%	4%	17%	12%	4%	4%	16%
Inflation rate 2002: don't know	82%	90%	65%	79%	88%	90%	68%

Source: FinScope (2003, Q38,39). School leaving refers to matriculation certificate.

The problem, however, was coordination failure: there was no overall view of the problem, and of how the different programmes could complement each other. This is because the issue does not fit neatly into institutional arrangements created by the Setas (Sectoral Education and Training Authorities), nor into individual product compartments such as home loans or micro lending. Financial literacy requires a consistent, broader framework that embraces them all.

There is also no agreed means of monitoring the impact of different programmes, and so resources can be wasted. Improving financial literacy will require a multi-faceted strategy over a prolonged period; and it is connected to progress in other areas of schooling and adult education.

In this light, the commitment made by the financial sector to a small levy of 0,2% of profits, to fund financial literacy or consumer education (see Box A.1) could be a significant step forward. It releases a relatively sizeable flow of

Box A.1: **Charter commitment to financial literacy**

8.4 Each financial institution commits, from the effective date of the charter to 2008, to annually invest a minimum of 0,2% of post-tax operating profits in consumer education. Consumer education will include programmes that are aimed at empowering consumers with knowledge to enable them to make more informed decisions about their finances and lifestyles.

resources—over R25m a year from the Big Four banks alone, based on reported 2002 profits—over a prolonged period of time. However, without proper co-ordination around how the money is spent, the opportunity to use it productively could be missed.

Endnote

1   ECI (2004).

Glossary

2015 Millennium Development Goals: At the United Nations Millennium Summit in September 2000, world leaders placed development at the heart of the global agenda, setting clear targets for reducing poverty, hunger, disease, illiteracy, environmental degradation, and discrimination against women by 2015.

AMPS: (All Media & Products Survey) biannual large-scale survey managed by the South African Advertising Research Foundation but undertaken, on contract, by private market research agencies that use LSM categories to survey the population.

angel finance: loans from family and friends.

apex lender: wholesale funder of retail lending institutions.

assistance business: a sub-category of life assurance that includes funeral policies.

basic bank account: a new class of basic transaction account co-branded by private sector banks that adopt it, with restricted functionality and reduced fees (no monthly fee; and the same flat charges for transaction fee regardless of bank).

card and PIN collection: retention of a borrower's debit card and PIN number as security, or to collect micro-loan repayments, by cash lenders.

cash back: cash from a merchant deducted via a debit card.

community bank: variously defined, e.g. a bank that takes its deposits from friends, neighbours and customers and makes loans in the community. A bank that is locally owned and managed. In SA, a co-operative or mutual bank, or one that operates under the South African Reserve Bank's Village Bank or Stokvel exclusion relating to 'common bond'. Ownership relates to the users, and the supervision requirements are less onerous.

consumer credit: credit for consumption.

conventional bank: regulated by the current Banks Act in SA, meeting the capital and liquidity requirements imposed by the Act.

core bank: restricted commercial bank similar to a savings and loan bank specialising in deposit-taking and payment activities. It is limited to a core of activities. It can take and use funds for a variety of purposes, including loans and advances.

cession: transferring rights to a claim.

credit bubble: when the rate of credit extension to a particular market exceeds the long-run debt-bearing capacity of that market, measured at the time the credit is granted.

credit bureau: an agency that compiles and distributes credit and personal information to creditors.

credit gap: unavailability of loans of R10 000–R100 000 in the housing finance arena.

demarcation debate: the debate on where to draw the line between insurance and medical coverage.

demonstration effect: when one player demonstrates a viable model that others follow.

derivative instrument: a financial instrument that derives its value from some other financial asset instrument.

deposit insurance: a mechanism to stabilise the banking system; usually a guarantee scheme for deposits, based on legislation such as the central bank law, the banking law, or the constitution.

financial intermediation: intermediation between the providers and users of financial capital.

financial summary measure (FSM): based on factors related to financial-service usage and profile, which is designed to complement LSMs in financial services.

fixed-rate mortgage: mortgage with a rate set for a specified period

Grameen principles: principles based on the belief that the poor can be creditworthy. The most significant pioneer of these principles was Mohammed Yunus, who started the Grameen Bank in Jobra, Bangladesh, in 1976.

group insurance schemes: schemes that cover defined groups of people, usually employees in a workplace.

group loan: a loan made to a group of people, for instance stokvel members or employees in a workplace.

incremental housing: formal freestanding units built under the Reconstruction and Development Programme and site-and-service housing, usually owner-built on a state-subsidised serviced site.

informal business: a business which has no separate legal persona and which is not registered for VAT or other taxes or levies.

living standards measure (LSM): a basic market segmentation algorithm, which categorises a respondent into one of ten groups, according to observable characteristics, largely to do with durable-goods ownership.

magstripe: the magnetic stripe containing encoded information found on the back of an ID card, like an ATM or credit card.

micro finance: all forms of financial services offered at the low end of the market.

micro lending/credit: micro loans for any purpose. Purist definition: micro credit offered by pro-poor, not-for-profit lenders to micro enterprise.

mortgage loan: loan made against the security of fixed property.

mutual bank: a bank that is owned by its depositors.

narrow bank: savings bank. It takes deposits and engages in credit payment activities but only invests in low-risk assets with high liquidity. It is prohibited from lending to the private sector.

payroll-deducted lending: loans granted against employer deduction of monthly payments from salary.

peer pressure/peer sanction: a member's eligibility for a loan and willingness to pay being dependent on the savings group to which he belongs.

pension-backed home loan: a loan made to fund housing, against the security of a retirement fund.
persal: state salary system for civil servants.
point-of-sale device: an electronic device for recording sales information at the time and place a card transaction occurs.
productive credit: credit for enterprises.
retail lending: selling goods on a monthly 'on account' basis.
securitisation: bundling of loan assets and sale of these as asset-backed securities.
solidarity group lending: peer-group lending schemes. Members receive loans and then make regular weekly or monthly payments, with all group members providing a mutual guarantee of loan repayment. This method differs from rotating savings and credit associations, in which group members make regular deposits and then take turns in receiving the total amount of the deposits.
transaction banking: the service offered by banks which allows day-to-day transactions, in particular electronic payments to and from accounts; this category includes current accounts and most debit and ATM-card accounts.
transactional capability: access to transaction banking.
usury rate ceiling: threshold loan size above which the Usury Act applies.
variable-rate mortgage: mortgage with a rate that varies in line with changes in the pattern of interest rates.
wellness interventions: products that allow HIV carriers and AIDS sufferers to obtain effective treatment.

References

ACNielsen. (2002). *Futurefact Marketscape Survey 2002.*

Adler, T. and M. Oelofse. (1996). 'The Housing Subsidy Scheme.' In K. Rust and Rubinstein (eds.), *A Mandate to Build: Developing Consensus around a National Housing Policy in South Africa.* Ravan Press, Randburg.

Aizcorbe, A. et al. (2003). 'Recent Changes in US Family Finances: Evidence from the 1998 and 2001 Survey of Consumer Finances.' *Federal Reserve Bulletin*, 88.

AMPS

Angela Motsa & Associates. (2003). 'African Craft Market: An Impact Evaluation.' Available via www.finmarktrust.org.za/research.

Angela Motsa & Associates. (2004). 'Background Paper: A Review of Key Documents on SMME Finance 1994–2004.' Available via www.finmarktrust.org.za/research.

Anicap Venture Partners. (2003). 'A Review of DTI's SME Financial Assistance Programmes and Its Proposal to Create a New Integrated Financial Institution (IFI).' Available via www.finmarktrust.org.za/research.

Barnard Jacobs Mellet. (2003). 'Financial Sector Focus.' Research document circulated to clients.

Bathuthukazi Consultancy cc. (2000). 'Research into Appropriate Finance Products for Enterprises in Various Industries.' Khula Operations Division.

Baumann, T. (2001). 'Microfinance and Poverty Alleviation in South Africa.' Bay Research and Consultancy Services.

Baumann, T. (2002). 'The Pro-Poor Microfinance Sector in SA.' Available via www.finmarktrust.org.za/research.

Baumann, T. (2003). 'Doing Pro-Poor Microcredit in South Africa: Cost Efficiency and Productivity of South African Pro-Poor MFIs.' Available via http://www.cmfnet.org.za.

Baumann, T. (2004). 'The Developmental Microfinance Sector in SA – Update 2004.' Bay Research and Consultancy Services. Available via www.finmarktrust.org.za/research.

Bell, R., A. Harper & D. Mandivenga. (2002). 'Can Commercial Banks Do Microfinance? Lessons from the Commercial Bank of Zimbabwe and the Co-operative Bank of Kenya.' *Small Enterprise Development Journal*, 13.4.

Belski, E. & A. Calder. (2004). 'Credit Matters: Low Income Asset Building Challenges in a Dual Financial System.' Working Paper Series, Joint Center for Housing Studies, Harvard University, Boston.

Berenbach, S. & C. Churchill. (1997). *Regulation and Supervision of MicroFinance Institutions.* MicroFinance Network Occasional Paper No. 1. Available from www.accion.org.

Berry, C. (2004). 'To Bank or Not to Bank?' Working Paper Series, Joint Center for Housing Studies, Harvard University, Boston. Available via www.jchs.harvard.edu/babc.

Bureau of Market Research (BMR). (2001). *Impact Assessment Study on Khula Products.*

Cadogan, P. (2002). *Operational and Financial Sustainability Problems Faced by SA Micro Finance Institutions: The Case of Provident South Africa*. Micro Enterprise Alliance, Johannesburg.

Calderon, C. & L. Liu. (2003). 'The direction of causality between financial development and economic growth.' *Journal of Development Economics*, 72.

CGAP. (2003). *Phase 3 Strategy*. CGAP, Washington, DC. Available via www.cgap.org.

Christen, R. (2001). *Commercialization and Mission Drift: The Transformation of Micro Finance in Latin America*. CGAP Occasional Paper No. 5. CGAP, Washington, DC.

Christen, R. & D. Pearce. (2004). 'Lessons learned from Nkwe Enterprise Finance.' Available via www.finmarktrust.org.za/research.

Christensen, C. (1997). *The Innovator's Dilemma*. Harvard Business School, Boston.

Christensen, C. (2003). *The Innovator's Solution*. Harvard Business School, Boston.

Churchill, C. (ed.). (1997). *Regulation and Supervision of MicroFinance Institutions: Case Studies*. MicroFinance Network Occasional Paper No. 2. Available from www.accion.org.

Claessens, S., T. Glaessner & D. Klingbiel. (2001). 'E Finance in Emerging Markets: Is Leapfrogging Possible?' Finance Sector Discussion Paper 7, World Bank. Available via www.econ.worldbank.org.

Coetzee, G., & W. Grant. (2001). 'Micro-finance in South Africa in the Last Decade: The "Silent" Revolution.' Presentation at Frankfurt Seminar. Available on Community Finance Network website.

Cole, S. and M. Ward. (2004). 'SA Home Loans: Bank Bashing is Good for Business!' Case study. Wits Business School, University of the Witwatersrand, Johannesburg.

Collins, D. (2004). 'Financial Diaries Project: Dissemination Workshop.' Presented 13 February 2004, Centre for Social Science Research, University of Cape Town.

Daley-Harris, S. (2002). *State of the Microcredit Summit Campaign Report 2002*. Available from www.microcreditsummit.org.

Daley-Harris, S. (ed.). (2002). *Pathways out of Poverty*. Kumarian Press, Bloomfield, Connecticut.

Dallimore, A. & M. Mgimeti (2002). 'Democratic Banking in the New South Africa.' DRA, Durban.

Dallimore, A. (2003), 'Savings versus Credit: Comparing Coping Strategies of Poor Households in Rural KwaZulu-Natal.' Available via www.finmarktrust.org.za/research.

Damane, W., & L. Xate. (1999). 'A Review Study on Access to Finance for SMMEs in South Africa (Khula, Banks and RFIs).' Funded by UNOPS and Kellogg Foundation, for the Department of Trade and Industry.

Deloitte. (2003). 'Transaction Banking Report.' Unpublished paper commissioned by FinMark Trust.

Department of Housing. (1994). *White Paper: A New Housing Policy and Strategy for South Africa*. Government Gazette Notice 1376 of 1994. Department of Housing, Pretoria.

Department of Housing. (2004). *ABC of Housing*, 4.1. 31 March.

Department of Trade and Industry (DTI). (1998). *Financial Access For SMMEs: Towards a Comprehensive Strategy*. Draft discussion document. Available from www.cmfnet.org.za.

De Ridder, J. (2004). 'The Role of Micro Finance in Meeting SA's Housing Challenge.' Presentation to the NHFC Breakfast Meeting, February.

Driver, A., E. Wood, N. Segal, and M. Herrington. (2001). *Global Entrepreneurship Monitor: 2001*. Graduate School of Business, University of Cape Town.

Du Plessis, P. (1998). *The MicroLending Industry in SA 1997*. Micro-Lenders Association, July 1998.

Dymski, G. (2003). 'Banking on Transformation: Financing Development, Overcoming Poverty.' Paper prepared for seminar at Instituto de Economia, Universidade Federal do Rio de Janiero, 15 September.

ECI Africa . (2000). 'Examination of Costs and Interest Rates in the Small Loans Sector.' *Government Gazette* 21381, 21 July.

ECI Africa. (2000). 'Review of Sectoral Opportunities for MSE Growth.' Micro Enterprise Alliance, Johannesburg.

ECI Africa . (2001), 'Private Equity and Capitalisation of SMMEs in South Africa: Quo Vadis?' Working Paper No. 34, Social Finance Programme, International Labour Organisation, Geneva.

ECI Africa. (2003a). *Third-Tier Banking Report. Lessons Learned and the Way Forward for Member-Based Financial Institutions in South Africa*. Available via www.finmarktrust.org.za/research.

ECI Africa. (2003b). *Analysis on the Application of Borrowed Funds*. Micro Finance Regulatory Council. Available via www.mfrc.co.za.

ECI Africa. (2003c). *The Effect of HIV/AIDS on the Micro-Finance Sector in South Africa and Implications for the MFRC*. Micro Finance Regulatory Council. Available via www.mfrc.co.za.

ECI Africa. (2004). *Financial Literacy Scoping Study and Strategy Report*. Available via www.finmarktrust.org.za/research, May.

ECI & DPRU. (2001). *Report on Impact of Credit and Indebtedness of Clients*. April. Available from www.mfrc.co.za.

Economist. (21 February 2002). 'South African Banks and Microfinance: Never a Micro Lender Be.'

Economist. (29 August 2002). 'Hunting the Loan Sharks' about US Regulatory Attacks on Predatory Lenders.'

Falkena H., I. Abedian, M. von Blottnitz, C. Coovadia, G. Davel, J. Madungandaba, E., Masilela, S. and Rees S. (2002). *SMEs' Access to Finance in South Africa – A Supply-Side Regulatory Review*. Task Group of the Policy Board for Financial

Services and Regulation. Available at www.finforum.co.za.

Falkena et al. (2003). *Establishing Core and Narrow Banks and their Competitive Impact on Fully Fledged Banks in SA*. Report of the Task Group of the Policy Board for Financial Services and Regulation.

Federal Reserve Board. (2003). 'Survey of Consumer Finances.' *Federal Reserve Bulletin*.

Ferguson, B. & E. Haider. (2000). 'Mainstreaming MicroFinance of Housing.' Inter-American Development Bank.

Financial Mail (17 January 2003). 'Home Enriching Home'.

Financial Sector Charter. (2003). Available from www.banking.org.za.

Financial Services Authority. (2000). *In or Out? Financial Exclusion: A Literature and Research Review*. Consumer Research 3, FSA, London.

FinMark Trust. (2003). *Vision 2010*. Johannesburg.

FinScope. (2003). Details available via www.finscope.co.za

FinScope BNLS (2004).

Fisher, T. & M.S. Sriram. (2002). *Putting Development Back into MicroFinance*. Vistaar Publications, New Delhi.

Foxcroft, M., E. Wood, J. Kew, M. Herrington, & N. Segal. (2002). *Global Entrepreneurship Monitor: South African Executive Report*. Graduate School of Business, University of Cape Town.

Gardner, D. (2003). 'Getting South Africans under Shelter: An Overview of the South African Housing Sector.' HFRP Web Resource Document No. 1.

Genesis Analytics. (2003a). *Access to Financial Services in Botswana*. FinMark Trust Research Paper No. 1. Available via www.finmarktrust.org.za/research.

Genesis Analytics. (2003b). *Access to Financial Services in Lesotho*. FinMark Trust Research Paper No. 2. Available via www.finmarktrust.org.za/research.

Genesis Analytics. (2003c). *Access to Financial Services in Namibia*. FinMark Trust Research Paper No. 3. Available via www.finmarktrust.org.za/research.

Genesis Analytics. (2003d). *Access to Financial Services in Swaziland*. FinMark Trust Research Paper No. 4. Available via www.finmarktrust.org.za/research.

Genesis Analytics. (2003e). *Account for Life*. Available via www.finmarktrust.org.za/research.

Genesis Analytics. (2003f). *African Families, African Money – Bridging the Money Transfer Divide*. Available via www.finmarktrust.org.za/research.

Genesis Analytics. (2003g). *Legislative and Regulatory Obstacles to Mass Banking*. Available via www.finmarktrust.org.za/research.

Genesis Analytics. (2004a). *A Survey of the SADC Region: SA Financial Institutions, Regional Policies and Issues of Access*. Available via www.finmarktrust.org.za/research.

Genesis Analytics. (2004b). *Making Insurance Markets Work for the Poor*. Available via www.finmarktrust.org.za/research.

Genesis Analytics. (2004c). *Point of Sale: The SA Landscape*. Available via www.finmarktrust.org.za/research.

Genesis Analytics. (2004d). *South Africa Savings Workshop: Policy Going Forward*. National Treasury, Pretoria.

Global Entrepreneurship Monitor. (GEM). (2003).

Gulli, H. (1998). *Micro-Finance and Poverty*. Inter American Development Bank, Washington, DC.

Hawkins, P. (2003a). *South Africa's Financial Sector Ten Years On*. Trade and Industry Policy Strategies, August.

Hawkins, P. (2003b). *The Cost, Volume and Allocation of Consumer Credit in South Africa*. Credit Law Review. Department of Trade and Industry, Pretoria.

Hirschland, M. (2003). 'Serving Small Depositors: Overcoming the Obstacles, Recognizing the Trade-offs.' *MicroBanking Bulletin*, 9. Available via www.themix.org.

HM Treasury. (1999). *Access to Financial Services*. Report of PAT. 14 November.

Hodge, J. (2002). 'Extending Telecoms Ownership in SA: Policy, Performance and Future Options'. University of Cape Town.

Holden, P. & V. Prokopenko. (2003). 'Financial Development and Poverty Alleviation: An Overview.' *Labour Markets and Social Frontiers*, 3. SARB, Pretoria.

Intelligence. (January 2004). 'Mobile Commerce: State of the Art.'

Jackelen, H. (2002). 'Property, Economic Citizenship and Savings as a Human Right.' Paper delivered at SA Savings Symposium, Johannesburg.

Khula Enterprise Finance. (various). *Annual Reports 1998, 1998/99, 2000, 2001, 2002, 2003*. Available via www.khula.org.za.

Khuzwayo, W. (2003). 'Social Grants Make Banking Sense.' *Business Report*, 27 April.

Kooi, P. (2002). 'Development of the MicroFinance Sector.' Paper delivered at MicroEnterprise Alliance Workshop, Johannesburg, 7 August.

KPMG. (2004). *Comparative Study on Banking Access for the Underbanked*. Available via www.finmarktrust.org.za/research.

Kumar, A. (2003). *Brazil: Access to Financial Services*. Latin American and Caribbean Region, World Bank.

Labie, M. (1995). *Credits to Small Businesses and Microenterprises*. ADA, Luxembourg. Available on www.microfinancegateway.org.

Lehlohla, P. (2002). *The Contribution of Small and Micro Enterprises to the Economy of the Country: A Survey of Non-VAT-Registered Businesses in South Africa: Part 1 – Summary and Tables*. Statistics South Africa, Pretoria.

Ligthelm, A. (2002). 'Characteristics of Spaza Retailers: Evidence from a National Survey.' *BMR Research Report*, No. 305. BMR, Pretoria.

Littlefield, E., et al. (2002). 'Water, Water Everywhere but not a Drop to Drink.' CGAP Donor Brief, No. 3. Available from www.cgap.org.

Littlefield, E, J. Murduch & S. Hashemi. (2003). 'Is MicroFinance an Effective Strategy to Reach the Millenium Development Goals?' Focus Note, No. 24. Available via www.cgap.org.

Mail & Guardian. (21–27 May 2004). 'Bond not for rural poor.'

Mashiya, N.S. (2001). 'The Role of Commercial Banks in Financing Small, Medium and Micro-Enterprises in Soweto.' (abstract). Vista University.

McKee, K. (2001). 'Light Bulbs, Heresies and Predictions – Observations from a "Fundamentalist".' Talk given at Frankfurt New Development Finance Seminar, 7 September.

Meagher, P. and B. Wilkinson. (2001). 'Filling the Gap in South Africa's Small and Micro Credit Market: An Analysis of Major Policy, Legal, and Regulatory Issues.' Submitted to the Microfinance Regulatory Council of South Africa, IRIS Center, University of Maryland. Available via www.mfrc.co.za.

MERG. (1993). *Making Democracy Work*. Macro-Economic Research Group, Centre for Development Studies.

MicroBanking Bulletin. (2002). Issue 8, Washington DC. Available via www.themix.org.

Micro Finance Regulatory Council. (2002). *Unregistered Lender Report*. Available via www.mfrc.co.za.

Micro Finance Regulatory Council. (2003). 'Submission to the Portfolio Committee on Finance on Indebtedness.' 17 June. Available via www.mfrc.co.za.

Micro Finance Regulatory Council. (2004). *Statistics Regarding the Micro-Lending Industry*. Press release, 25 May.

Micro Lenders Association. (2002). 'MLA Survey Data Analysis.' Unpublished survey by J Jackson Consulting.

MicroSave Africa. (2003). 'Project Proposal: MicroSave Africa III.' MicroSave Africa, Nairobi.

Mortgage Indemnity Fund. (1998). *Closure Report*.

Moss, D. (2002). *When All Else Fails: Government as Ultimate Risk Manager*. Harvard University Press, Cambridge.

Moyo, S., D. Musona, W.T. Mbhele, & G. Coetzee. (2002). 'Use and Impact of Savings Services among Low Income People In South Africa.' MicroSave-Africa, March. Available on www.microfinancegateway.org.

NHFC. (2001) *Annual Report*.

NHFC. (2003a). *Primary Market Monitor Bulletin*, 1.4. Available via www.nhfc.co.za.

NHFC. (2003b). *Corporate Impact Report*.

NHFC (2003c). *Annual Report*.

Nichter, S., L. Goldmark & Fiori, A. (2002). 'Understanding Microfinance in the Brazilian Context.' PDI/ BNDES. Available via www.microfinancegateway.org.

Ntsika Enterprise Promotion Agency. (1999). *State of Small Business in South Africa, 1998*. Ntsika, Pretoria.

Ntsika Enterprise Promotion Agency. (2001). *State of Small Business Development in South Africa Annual Review*. Ntsika, Pretoria.

Ntsika Enterprise Promotion Agency. (2003). *The Small Business Monitor*, 1.1.
Nurcha. (2003). *Annual Report*. Nurcha, Johannesburg. Available via www.nurcha.org.za/financial matters.
Orford, J., E. Wood, C. Fischer, M. Herrington, & M. Segal. (2003). *Global Entrepreneurship Monitor: South African Executive Report*. Graduate School of Business, University of Cape Town.
Paulson, J., & J. McAndrews. (1998). 'Financial Services for the Urban Poor: South Africa's E Plan.' World Bank Working Paper. Available via www.econ.worldbank.org.
Porteous, D. (2001). 'Micro Lending Industry: Market Sizing for the Future.' Updated March 2002. Available from African Bank Investments Investor Relations, www.africanbank.co.za.
Porteous, D. (2002a). 'State's Role Is the Key to the Future of the Micro-Lending Industry.' *Business Times*, 3 February.
Porteous, D. (2002b). 'Has There Been a Credit Bubble in SA?' Paper presented at the Development Finance Conference, University of Cape Town.
Porteous, D. (2002c). 'Industry Position Paper.' Unpublished paper, FinMark Trust.
Porteous, D. (2003a). 'Is Cinderella Finally Coming to the Ball? SA Micro Finance in Broad Perspective.' Available via www.finmark.org.za.
Porteous, D. (2003b). 'Is the Mortgage Instrument Relevant to Low Income Housing? The Key Question for Relevance.' Presented to NHFC Breakfast Forum, September. Available via www.finmarktrust.org.za/research.
Porteous, D. (2003c). 'The Demand for Financial Services by Low Income South Africans.' Available via www.finmarktrust.org.za/research.
Porteous, D. (2003e). 'The Landscape of Access to Financial Services in South Africa.' *Labour Markets and Social Frontiers* No.3. SARB, Pretoria.
Porteous, D. & K. Naicker. (2003). 'South African Housing Finance: The Old is Dead – Is the New Ready to be Born?' In F. Khan & P. Thring. (eds.). *Housing Policy and Practice in Post-Apartheid South Africa*. Heinemann, Sandown.
Pralahad, C.K. & A. Hammond. (2002). 'Serving the World's Poor Profitably.' *Harvard Business Review*, September.
Presidency. (2003). *Towards Ten Years of Freedom*. Presidency, Pretoria. Available at www.gcis.gov.za/docs/publications/10years.htm.
Prinsloo, J. (2000). 'The Saving Behaviour of the South African Economy.' SARB *Occasional Paper* No. 14, November.
Prinsloo, J. (2003). *Saving, Capital Flows and Economic Growth: South Africa's Experience*. Presentation at the Savings Policy Round Table, Pretoria, 2 December.
Reddy, C. (2003). *An Overview of BEE financing in SA*. BusinessMap Foundation. Available via www.businessmap.org.za.
Reinke, J., (1996). 'Alternative Models for Micro-credit in South Africa: Theoretical Foundations and Two Case Studies.' *Savings and Development*, 3.

Renaud. (2003). *South African Housing Finance in World Context.* Paper delivered to NHFC Symposium, 1 October.

Rhyne, E. (2001). *Mainstreaming Microfinance.* Kumarian Press, Bloomfield, Connecticut.

Rogerson, C.M. (1997). *SMMEs and Poverty in South Africa.* Input Report for the National Project on Poverty and Inequality, May 1997.

Roth, J. (2000). 'Informal Micro-Finance Schemes: The Case of Funeral Insurance in South Africa.' ILO Social Finance Unit Working Paper 22.

Roussos, P., and D. Ferrand. (1999). *Review of the Microfinance Sector in South Africa.* DFID SA.

Rust, K. (2001). *Investigation into Constraints on the Delivery of Rental Housing in South Africa.* Unpublished report prepared for Nurcha, Johannesburg.

Rust, K. (2002a). *We're All Here – Now Where's the Party? Understanding Logjams around Housing Finance.* HFRP Occasional Paper 1.

Rust, K. (2002b). *Competition or Co-operation? Understanding the Relationship between Banks and Alternative Lenders in the Low-income Housing Finance Sector.* HFRP Occasional Paper 4.

Rust, K. (2003a). 'No Shortcuts: South Africa's Progress in Implementing its Housing Policy 1994–2002.' Institute for Housing in Southern Africa.

Rust K. (2003b). *Sink or Swim. Progress Made in the Relationship between Banks and Alternative Lenders in South Africa's Low Income Housing Finance Sector.* HFRP Occasional Paper 9.

Rust, K. (2004a). *Doing it for Themselves. Hope and Challenges in Incremental Housing.* HFRP Occasional Paper 3.

Rust K. (2004b). 'The State of Access to Housing Finance in 2004: Broad and Deep but How Thick is It?' Available via www.finmarktrust.org.za/research.

Rutherford, S. (2000). *The Poor and Their Money.* Oxford University Press, Delhi.

Rutherford, S. (2002). 'Money Matters: Conversations with Poor Households in Bangladesh about Managing their Money.' Finance and Development Research Programme Working Paper Series No. 45, IDPM, University of Manchester. Available via www.man.ac.uk/idpm.

Ruthven, O. & S. Kumar. (2002). 'Fine Grain Finance: Financial Choice and Strategy among the Poor in Rural North India.' Finance and Development Research Programme Working Paper Series No. 57, IDPM, University of Manchester. Available via www.man.ac.uk/idpm.

SADC Secretariat. (2001). *SADC Regional Indicative Strategic Development Plan.* Available at http://www.sadc.int/index.php?lang=english&path=about/risdp&page=index.

SA Institute of Race Relations.(2002). *SA Survey 2001/2.*

Sandler, R. (2002). 'Review of Medium and Long-term Retail Savings.' Available at http://www.hm-reasury.gov.uk/newsroom_and_speeches/press/2002/press 2002_sand.cfm.

SA to Z. (2002). *Analysis on Stokvels and Burial Societies*. Available via www.finmarktrust.org.za/research.

Schoombee, A. (1999). 'Linkage Banking for Micro-enterprises in SA.' *SA Journal of Economics*, 67.3.

Schoombee, A. (2003). 'South African Banks and the Unbanked: Progress and Prospects.' *SA Journal of Economics*, 71.

Seward, J. (2002). 'The Development and Reform of Postal Banking Systems in Europe and Asia.' Draft paper. Financial Sector Development Department Europe and Central Asia.

Shiller, R. (2003). *The New Financial Order*. Princeton Press, Princeton.

Shisaka. (2003). *Element 4: Private Sector Engagement with Government's Housing Programme*. Prepared under Mega-Tech Inc's prime contract with USAID.

Shisaka. (2004). *Phase Three Report: Findings, Conclusions and Implications, Workings of Township Residential Property Markets*. Available via www.finmarktrust.org.za/research. or www.finmarktrust.org.za/themes/trpm.

Shreiner, M. (1999). 'Aspects of Outreach: A Framework for the Discussion of the Social Benefits of MicroFinance.' Center for Social Development, Washington University, St Louis, Missouri. Available via www.microfinance.com.

Smith, D.A. (2003). 'Using Tax-Relief Incentives (TRIs) to Stimulate Affordable Housing; With Commentary on the Proposed Urban Generation Tax Initiative.' Available via www.finmarktrust.org.za/research.

South African Reserve Bank (2002). *Quarterly Bulletin*.

South African Reserve Bank. (2003). *Financial Development and the Unbanked*. Issue of *Labour Markets and Social Frontiers*, 3.

Staschen, S. (1999). 'Regulation and Supervision of Microfinance Institutions in South Africa.' Eschborn: GTZ. Available on www.microfinancegateway.org.

Statistics South Africa. (2003a). *Labour Force Survey*. March 2003

Statistics South Africa. (2003b). *Census 2001*. Pretoria.

Strauss Commission. (1996). *Final Report of the Commission of Enquiry into the Provision of Rural Finance Services*. Available via www.polity.org.za/govdocs/commissions.

Thomson, R. & D. Posel. (2002). 'The Management of Risk by Burial Societies in SA.' *SA Actuarial Journal*, 2.

Tomlinson, M. (1997). *Mortgage Bondage? Financial Institutions and Low-cost Housing Delivery*. Social Policy Series, Research Report 56. Centre for Policy Studies.

UCT Unilever Institute of Strategic Marketing. (2003). *Stokvels: Making Social Cents?* Available via www.unileverinstitute.co.za/stokvels.asp.

UNDP. (2004). *South Africa: Human Development Report 2003*. Oxford University Press, Cape Town.

USAID. (1995a). *Micro-enterprise Development Policy Paper*. Washington, D.C. 20523.

Van de Ruit, C. (2001). 'Micro-finance, Donor Roles and Influence and the Pro-poor Agenda: The Cases of South Africa and Mozambique.' Draft paper, Donor Funding Conference, 30 October.

Van Greuning, H., J. Gallardo & B. Randhawa. (1999). *A Framework for Regulating MicroFinance Institutions*. Policy Research Working Paper No. 2061, World Bank.

Van Rooyen, O. and S. Mills. (2003). *Banking on the Poor: A Review of the Kuyasa Fund*. HFRP Occasional Paper No. 8.

Visa. (2003). *The Virtuous Cycle: Electronic Payments and Economic Growth*.

Vulindlela Development Finance Consultants. (2004). 'Background to the SA Market for Microfinance.' Unpublished paper.

Wadula, P. (2003a). 'Khula may Become Retail Finance Agent.' *Business Day*, 4 February.

Wadula, P. (2003b). 'Ntsika Restructures To Change Perceptions of Small Business Sector.' *Business Day*, 13 March.

Wadula, P. (2003c). 'Fate of Empowerment Fund Raises Questions.' *Business Day*, 20 August.

Wadula, P. (2003d). 'State pulls plug on empowerment agency.' *Business Day*, 14 August.

Wadula, P. (2003e). 'Khula Puts Plans to Enter Retail Finance on Hold.' *Business Day*, 30 September.

Wilkinson & Meagher. (2001). 'Filling the Gap in South Africa's Small and Micro Credit Market. An Analysis of Major Policy, Legal and Regulatory Issues.' Institute for Informal Sector Research, University of Maryland.

Wimaladharma, J., D. Pearce & D. Stanton. (2004). 'Remittances: The New Development Finance?' *Small Enterprise Development Journal*, March.

Wright, G. (ed.) (2000). *Savings in Africa: Remembering the Forgotten Half of MicroFinance*. MicroSave-Africa, Nairobi.

Xaba, J., P. Horn, & S. Motala. (2002). 'The Informal Sector in Sub-Saharan Africa, Employment Sector 2002.' Working Paper on the Informal Economy, Employment Sector, International Labour Office, Geneva.

Yunus, M. (2003). 'Grameen Bank II: Designed to Open New Possibilities.' Available at Grameen Bank website

Newspapers and Magazines Cited

Business Day
Business Times
Financial Mail
Intelligence
Mail & Guardian
The Economist

Index

Absa 19, 132, 136; regionalisation of 172, 174; *see also* AllPay
access to financial services 3–6, 8–10, 13, 16–20, 63, 93, 121, 171, 180, 188–90; affordability 37–8; by SMMEs 100–20; effective 13–15, 26, 35–9, 44, 159; expanded 39, 43, 69, 171, 181, 190–2, 222; geographic 36–7, 41, 50; in BLNS countries 175–80; lack of access 5–6, 32, 110, 193; legislative obstacles 39–40; product features 38–9; via cellphones 41–2; *see also* credit; insurance; savings; transaction banking
Accumulating Savings and Credit Association (ASCA) 87
affirmative procurement 107, 114; *see also* black economic empowerment (BEE)
affordable housing 121, 130, 133–6, 146–7, 163, 165–6
African Bank Investments Limited (Abil) 19, 81–2, 84, 96–9, 104, 115
African Contractor Finance Corporation (ACFC) 98, 107, 114–17
African Economic Community (AEC) 219
African Life Assurance (ALA) 174–5, 182–3
African National Congress (ANC) 2, 6–7, 102, 114
African Trade Insurance Agency 219
African Union 219
Ahmed, Rashid 94–5
All Media and Products Survey (AMPS) 14, 16, 22–3, 29, 32, 58, 61, 78, 153–5
AllPay 28–31, 50–1
Altfin 96
Anicap Venture Partners (AVP) 214
anti-money laundering (AML) 39–40
anti-retroviral therapy (ART) 159, 165
armchair banking 173–4
Arnold, Mike 52
Association of Black Securities and Investment Professionals (Absip) 7–9, 18–20
Association of Collective Investment Schemes 18
attitudes towards: banks 34–5; informal saving associations 64–5; savings 57, 59–61; starting a business in South Africa 109–10; technology 33–4
automated teller machines (ATMs) 1, 13, 15, 30–1, 34, 43–4, 47, 51–2, 55, 142, 186; cards 21–4, 29, 33, 37, 54–5; mini ATMs 37, 43, 52

BoE 12, 71–2, 77, 146
BancoSol (Bolivia) 88, 104, 143
bank accounts 21–9, 31–2, 39–41, 43–4, 66, 91, 185, 189; savings 54, 57–9, 60–2, 64, 68–9; transaction 21–56, 58, 68, 109
bank failure 12, 34–5, 77, 84, 145; *see also* Saambou
banked people 21–8, 41, 82, 154, 157, 199; savings by 60–1, 63; use of public transport by 36–7; *see also* previously banked people; unbanked people
Banking Council of South Africa 9, 18–19, 33, 105, 131
banking system, public trust in 34–5
Banks Act 40, 42, 144, 196
Baobab Solid Growth Ltd 81–2, 96–7
Barclays 170, 172, 180
basic bank account (BBA) 20–1, 32–3, 40–1, 53, 142
Baumann, Ted 87, 89–90, 102, 105
Bhenka Financial Services 52
Big Four 12, 19, 33–4, 105, 140, 174, 189, 223
Black Business Council 18
black economic empowerment (BEE) 8–10, 18–20, 103, 106–7, 136, 191, 197, 210–11, 214
Black Empowerment Commission (BEC) 103
Bond Exchange of South Africa 18
Botswana, Lesotho, Namibia and Swaziland (BLNS countries) 171, 175–6, 189, 216
Bradley, Andrew 57
Broad-Based Black Empowerment Act (2004) 103
building societies 139
Bungane, Kennedy 18–20

Burbidge, John 182–3
Bureau of Market Research (BMR) 14, 109, 213
burial societies 9, 15–16, 26, 40, 58, 60–5, 150, 155–61, 167–9, 177, 190, 194
Business Day 161, 174, 214

Caixa Econômica Federal (Brazil) 32, 189
Capitec Bank 32
Cash Paymaster Services (CPS) 28–31, 50
cash transactions 21, 28–30, 33, 37, 40–3, 109–10, 150; lending 81–3; social grant payouts 50–2
CashBank 80, 104, 129, 143–8, 187
cellphone banking 2, 34, 40–4, 47, 55, 174, 187–9
charges, access and terms (CAT) 160
Charter *see* Financial Sector Charter (FSC)
Charter Council 18, 185–6
Chemel, Charles 47
Christensen, Clayton 187
Collins, Daryl 67, 73
Comesa Bankers' Association 218
Committee of Insurance, Securities and Non-banking Financial Authorities (Cisna) 220
Common Market for Eastern and Southern Africa (Comesa) 218–20
Common Monetary Area (CMA) 170, 216
Community Bank 30–1, 104, 139–42; Foundation 140–1
Community Reinvestment Bill (CR Bill) 7–8, 129
Consultative Group to Assist the Poorest (CGAP) 88–9
Consumer Credit Association 94
Consumer Credit Bill 85, 92, 95, 189
consumer education 30, 46, 94, 185, 223; *see also* financial literacy
consumer protection 39–40, 85, 93–4, 189–90
Cooper, Derek 7, 191
Co-operative Banks Act 40
Coovadia, Cas 139–42
cost of banking 12, 33, 37–41, 43–4, 47, 52, 54–5, 58, 62, 91, 97

counter-terrorist finance (CTF) 39–40
credit 10, 15–17, 39, 57, 70, 77, 80, 85, 89, 91, 176, 189–90, 217; access to 85–7, 93, 98, 109, 114; bubble 203–7; card 22–3, 43; consumer 92, 206–7; rates 203–4; retail 80–1, 203–4; *see also* housing finance, micro credit; micro lending
Credit Law Review 85
Creighton, Denis 130

Dallimore, Anthea 197–9
Davel, Gabriel 93–5
De Klerk, FW 2
De Ridder, Johan 115–17, 133
debit cards 1, 15, 23, 43, 55, 186; as used by cash lenders 81–3; *see also* Sekulula debit card
debit orders 32, 150, 154
Dedicated Banks Bill 40, 188–9
Department of: Housing 7, 129; Social Development 53, 196; Trade and Industry (DTI) 18–19, 77–8, 83, 85, 91–3, 103, 112, 207, 212, 214
developed countries 5, 28, 31, 100, 112
developing countries 4, 28, 31–2, 39, 42, 100, 110–11, 139, 142–3, 161, 183, 189–90
Development Bank of Southern Africa (DBSA) 71, 114, 140, 143
development finance institution (DFI) 185, 190–1
Du Plessis, Barend 139
Du Plessis, PG 82–3

E Plan 30–1, 46–9, 58, 140; *see also* Standard Bank
Eastern and Southern African Anti-Money Laundering Group (ESAAMLG) 220
Eastern and Southern African Banking Supervisors Group (ESAF) 220
Eastern and Southern Trade and Development Bank 218
Ebony Consulting International (ECI) 87, 158, 223
economic growth 2, 4–6, 80, 100, 111, 184, 200

electronic transactions 21, 31, 42, 44, 91, 150; *see also* automated teller machines (ATMs); cellphone banking; E Plan; Internet banking
entrepreneurship 100, 109–12, 210; *see also* small, medium and micro enterprises (SMMEs)
Erwin, Alec 19
Europay, Mastercard, Visa (EMV) smart-card 33, 43

Finance and Investment Protocol (FIP) 217–18
Financial Action Task Force (FATF) 220
Financial Advisory and Intermediary Services (FAIS) Act 40, 161
financial co-operatives 9, 20, 40, 66, 87, 177, 196–7
Financial Diaries of the Poor 27, 61, 64, 67, 69, 73–6
financial institutions 5–9, 66, 104, 170–83, 191; problems in BLNS countries 178–80; regionalisation of 5, 170–6, 180
Financial Intelligence Centre Act (FICA) 39–40
financial literacy 20, 185, 222–4; *see also* consumer education
Financial Mail (FM) 18, 20
Financial Sector Campaign Coalition (FSCC) 7
Financial Sector Charter (FSC) 1, 3–4, 8–10, 13–15, 18–21, 101, 106, 159, 185–6, 188, 191, 224; and housing finance 121, 129–30, 137, 149; and insurance 150–1, 158–62; commitment to SME development 106–7, 211; targets 33, 35–6, 44, 52, 63, 68, 191; transactions access definitions 35–9
Financial Services Association (FSA) 196–7
Financial Services Board (FSB) 155, 223
financial services sector 2, 4–5, 7–9, 12, 89, 92, 100, 107, 130, 209, 221; first-order 10, 13–15, 35, 159; retail 10, 15–16, 173, 176, 180, 189; *see also* financial institutions; tiered banking

financial summary measure (FSM) 15
financial system 1, 11, 82, 170, 175, 184, 190, 222; globally 88–9
FinaSol 196–7
FinMark Trust 15, 28, 38, 40, 67, 102, 105, 132, 135, 171, 175, 188, 223
FinScope (2003) 14–16, 23–4, 26–8, 33–4, 36, 59–61, 65–6, 78, 100, 109, 152, 154, 156, 175–7, 185, 194, 222; BLNS 176, 178
Flexi Banking 31; *see also* Absa
First National Bank (FNB) 19, 29, 37, 70, 82, 197; mini ATMs 37, 43, 52; regionalisation of 172, 174; Social Grant Payment product 52
foreign bank immigration 12, 170–3, 175, 180
Freedom Charter 6
Futurefact 65–6, 156

Gateway Home Loans 129, 135–6, 147–9, 187
Genesis Analytics 28, 40, 42, 158, 160, 175, 183
Geographic Information Systems (GIS) 14
Get Ahead Foundation 119, 139–40; *see also* Rural Finance Facility (RFF)
Global Entrepreneurship Monitor (GEM) 109–12, 209–10, 213
Glover, Christine 143–6
GoBanking 43
gooi-gooi see stolvels
Grameen Bank (Bangladesh) 87–8, 139–40; influence on policies and loans 93–4, 118
gross domestic product (GDP) 21, 57, 102, 121–2, 153, 200–1, 219
Group Credit Company (GCC) 80, 104, 143–6, 187
Grow with Us 32, 55

HIV/AIDS epidemic 28, 136, 201; and insurance 151, 157–9, 161–2, 164–5
Hawkins, Penny 131
Hock, Chris 118–20
Hoffmann, Jenny 54–6

Home Affairs National Identification
    System (HANIS) 33, 43–4
home improvements 61–2, 122, 131–2
Home Loan and Mortgage Disclosure Act
    (2000) 7, 129
Home Loan Guarantee Company (HLGC)
    131, 136, 159, 162–6, 187
home ownership and housing markets 2,
    122–5, 130, 137; government policy
    and interventions 125–32; *see also*
    township housing
Housing Amendment Act (2001) 125
housing finance 1–3, 5, 7–8, 10, 17, 85, 87,
    96, 104, 112, 121–49, 164, 184, 188–9,
    191; access to 121, 132, 166; credit gap
    122, 129, 132–6, 147; for first-time
    home buyers 121–2, 146; for low-
    income market 143–9; government
    policy and interventions 125–32;
    products 131–2; securitisation 121,
    129, 135–6, 147, 149; *see also* African
    Contractor Finance Corporation
    (ACFC); CashBank; Gateway Home
    Loans; Rural Finance Facility (RFF)
Housing for HIV Foundation 164–5
Housing White Paper (1994) 125–6
human capital investment 5, 112, 223
Hurst, Archie 141

Independent Development Trust (IDT)
    80, 96, 118, 140; Finance Company
    (IDTFC) 80, 84, 96, 98, 114, 190–1
Industrial Development Corporation
    (IDC) 140, 202, 214
innovations 30, 32, 41, 44, 49, 52, 121, 129,
    145, 148, 151, 159, 162, 164–5, 174,
    180, 186–7, 189, 192, 204–5
insurance 5, 10, 15, 20, 26, 39, 58, 109,
    150–69; and HIV/AIDS 157–9, 161–2;
    collection of premiums 150, 154, 161;
    effective access to 151, 159–61; funeral
    153–4, 158, 182; group schemes 150–1,
    161; life 60–2, 150–1, 154–5, 158,
    160–2; perceived risks and coping
    strategies 151–2, 161; products 160–1;
    regionalisation of 174–5, 182–3; risk
    pool 150–1, 161; short-term 151,
    153–5, 160–1; usage 152–5, 158, 160;
    see also burial societies
Integrated Financial Institution (IFI) 103
International Finance Corporation (IFC)
    182–3
International Fund for Agricultural
    Development (IFAD) 196
International Monetary Fund (IMF) 201
Internet banking 12, 42
Investec 19
investment 7, 20, 58, 61–3, 109, 122, 184
Ithala 31–2, 40, 186, 189

JSE Securities Exchange 12, 18, 81
Jackelen, Hank 88, 139–40
Japp, Stephen 70–2
job creation 4–5, 89, 100, 102, 111, 114
Job Summit (1998) 130, 149
Johannesburg Housing Company 132

Kganyago, Lesetja 20
Khyula Enterprise Finance Limited
    (Khula) 7, 82, 84, 103, 105–6, 118,
    190–1, 212–14
King Finance 80, 96, 114–15
Kirk, Ian 161
Kirkinis, Leon 96–9
Kotze, Dirk 50–2

Labour Force Survey (LFS) 101
Land Bank 214
Lea, Charlene 163–6
Life Offices Association (LOA) 9, 18–19, 155
living standard measure (LSM) 15, 154;
    LSM 1–5 10, 14, 20, 25, 33, 35–6, 54,
    57–8, 63, 66, 158; LSM 5–7 182; LSM
    6–10 24–5, 60, 123, 223
living standards 3
Lukhele, Andrew 70–2

Macro-Economic Research Group
    (MERG) 6
Makhulong Home Loan 147–8; *see also*
    Gateway Home Loans
Mali, Lincoln 46–8

Mandela, Nelson 6
Manuel, Trevor 19, 191
Marang Financial Services 105
Marcus, Gill 19
Maree, Jacko 18–20
Masakhane campaign 125–6
mass market 4, 29–31, 46, 48, 54, 58, 80–1
Mastercard Maestro 23, 42, 47
Mboweni, Tito 19
Metropolitan Life 175
micro credit 1, 9, 17, 31–2, 77–99, 112, 186–7, 189–91; *see also* micro lending
Micro Credit Summit (1997) 88
micro finance 67–8, 77–8, 88, 92–5, 217; by large banks 104–6; for housing 133–4; regulatory environment 83, 91, 95; *see also* small, medium and micro enterprises (SMMEs)
Micro Finance Institution (MFI) 89
micro finance organisations (MFOs) 84, 87, 89–90, 104–5
Micro Finance Regulatory Council (MFRC) 78, 83–6, 93–5, 158, 187, 189, 207, 223
micro lending 77–99, 122, 176, 204, 206–7; history in South Africa 78–85; in South Africa today 85–7, 90; international 87–90, 176; *see also* micro credit
Micro Lenders Association (MLA) 84
MicroSave-Africa 67
Mining Charter (2002) 7, 18
Mogase, Mutle 19–20
Monetary and Fiscal Policies Harmonisation Programme 218
money guarding 76
Mortgage Indemnity Fund (MIF) 125–6, 129
mortgage markets 121–3, 125, 129, 131, 134–6, 141, 149; high end of 148; in townships 125, 145, 147–8; top-up 163, 165
Moss, David 161
Motloba, Modise 19–20
Moyo, Peter, 19, 67
mutual banks 66, 144
Mutual Banks Act 40, 88, 142

Naicker, Keith 132
National Department of Agriculture (NDA) 197
National Economic Development and Labour Council *see* Nedlac
National Empowerment Fund (NEF) 103, 214; Act, 1998 214
National Housing Accord 125
National Housing Finance Corporation (NHFC) 7, 82, 119, 127–9, 132, 135–7, 147–8, 190–1
National Loans Register (NLR) 78, 91, 94–5
National Manufacturing Advisory Centre (Namac) 191, 212
National Payment System 32–3, 40, 42
National Small Business Act (1996) 209, 212
National Stokvels Association of South Africa (Nasasa) 70–2; *see also* stokvels
National Treasury 8, 10, 20, 57, 86
Nedcor 19, 82, 145; regionalisation of 174; *see also* GoBanking
Nedlac Financial Sector Summit (2002) 7, 9, 18, 33, 91, 191
network effects 44, 128; 185, 188
New Partnership for Africa's Development (Nepad) 170, 219
non-government organisations (NGOs) 9, 80–1, 87–8, 98–9, 105, 119, 132, 143, 187, 223
Ntsika Enterprise Promotion Agency (Ntsika) 191, 210, 212

Old Mutual 170, 174, 214, 223

payroll deductions 31, 82, 96, 98, 114, 118, 128, 145, 154, 176, 204, 206; *see also* Persal facilities
People's Benefit Scheme (PBS) 70–2
Persal facilities 77, 81, 83, 86, 205
personal identification number (PIN) 28, 204
point of sale (POS) 22–3, 37, 43, 51, 55
Policy Board for Financial Services and Regulation 105, 112
Porteous, David 132, 147–9

Posel, Debbie 156
PostBank 6, 16, 23, 31, 40, 61–2, 186, 189
poverty 25–6, 58, 68, 112, 122, 130;
    alleviation 5, 20, 28, 89, 91–2, 112,
    210–11, 219
Preferential Trade Area for Eastern and
    Southern Africa (PTA) 218
Prevention of Illegal Eviction Act 164
previously banked people 24–6, 41; *see also*
    banked people; unbanked people
Prinsloo, Johan 200–1
Prodem (Bolivia) 87–8, 143
properties in possession (PIP) 134

Quattro Trading 105

Reconstruction and Development
    Programme (RDP) 6, 124–5, 132
record of understanding (RoU) 7, 125–6,
    129
Red October campaign 7, 9
Rees, Gerry 50–2
Regional Indicative Strategic Development
    Plan (RISDP) 217–18
Registrar of: Banks 142, 144, 196;
    Co-operatives 197
remittances 28–9, 31, 33, 41, 44, 52
retail financial intermediary (RFI) 103,
    212–13
retail lending 80–1, 189
retailers 37, 40, 98, 109; *see also* point of
    sale (POS)
retirement funding 57, 60–1, 63; *see also*
    savings
Rotating Savings and Credit Association
    (Rosca) 73, 177, 193
Roth, Jim 167
Rural Finance Facility (RFF) 118–20, 187,
    213
Rural Housing Finance (RHF) 118–19
Rural Housing Loan Fund (RHLF) 84, 128
Rutherford, Stuart 66–7, 76

Saambou 12, 34, 77, 82, 84, 97–8, 145, 147,
    205
Samie, Adam 19

Sanlam 214
Santam 175
savings 5, 9–10, 15, 26, 31, 57–76, 109, 199,
    201, 217; account 54, 57–62, 64, 68–9;
    attitude towards 57, 59–61; book 23,
    31, 33; by the poor 66–9; clubs 63–6;
    contractual 63, 201; formal means of
    57–8, 61, 65, 68; home improvement
    as 61–2, 122; household 57–8, 68–9,
    201–2; informal means of 57–8, 61,
    63–6, 68; instruments of 60–1, 68;
    mobilisation of 31, 33, 189–90; rate
    of 200–2; *see also* E Plan; stokvels
Schachat, Gordon 96–7
Schoombee, A 103–4, 213–14
Sectoral Education and Training Authority
    (Seta) 223
Sekulula debit card 29, 51–3
Servcon 130
Shiller, Robert 161–2
Simplus 42
Sizanani-Sizabantu Scheme 105–6
Slovo, Joe 125
small and medium enterprises (SME) 85,
    100–2, 112, 140, 209–12, 215, 217;
    black 106–7; Charter commitments to
    106–7; financial needs 107–8; private-
    sector initiatives 105–7
Small Business Development Corporation
    214–15
Small Enterprise Foundation (SEF) 80, 94,
    105, 139–40
small, medium and micro enterprises
    (SMMEs) 1, 3–5, 111–12; definitions
    208–11; finance 2, 7–8, 17, 78, 82,
    100–20, 184, 188–9, 191; government
    support initiatives 102–3, 212–15;
    private-sector initiatives 103–5; size
    and financial needs 101–2, 107–11
smart card (SIM card) 42–3, 50–1
Smartsave 31
social grants 2, 28–31, 41, 44, 91; pay-
    ments 41, 50–3, 198–9
Social Security Act 52
South African Advertising Research
    Foundation (SAARF) 14

South African Communist Party 7
South African Home Loans (SAHL) 135, 148–9
South African Reserve Bank (SARB) 54
South African Short-Term Insurance Association (SAIA) 18–19
South African Social Security Agency 29, 52
South African Special Risks Insurance Association (Sasria) 165
Southern African Customs Union (SACU) 170, 175–80, 216, 220–1
Southern African Development Community (SADC) 170, 181, 216–20
Sowazi, Nkululeko 163
Stanbic Africa 173
Standard Bank 7, 19, 29, 82, 191, 223; Community Banking Project 104; regionalisation of 171–4; *see also* E Plan
Standard Chartered 170, 173, 180
Sate of Micro Credit Summit Campaign 2002 89
state–private sector relations 2, 6–10, 90, 165, 188–92, 214–15; lack of coordination between 184–5; regards housing finance 125–6, 129–30, 136–7, 147–8
Statistics South Africa 101, 109
stokvels 9, 15–16, 26, 40, 57–8, 60–6, 68, 70–5, 88, 143, 157, 193–5; different kinds 193–4; procedure at meeting 73–5; profile of members 156; similar organisations 143
Su Casita (Mexico) 135
suitcase banking 173–4

Teba Bank 29–30, 32, 40, 54–6; *see also* Grow with Us
technology 1, 41–2, 52, 55, 92; attitude towards 33–4
Theta Group 81, 96–7
Thomson, Rob 156
tiered banking 9, 20, 40, 66, 104, 188–9
Towards a Ten Year Review 3, 100, 209
township housing 7, 121, 123–5, 130, 136, 184; lack of secondary market 123–4, 131–2, 134, 136

Township Residential Property Markets project 109, 112
transaction banking 10, 15, 21–56, 92, 186–7; electronic 21, 31, 55; FSC targets for 35–9; growth of low-end 29–35; via cellphones 41–2, 188
transformation 2, 5–8, 10, 100, 191, 210–11
TransUnion ITC 16, 87, 94
Tucker, Bob 46, 139–40

UCT Unilever Institute of Strategic Marketing 62, 64, 193–5
umgalelo see stokvels
Umsobomvu Youth Fund (UYF) 214
unbanked people 5, 21–7, 30, 37, 42, 44, 199; 'banking' them 33–4, 40–1; remittance to 28–9; saving by 60–1, 63; *see also* banked people; previously banked people
unemployment 25–6, 77, 109–10, 130
Unity Financial Services 96
Unibank 31, 82, 84, 98, 142, 147, 205
unit trusts 62–3, 153
Unlawful Occupation of Land Act 164
Urban Foundation 80, 143
urbanisation 80, 136
usage of financial services 13–17, 22–3, 26, 36, 68; in BLNS countries 175–80
Usury Act 80, 83, 85; exemption from 77, 81, 85, 94, 189; revised Usury Act Exemption notice (1999) 83, 88, 91–3

Value Added Tax (VAT) 209
Vermeulen, Philip 114–15
village banks 66, 87, 196–9
Vision 2010 188
Vulindlela 112

White Paper on Small Business (1996) 208–9
wireless communications 21, 32, 43, 55, 187; *see also* cellphone banking
World Bank 30, 42, 48, 88–9
Wright, Graham 67–8

Yunus, Mohammed 87